Best Football Drills

The Drill Book for Winning Football Teams

DILLON HESS

To Tom Landry,

*the Best Football Coach
there has ever been*

Table of Contents

Introduction	1
Drills	
Physical Performance Drills	11
Skill Drills	89
Execution Drills	225
Index	271
About the Author	279

Introduction

Who is this book for?

The Best Football Drills book is for football coaches and football players who want to get the most out of their practice time. The way you win a football game is to win multiple practices leading up to the game. This book equips players and coaches with the drills, tips, and techniques needed to plan and execute successful practices.

Whether you are a head coach leading an entire team, or an individual player looking to get the upper hand on your competition, this book will provide you with a plethora of proven and effective football drills.

Categories

This book categorizes all of the football drills into three main branches of categories, namely Physical Performance Drills, Skill Drills, and Execution Drills.

These three drill categories each specialize in certain traits that allow football players to focus on and develop many different skills, talents, and abilities. Improvements on the practice field will translate to success on the game field.

Physical Performance Drills:

Physical performance drills are the drills that increase a player's physical attributes. For example, physical performance drills might develop a player's strength, agility, speed, and/or conditioning.

Performing on the football field requires an incredible combination of speed, agility, and other physical feats, all while performing complex tactical tasks. The stronger and faster a player is, the better off he is going to be in the heat of competition on the football field.

Skill Drills:

The Skill Drills category contains the most drills out of the three main categories in the book. Football is a game where players all across the field have different skills and techniques that are required for each play and assignment. Therefore, it is important that each player is equipped to perform the skills needed for their team to have success.

The Skill Drills section demonstrates many different drills that focus on specific skills, techniques, and football fundamentals. When repeatedly practiced, these skill drills will increase the ability of players to perform in the game.

Execution Drills:

Execution drills represent the culmination of individual skill drills put into practice in a team setting. Executing as a team in a game situation is when the players get to have fun putting everything they have been practicing together. After working hard on physical fitness and specific skill development, executing football assignments as a team becomes the most rewarding aspect of any practice.

Players may be successful individually, but it is all worthless unless everybody is properly working together and executing as a team. The execution drills in this book put all the fitness and skill developments into practice by having the team execute what they have learned in a game like scenario.

Equipment

Although this book aims to provide drills that require as little equipment as possible, there are many drills that are better performed when certain types of equipment are used.

If you don't have a particular type of equipment readily available to you, you will often still be able to implement a modified version of the drill in your practice.

CONE   BLOCKING PAD   TACKLE DUMMY

Techniques

There are seven specific techniques outlined in this book that focus on particular football fundamentals. Drills focus on various techniques to help players from positions all across the field on both sides of the football.Developing the ability for players to perform specific techniques in practice will increase their ability to have success in their assignments and responsibilities in the game.

Passing Drills: Passing Drills are exclusively geared for the quarterback position and can range from individual drills to team-oriented drills. Developing all of the areas of the passing game is critical for an offense to be able to move the ball through the air.

Catching Drills: There are two halves to the passing game. First, the throw, secondly, the catch. Working on catching drills will help receivers, tight ends, running backs, and sometimes even defensive backs perform at a higher level when the ball is in the air coming their way.

Ball Carrying Drills: There are endless possibilities of situations that a ball carrier will face while running the ball on the football field. The ball carrying drills in this book will teach running backs, fullbacks, and quarterbacks the correct techniques for running with the football and how to respond in the most common scenarios a ball carrier will encounter.

Blocking Drills: An offense will never be able to move the football if the players up front are not able to block the defense. Blocking drills teach the offensive lineman and other players how to perform the best blocking maneuvers to fend off the defense.

Tackling Drills: The most important thing for a defense to do on any given play is to tackle the player with the ball. Tackling drills focus on the techniques and fundamentals involved with executing the most violent, and most fun aspect of playing defense.

Pass Defending Drills: A defense that gets torched through the air will never have a chance of stopping the offense. Pass defending drills equip defensive backs with the tools needed to defend against receivers and prevent pass completions.

Footwork Drills: Football is a game of inches. If a player's footwork is a step slow, or a step misplaced, then it can spell doom for the entire play. Footwork drills not only develop quickness and agility, but they also focus on the correct steps and movements a player should take in particular situations to be as efficient as possible.

Difficulty

The difficulty rating provides a holistic indicator of how easy or hard it is to successfully implement a given drill in the course of a football practice.

Not only is the difficulty level determined by how difficult it is for players to learn the basic rules and responsibilities of the drill, but it also takes into account how difficult it is to successfully execute and develop all the skills and techniques that the drill requires. Some drills may be easy in principle, but may be much more difficult to master.

EASY   INTERMEDIATE   ADVANCED

Size

All of the drills in the book indicate the size of the drill through the means of an icon that communicates the minimum amount of players required to perform the drill. This is mostly determined by the number of players that it takes to complete one entire repetition of the drill.

Each drill can handle more players than the size icon indicates. The icon is purely meant to show the minimum amount of players required. For example, if a drill is marked as an individual drill, then it is certainly possible to set up the drill to have multiple individuals take turns rotating through the drill or even to have multiple individuals spread out and all perform the drill at the same time.

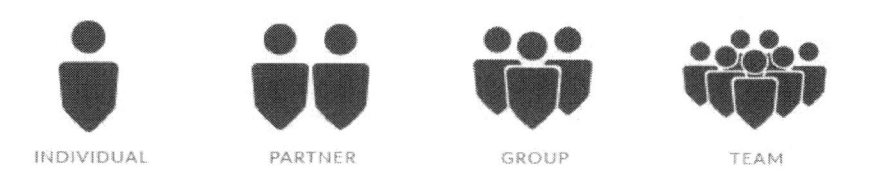

INDIVIDUAL   PARTNER   GROUP   TEAM

Contact Level

The game of football is a contact sport. The practice of football, however, does not always need to be a full-contact situation.

Each drill in this book has a contact level icon that indicates whether or not the drill has any sort of contact. Marking each drill with a certain contact level is meant to help players and coaches better filter through and decide which drills are the best fit for particular practice situations.

NO-CONTACT   CONTACT

Drill Type

Evaluation Drills: At the beginning of the season, coaches need to evaluate players in order to properly place them in the positions that will help benefit the team. Evaluation drills provide the platform for players to showcase their physical performance and football abilities in certain situations.

Speed Drills: What is more important in the open field than pure, raw speed? Speed drills help to develop a player's running speed to get him from point A to point B faster. The faster team with faster players has a big advantage over a slower team. Utilize the speed drills to increase player speed.

Agility Drills: Agility drills focus on quick movements and changes of direction that develop a player's quickness. Quickness on the football field is one of the most important physical attributes that a player can work on. Not only is it generally better in the sport of football for players to be quick than it is for them to be fast, but quickness is also an attribute that is more easily developed and improved. Whereas most athletes are born with a certain top speed, quickness is something that can more readily be improved through the use of agility and footwork drills.

Conditioning Drills: Conditioning is often one of the most overlooked aspects of a football player's training. It is important to be strong, fast, and quick, but if a player doesn't have the energy and endurance to keep pushing himself, then he will fall apart in later stages of the game. The conditioning drills in this book develop a player's stamina and keep him from getting winded when it matters most in a game.

Coordination Drills: Often times football is perceived as a game of brutish strength, but more often than not, some of the most critical situations in a game require detailed coordination and finely tuned maneuvers. The coordination drills in this book work to develop a player's coordination, mostly in the way that he utilizes his eye-hand coordination to handle the football.

Teamwork Drills: Football is the ultimate team sport. Eleven players playing eleven different positions all must work together in unison in order to successfully execute plays. The teamwork drills in this book specifically deal with teammates working together as a team to accomplish a given goal.

Competition Drills: The game of football is a competition. Why not bring some of that competition into football practice? Competition drills pit players against players. When players compete, they usually push themselves harder, and they learn skills that can only be taught and encountered in the midst of competition.

Final Words

All good football coaches know that players don't play better in the game than they do in practice. That is why it is incredibly important that you make the most of the time you have in practice to prioritize what your players spend their time working on.

Football teams have practices all throughout the week, but they only have one day a week where they actually play a game. Preparing for productive practices may be even more important than preparing for games. Make sure that your team is equipped with all of the best drills to maximize their development in practice, in order to maximize their results in games.

Successful drills lead to successful practices.

Successful practices lead to successful games.

Successful games lead to successful teams.

Start planning your team's success with the drills found in this book.

Drills

Physical Performance Drills

Pro Agility Shuttle

SETUP

Setup the drill by placing three cones 5 yards apart. These cones will indicate the boundaries of the drill. Technically, you do not need any cones if you already have yard lines that mark the field, but the players should be instructed which yard lines are the correct boundaries for the drill. The player should line up even with the middle cone with their feet straddling the line and their body facing the cones in front of them.

TECHNIQUES: **FOOTWORK**

EQUIPMENT: **CONE, TIMER**

DRILL TYPE: **PHYSICAL PERFORMANCE, EVALUATION, AGILITY**

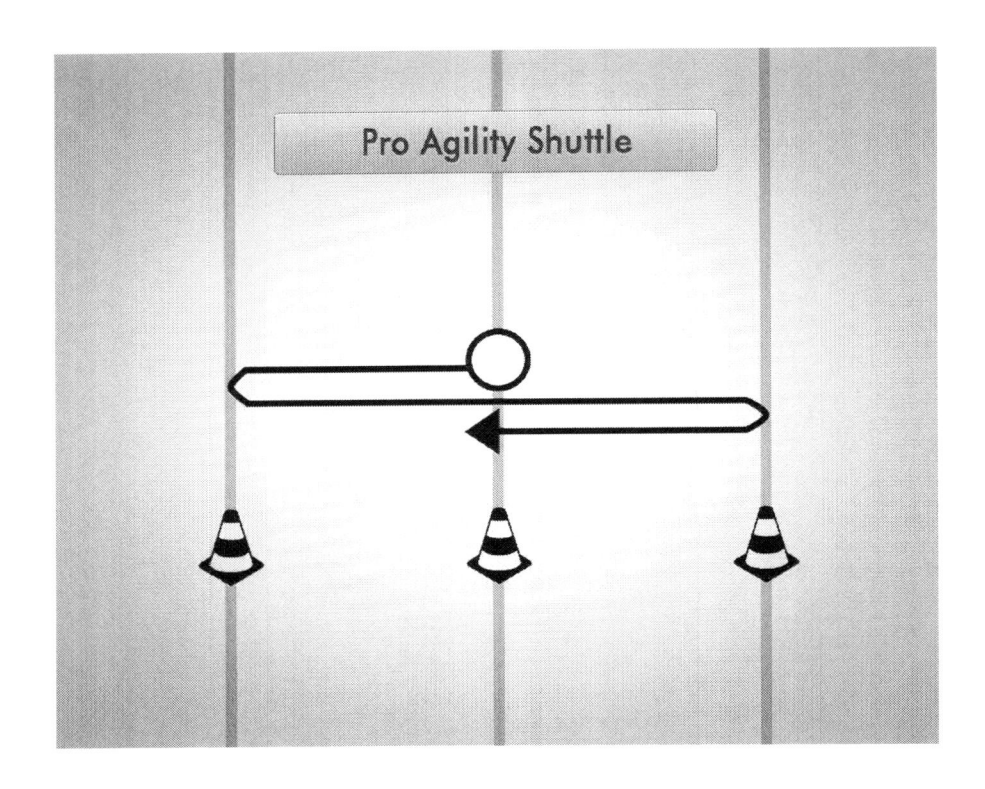

Pro Agility Shuttle

EASY | INDIVIDUAL | NO-CONTACT

PURPOSE

The primary purpose of the Pro Agility Shuttle is to evaluate a players quickness. Featuring two complete change of directions within a 20 yard span, this drill is the most popular way to measure a football player's quickness on the field.

This drill is also sometimes called the 20 Yard Shuttle, referring to the total amount of yards covered by the player in the drill.

DRILL DESCRIPTION

The player prepares for the drill by getting in an athletic stance while touching the center line with one of his hands. Upon bursting off of the center line the player quickly runs five yards to one side and touches the outside line with his hand. After completely changing direction, the player then runs ten yards and touches the other outside line with his hand. Then, turning all the way back around one more time, the player sprints five more yards through the center line to complete the drill.

If timing the player for evaluation, the timer starts as soon s the player's hand lifts off the ground and stops as soon as the player's body breaks the center line after the second turn.

Three Cone Drill

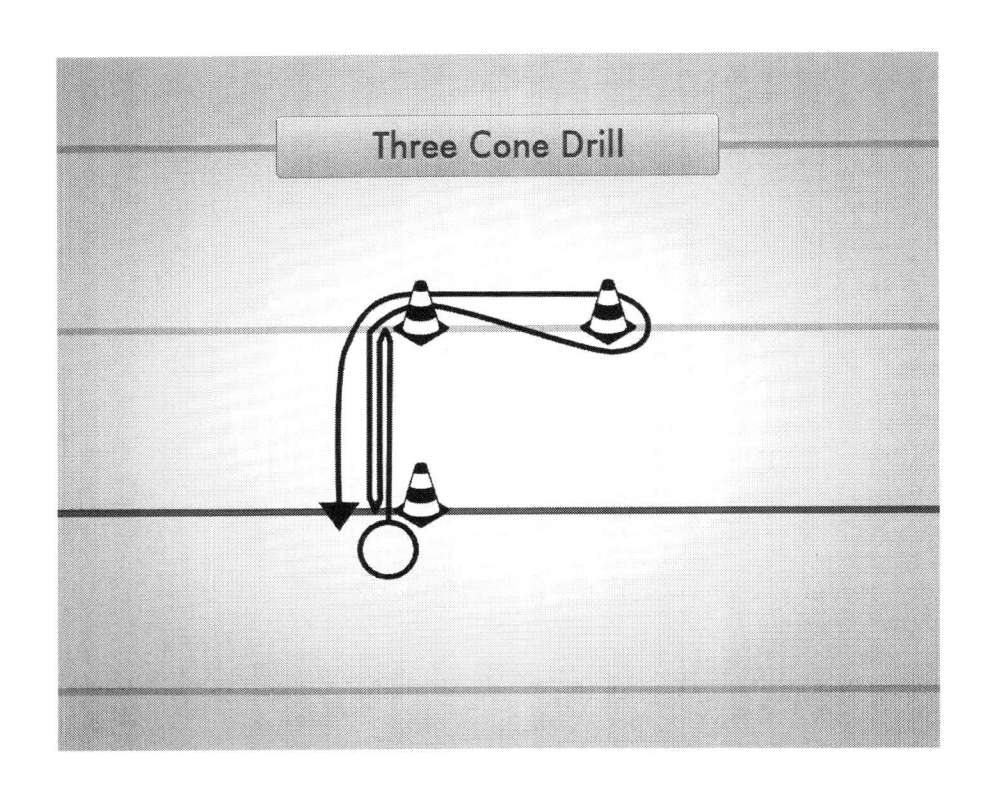

SETUP

Using three cones, place one cone on the starting line, the second cone five yards downfield, and the third cone five yards to the side of the second cone. This setup will allow both a right-hand turn and a left-hand turn without having to move any of the cones, simply by swapping which of the outside cones you utilize as the starting line.

TECHNIQUES: **FOOTWORK**

EQUIPMENT: **CONE, TIMER**

DRILL TYPE: **PHYSICAL PERFORMANCE, EVALUATION, SPEED, AGILITY**

Three Cone Drill

EASY | INDIVIDUAL | NO-CONTACT

PURPOSE

Football is not a game played in a straight line, therefore, it is imperative that players prepare for quickly turning while running on the football field. The NFL combine utilizes this drill to measure how fast defensive players can run around the offensive line and blitz into the pocket in order to sack the Quarterback.

DRILL DESCRIPTION

Also known as the "L Drill," the Three Cone Drill simulates a quick turn while on the run on the football field. The compact turns require precise footwork in order to swiftly maneuver through the drill.

Players sprint forward five yards, touch the line, and then turn and sprint back to the starting line. After touching the starting line, they then begin the L portion of the drill by sprinting back to the middle cone. Upon reaching the middle cone, they turn 90 degrees around the middle cone, come underneath and turn 180 degrees around the last cone, and then return to the starting line by running 90 degrees around the middle cone again and sprinting through the finish line.

The focus is for players to use their footwork to completely circle around each cone as closely and as quickly as possible without knocking any of the cones down. If a player takes too wide of a turn around the cones it will significantly increase the time it takes for him to cross the finish line.

Square Shuffle

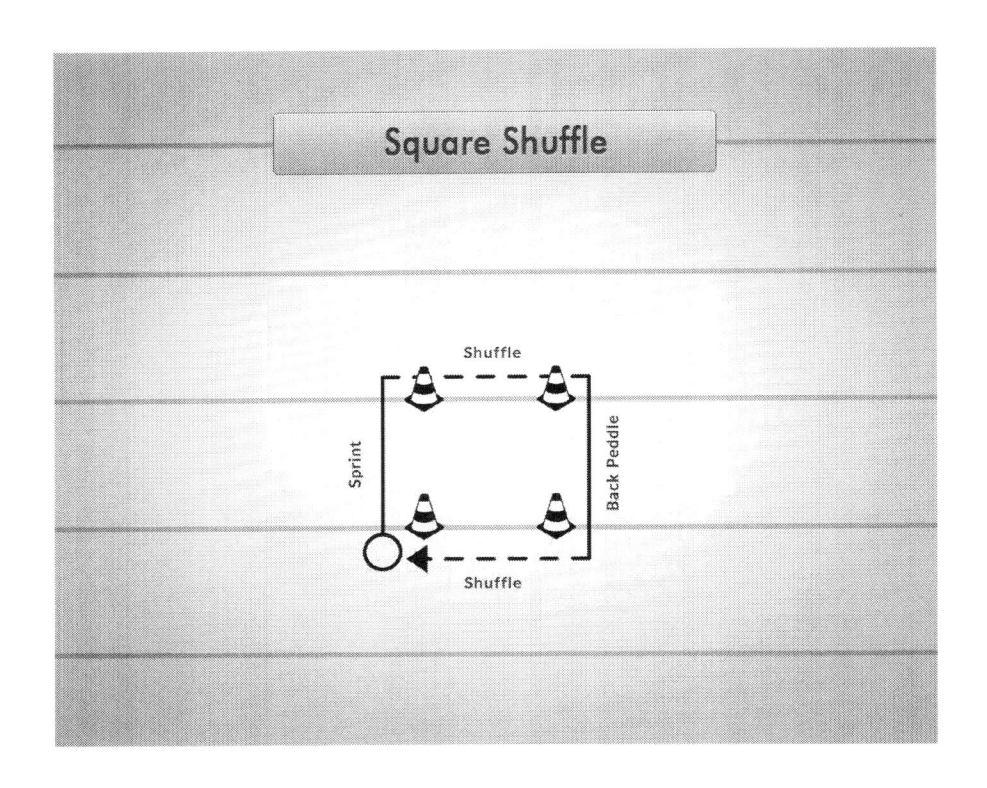

SETUP

Simply setup four cones to make a square that is 5 yards by five yards.

TECHNIQUES:	FOOTWORK
EQUIPMENT:	CONE
DRILL TYPE:	PHYSICAL PERFORMANCE, AGILITY

Square Shuffle

INTERMEDIATE | INDIVIDUAL | NO-CONTACT

PURPOSE

The Square Shuffle incorporates four different types of movements in order to improve player mobility and quickness. Featuring a sprint, a back peddle, and shuffles to each side, this drill quickly teaches athletes to rapidly navigate corners.

DRILL DESCRIPTION

Starting in one corner, players start the drill by sprinting forward up the side of the square. Players then pass around the cone by laterally changing direction by entering a side shuffle across the top of the square. After rounding that corner, players enter a back peddle down the side of the square. Finally, players enter one last side shuffle across the bottom of the square.

All in all, players always remain facing the same direction throughout the entirety of the drill while they change their movement type.

With a large group of players lined up to run this drill, you can increase the flow of traffic through this drill by having multiple players navigate the square at the same time. You can do this by sending the second player when the first player reaches the far corner. Then send the third player as soon as the first player passes in front of him at the starting/finish line. Players then continue this pattern of initiating the drill when a player passes in front of them at the start/finish line.

Five Cone Drill

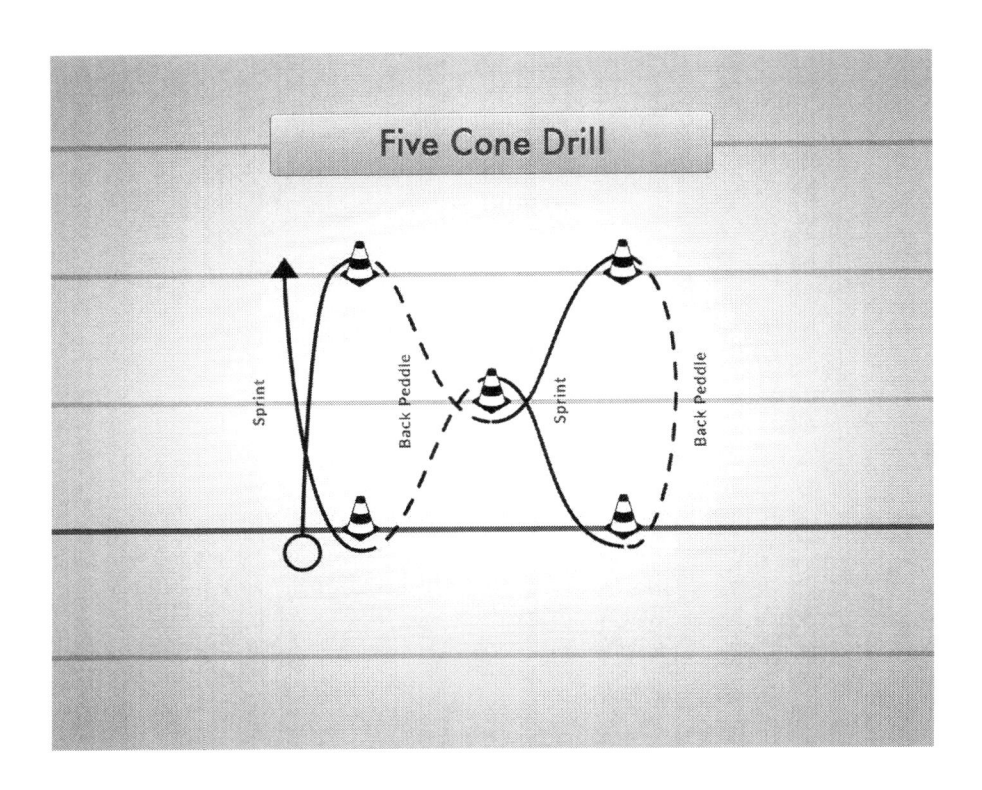

SETUP

Setup this drill with five cones by creating a square with four cones and placing the remaining cone directly in the middle. Technically the square can be any size, but ensure that all four sides are equal distance and that the cones clearly indicate the points at which the players will change direction.

TECHNIQUES:	**FOOTWORK**
EQUIPMENT:	**CONE**
DRILL TYPE:	**PHYSICAL PERFORMANCE, SPEED, AGILITY**

Five Cone Drill

INTERMEDIATE   INDIVIDUAL   NO-CONTACT

PURPOSE

The sport of football requires rapidly changing directions continually throughout the game. The Five Cone Drill provides a great practice situation to allow players to get used to alternating between a full spring and a full back peddle. Players will improve their ability to rapidly change direction through repetitions of this drill.

DRILL DESCRIPTION

Players change direction by alternating between sprinting forward and back peddling backward around each cone. Sprint to the first cone along the outside and then back peddle to the middle cone, then sprint to the far outside cone and back peddle down the side of the cones, then sprint to the middle, then back peddle around the starting cone before sprinting through the finish line one more time to finish the drill. (The diagram indicates a sprint with the solid lines, and a back peddle with the dashed lines.) Force your players to build their footwork coordination by going around each cone before changing their direction.

Each time the players go through this drill, they should alternate the side they start on so that they even out with angles they are working on.

You can also implement a condensed version of this drill by modifying the cones from a 10×10 yard square to a 5×5 yard square. This condensed version allows you to focus even more on quickness and the rapid change of direction.

Quick Cut Drill

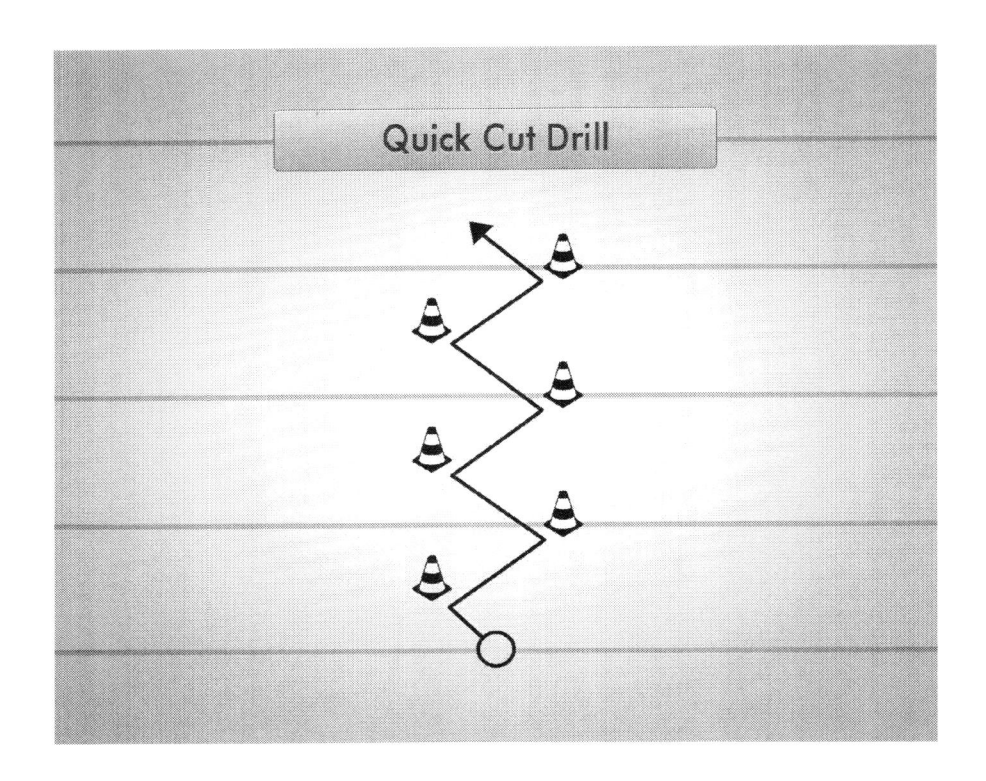

SETUP

Set up six cones in an alternating zigzag formation. There should be roughly three to five yards of diagonal space between each cone.

TECHNIQUES:	**FOOTWORK**
EQUIPMENT:	**CONE**
DRILL TYPE:	**PHYSICAL PERFORMANCE, AGILITY**

Quick Cut Drill

EASY   INDIVIDUAL   NO-CONTACT

PURPOSE

Focus on the footwork involved with making 90 degree cuts. This football drill is particularly useful for wide receivers to help them develop quick crisp route running.

DRILL DESCRIPTION

Each player entering this drill will have enter with a slow pace of about half speed while running in between cones. When arriving at the cone, however, their foot speed should increase as fast as possible as they quickly chop their feet to make a crisp 90 degree cut.

When preparing to make the cut, players have three quick jab steps, ending with their cut foot which explodes and propels them in the other direction.

It is important for the players to keep their feet under their body. If they extend one of their feet too far out, it will often cause them to slip and lose their footing. Focusing on this footwork will allow your players to ingrain better habits and make quicker cuts while on the field.

Figure Eight

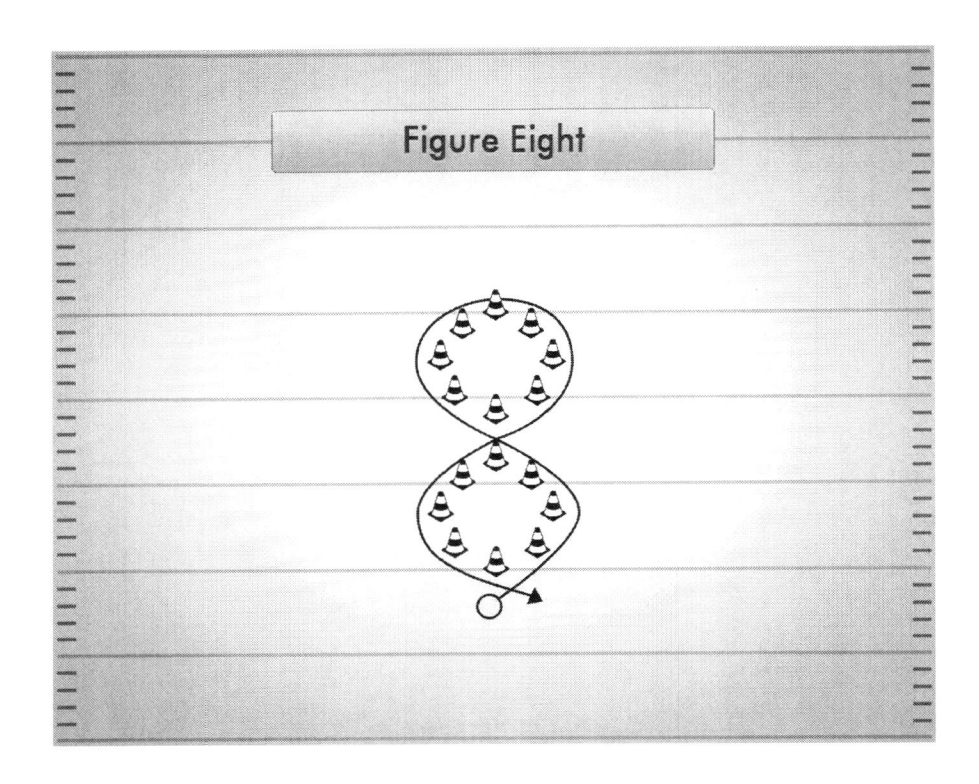

SETUP

Setup two circles of cones to indicate the boundaries of the figure eight. Make sure that there is a gap in between each of the circles so that that players have a path to run through the middle of the figure eight portion. You will need to ensure that there are enough cones to make the path curved so that there are no sharp angles.

TECHNIQUES:	FOOTWORK
EQUIPMENT:	CONE, TIMER
DRILL TYPE:	PHYSICAL PERFORMANCE, SPEED, AGILITY

Figure Eight Drill

INTERMEDIATE   INDIVIDUAL   NO-CONTACT

PURPOSE

Most agility drills focus on making hard cuts with sharp 90 degree angles. The Figure Eight drill, however, focuses on a very rounded type of agility. This specific type of agility prepares football players for a turning footwork maneuver that they will need to utilize throughout the course of a football game.

DRILL DESCRIPTION

Players go through this drill one at a time starting at the bottom end of the figure eight. As they spring around the cones, players should make the turns as close as possible to the cones without knocking any of them over. Throughout the course of these two full circles, the players will encounter two full 360 degree turns in order to improve that ability to make gradual turns on the football field.

Make sure that a player in line does not start the drill too early in order to avoid collisions in the middle of the figure eight.

To add a sprinkle of fun to this drill, you could time each player and declare their time to the team in order to encourage players to give this drill all of their effort in the name of competition.

Standing Broad Jump

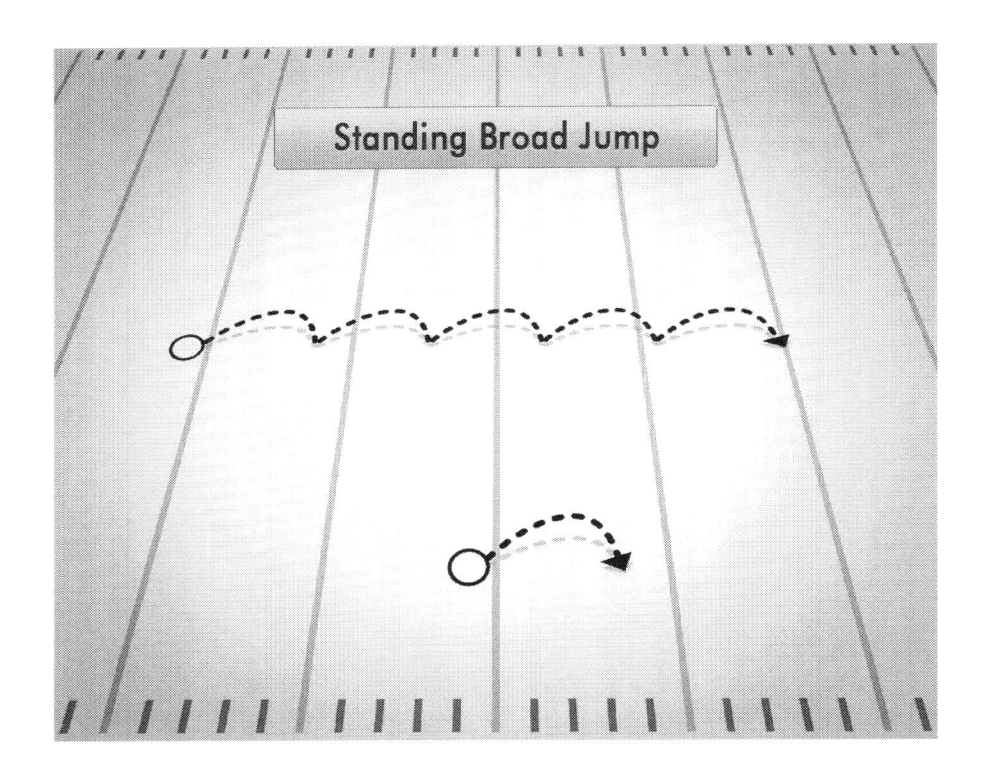

SETUP

Mark the starting line to ensure that all athletes are jumping from the same location. If using as an evaluation drill, prepare a measurement method to measure the length of each athlete's jump.

TECHNIQUES: FOOTWORK

EQUIPMENT: NONE

DRILL TYPE: PHYSICAL PERFORMANCE, EVALUATION

Standing Broad Jump

EASY | INDIVIDUAL | NO-CONTACT

PURPOSE

Predominantly used as a drill for purely evaluation purposes, this drill measures and develops the explosive power that each player possesses.

DRILL DESCRIPTION

If using as an evaluation, only one jump is needed. Players step up to the starting line with two feet even and shoulder width apart. Squatting down, they explode into a jump as far out as they can. Players should be instructed to stick the landing so that you can measure the jump to where their nearest back heel landed. This measurement displays the explosive power that each athlete possesses.

If used as a developmental drill, players can perform this drill together by spreading out on the starting line and beginning to jump forward downfield. This jump is the same standing broad jump, but is continually repeated after sticking each landing. There should be no steps in between jumps. Instead, after sticking the landing, players regroup and begin the next explosive jump as they continue jumping downfield. Several repetitions of this drill builds explosive power throughout the entire lower body as well as developing balance as the athletes must focus on solidly landing each jump without faulty steps.

Ladder Drill

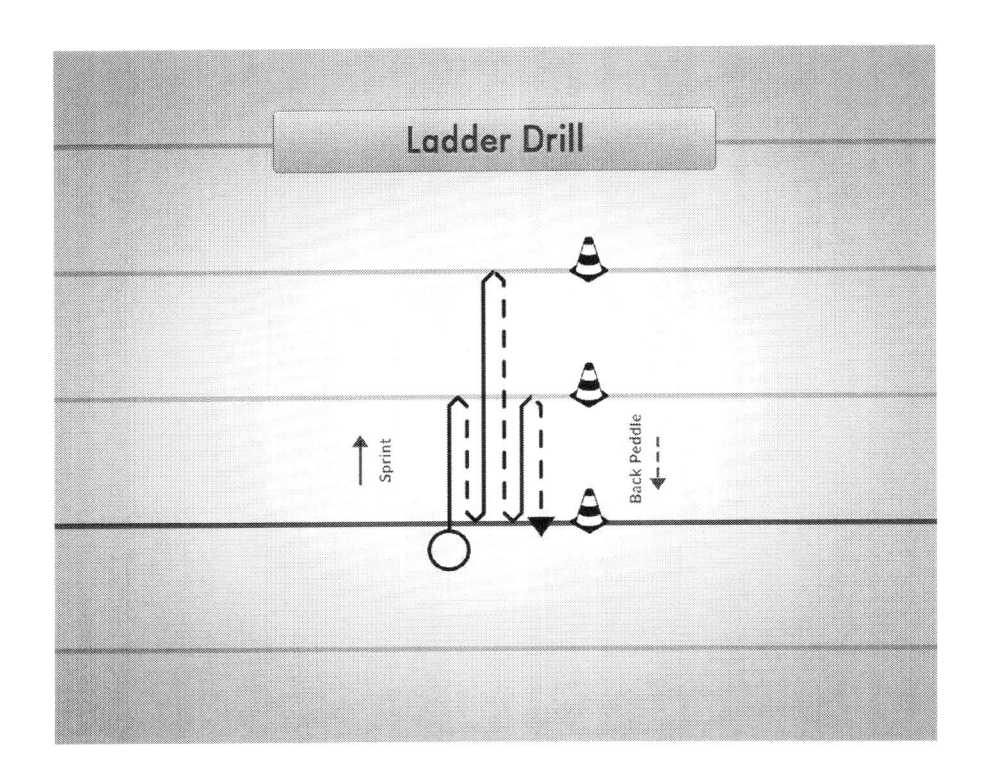

SETUP

Either use cones or yard lines to indicate the starting line, the 5-yard line, and the 10-yard line. This drill will only span these three lines that cover a total distance of ten yards. Multiple athletes can perform this drill at the same time in parallel.

TECHNIQUES:	FOOTWORK
EQUIPMENT:	CONE
DRILL TYPE:	PHYSICAL PERFORMANCE, SPEED, AGILITY

26

Ladder Drill

EASY | **INDIVIDUAL** | **NO-CONTACT**

PURPOSE

Develop starting and stopping speed and quickness. Players repeatedly accelerate for a total of six times throughout the course of one rep in order to build a faster burst of speed when coming off of the line of scrimmage or when changing direction on the field.

DRILL DESCRIPTION

The Ladder Drill begins with all athletes lined up on the starting line. Athletes begin drill by exploding off of the line as fast as possible. Once the drill has begun, there is a rapid succession of forward sprints and back paddles in a pattern of 5-10-5. In other words, the athletes will sprint to the first line (five yards away) and then back peddle to the starting line. Once back at the starting line, the athletes will again explode into a sprint for ten yards and then return to the starting line with a back peddle. Finally, there is one more forward and back for another five yard trip.

To focus on the initial explosion, you can begin the drill with a certain snap count or cadence in order to prepare players for an initial burst of acceleration during the course of a normal play.

By lining up the entire team, or group of players, to run this drill in parallel, you can build a sense of race and competition that provides extra motivation for your athletes to push themselves hard throughout the course of the drill.

Shuffle Shuttle

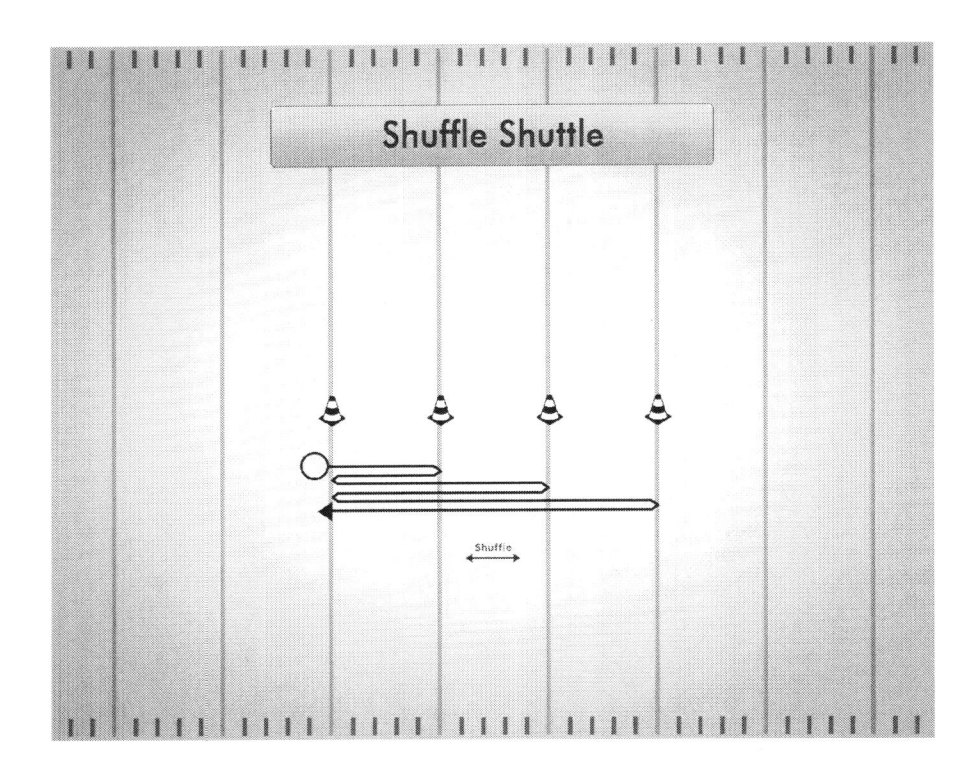

SETUP

Utilize a space of 15 yards by using 4 cones to mark out 3 sets of 5 yards. Each 5-yard increment will be used for a portion of the drill.

TECHNIQUES:	FOOTWORK
EQUIPMENT:	CONE
DRILL TYPE:	PHYSICAL PERFORMANCE, AGILITY

Shuffle Shuttle

EASY   **INDIVIDUAL**   **NO-CONTACT**

PURPOSE

Build lateral quickness in your players by developing their side to side shuffling ability. This will allow defensive players to better break down and make tackles on ball carriers, as well as, allowing your offensive players to better slide in front of the defenders they are trying to block. All in all, this drill builds the players ability to mirror the movements of the target opponent of the football field.

DRILL DESCRIPTION

Each participant lines up at the starting line facing the cones. Athletes should remember to keep their bodies facing the same direction of the cones throughout the entirety of the drill, as they are never supposed to turn their body.

Upon the start of the drill, athletes begin shuffling their feet as quickly as possible for five yards and then facing the same direction shuffle the opposite way back to the starting line. Athletes continue this pattern of shuffling back an forward in 5 yard, 10 yard, and 15 yard increments, always returning to the starting line. A foot should be placed on each line, before changing direction in order to ensure that athletes traverse the whole length of the drill without cutting themselves short.

For a proper shuffle, the athlete's feet should never cross over each other. Instead, the front foot reaches downfield and the back foot quickly regathers underneath the body and next to the front foot, without crossing over. This will ensure that the athlete doesn't develop a bad habit that leads to their feet getting tangled and tripped up over each other.

Gainer

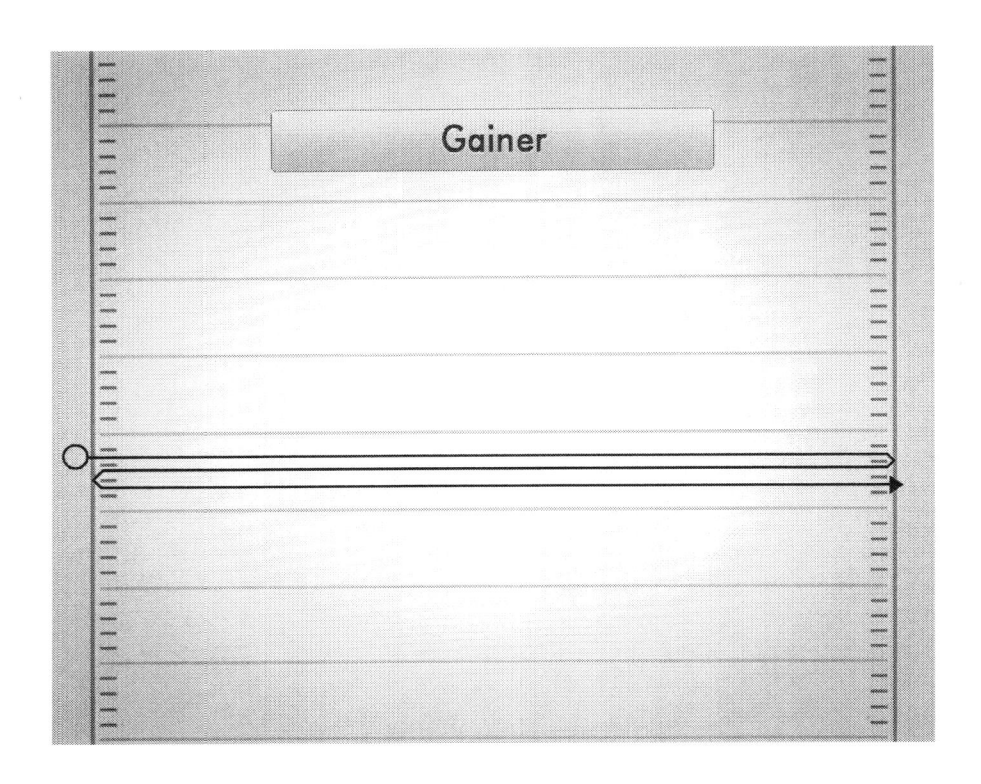

SETUP

Line your players up on one sideline. This conditioning drill will use the full width of the field so make sure it is clear of obstructions.

EQUIPMENT: NONE

DRILL TYPE: PHYSICAL PERFORMANCE, CONDITIONING

Gainer

| EASY | INDIVIDUAL | NO-CONTACT |

PURPOSE

Building endurance is an often overlooked attribute for a football team because it is less glamorous than other attributes. Nonetheless, it is a very necessary one. Running the consecutive lengths of the field will allow your team to GAIN endurance and have better conditioning.

DRILL DESCRIPTION

The Gainer is a classic conditioning drill that strengthens your team's endurance levels. With all participants lined up on one sideline, begin the drill by having them run to the other sideline. After touching the sideline with their hand, turn back around to the starting sideline. Once more touch that sideline and finish on the far sideline for three entire lengths of the width of the football field where they will recover until the next repetition of the drill.

Due to the fact that this is a conditioning drill, it is absolutely imperative that each player makes it across the entirety of the field and physically touches the far sideline with their hand before turning back around. This has three main purposes. 1) Squatting low enough to touch the line with your hand requires an extra movement and use of your leg muscles in order to have a greater effect for conditioning purposes. 2) If they do not reach all the way to the sideline, they are cheating themselves out of conditioning and will result in a weaker player that fatigues quicker. 3) Conditioning builds disciple, and cutting corners hurts both their physical strength, as well as, their mental strength.

40 Yard Dash

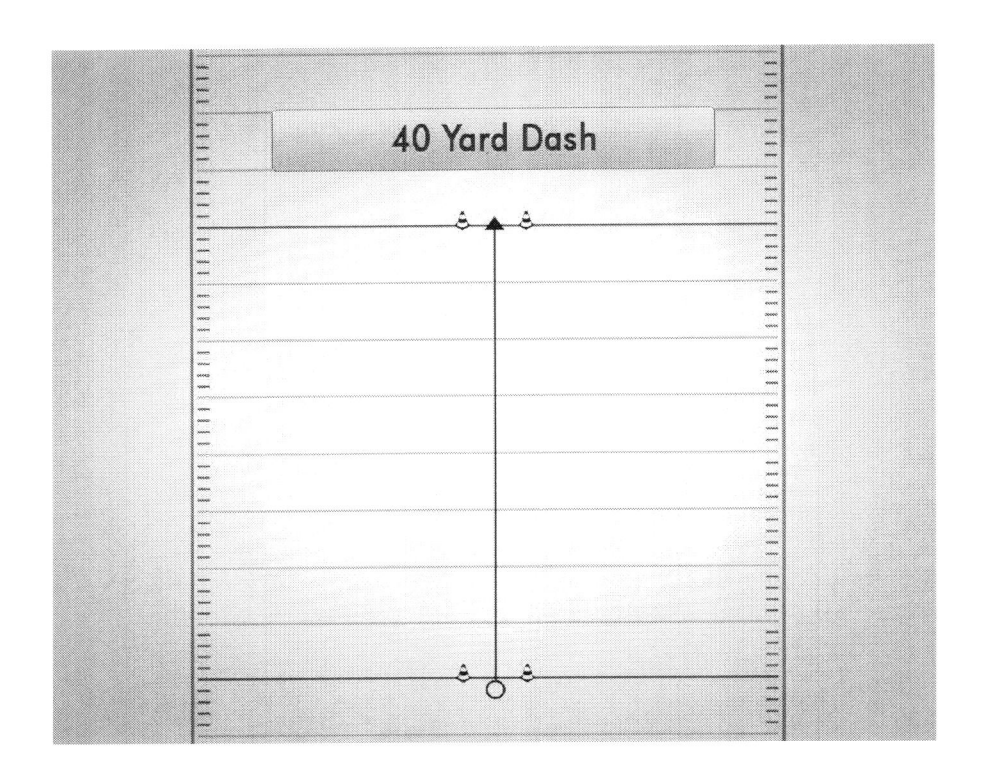

SETUP

Mark off 40 yards and indicate both the starting line and the finish line. If timing the drill, set up the timers even with the finish line.

EQUIPMENT: CONE, TIMER

DRILL TYPE: PHYSICAL PERFORMANCE, EVALUATION, SPEED

40 Yard Dash

EASY | INDIVIDUAL | NO-CONTACT

PURPOSE

Primarily used as an evaluation drill, the 40 Yard Dash measures the amount of time it takes an athlete to run 40 yards in a straight line. Both initial acceleration and full speed are an important aspect of this drill.

DRILL DESCRIPTION

At its core, the 40 Yard Dash is simply a straight line sprint that focuses both on acceleration and top speed. Unlike other football situations, however, this drill is no started by a snap count or some other sort of external command. Instead, this drill is begun voluntarily at the athlete's sole discretion. Therefore, the timer must closely watch the players first movement in order to begin timing the drill.

Advanced athletes will get in a three-point stance with their hand on the starting line and their feet moved as close as possible to the line in order to gain every inch of momentum towards the finish line at the very start.

The 40 Yard Dash is the most commonly used drill to measure an athlete's speed and is often the most talked about portion of the NFL combine.

Weave Drill

Backward — Forward | *Shuffle — Forward*

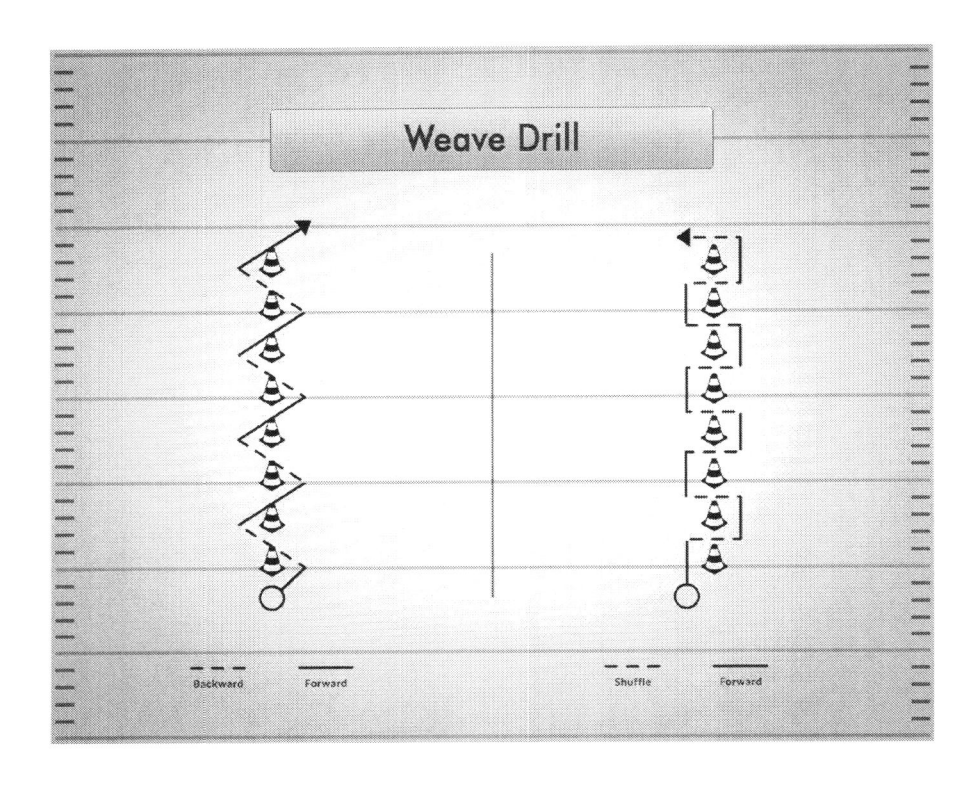

SETUP

Place eight cones in a straight line with two and a half yards of space in between them, which allows players to weave in between the cones.

TECHNIQUES:	FOOTWORK
EQUIPMENT:	CONE
DRILL TYPE:	PHYSICAL PERFORMANCE, SPEED, AGILITY

Weave Drill

INTERMEDIATE **INDIVIDUAL** **NO-CONTACT**

PURPOSE

Utilize this drill to work on player quickness and change of direction. When a player loses their footing on the football field because they try and fail to quickly change direction, it can ruin the entire play. This drill requires your players to build up the muscle memory it takes to quickly and safely change directions.

DRILL DESCRIPTION

There are two different versions of the weave drill that both feature different types of changes of direction.

The first version alternates players between a forward sprint to a backward back peddle. Each player takes a few quick steps forward, then opens up their hips to begin a back peddle at an angel. Due to the face that this drill alternates the angels of the turns, it requires players to open up their hips and work on a different angle of the footwork and agility.

The second version alternates players between a forward sprint and a sideways shuffle. Each player sprints forward in between cones, and after passing a cone, takes two shuffle steps to the side, before entering a sprint forward again past the next cone.

Clockwork Drill

SETUP

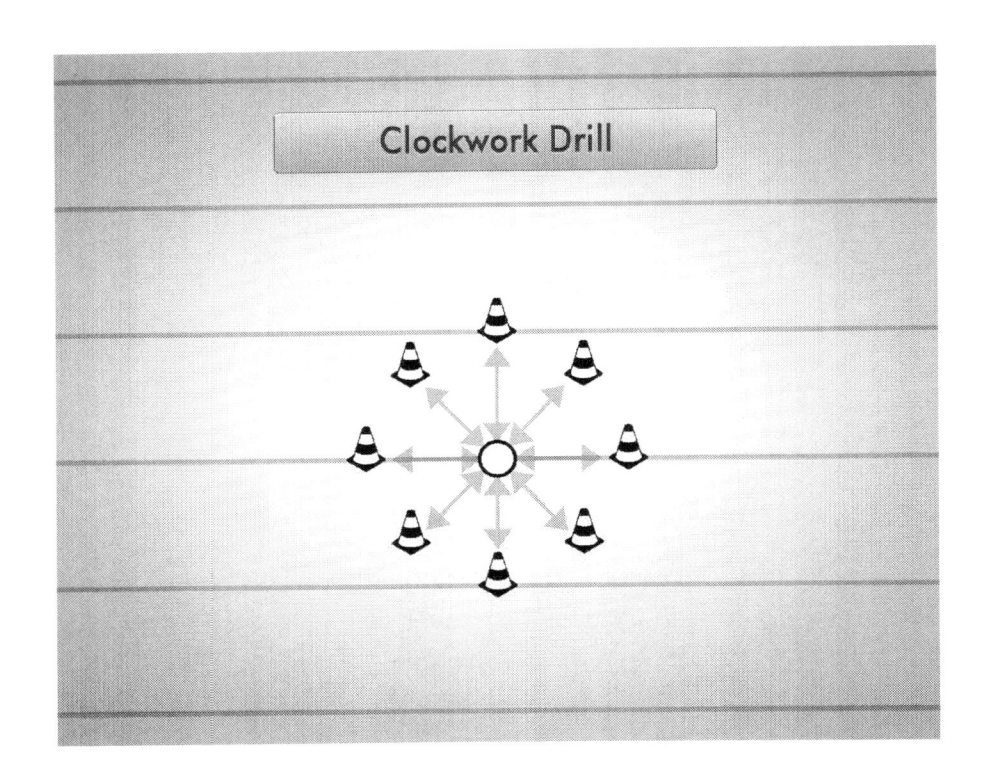

Place eight cones in a circle with a diameter of ten yards. The player begins this drill be standing in the middle of the circle.

TECHNIQUES: **FOOTWORK**

EQUIPMENT: **CONE**

DRILL TYPE: **PHYSICAL PERFORMANCE, AGILITY, CONDITIONING**

Clockwork Drill

INTERMEDIATE   **INDIVIDUAL**   **NO-CONTACT**

PURPOSE

This drill can be used towards the end of practice to work on both agility and conditioning.

DRILL DESCRIPTION

A player starts in the middle of a circle of cones and will traverse through the circle that makes his route look like the hands of a clock.

Starting in the middle, the player will run to the cone directly in front of him and then return to the center. After returning to the center he will change his angle and run to the next cone. Eventually, the player will touch each cone in a clockwise order and return to the center after each one. After he has made it all the way around the clock, the drill is complete.

Star Drill

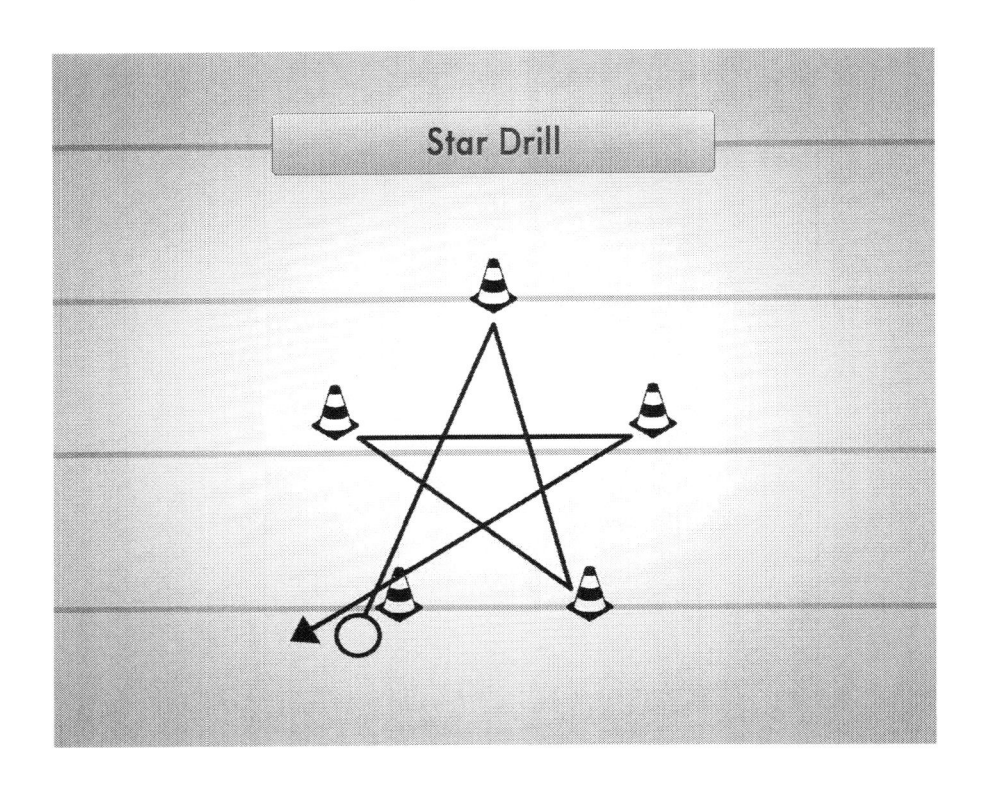

SETUP

Place five cones on the field in a pattern that marks the five outer points of a star. The start should have a height of 10 yards, which the markings of a football field will identify for you.

TECHNIQUES:	**FOOTWORK**
EQUIPMENT:	**CONE**
DRILL TYPE:	**PHYSICAL PERFORMANCE, SPEED, AGILITY**

Star Drill

ADVANCED   **INDIVIDUAL**   **NO-CONTACT**

PURPOSE

Build quickness by having players traverse through a star shaped course with many changes of directions.

DRILL DESCRIPTION

Line up each of the drill's participants behind the bottom left cone of the star. Make sure that players know the pattern that they will use to traverse the star.

Players will start in the bottom left and run to the top cone, quickly change direction, and go to the bottom right cone, then the far left cone, then the far right cone, then back across the face of the bottom left cone that they started from.

After the player has finished by crossed the face of the next player in line, then the next player should begin and continue until all players have gone once.

After all players have ran through the drill, switch the starting cone to the bottom right cone so that they will have to turn to the left for each change of direction to even it out.

T Drill

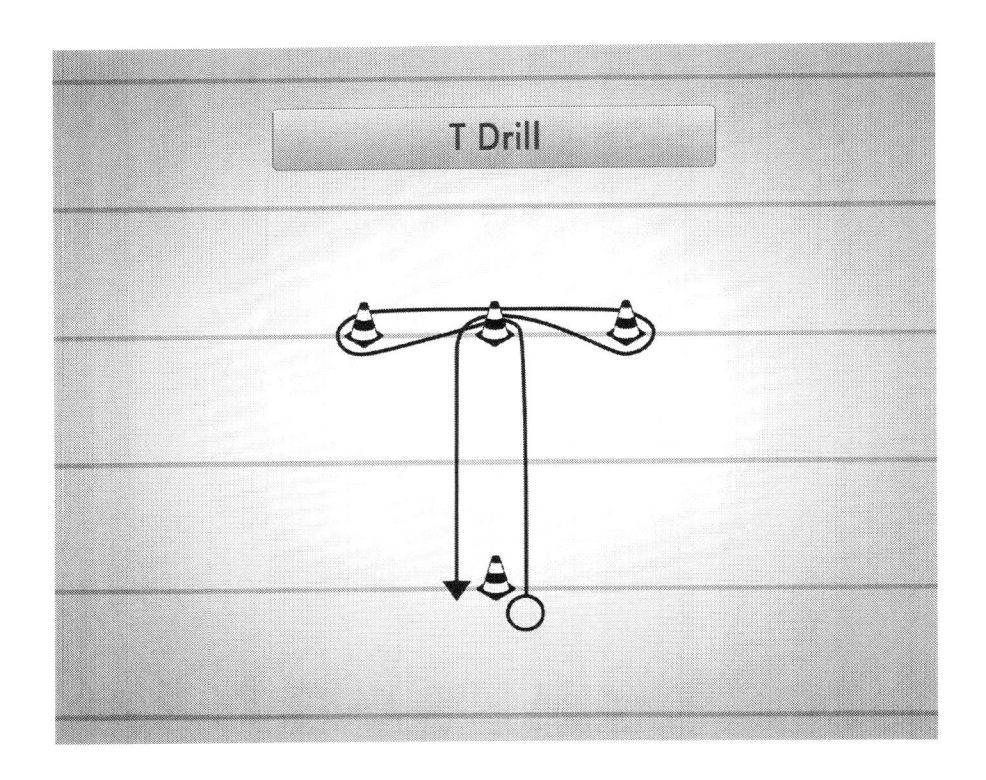

SETUP

Place four cones into a capital T. The height of the T should be ten yards, and the three cones forming the top of the T should each be three yards apart.

TECHNIQUES:	FOOTWORK
EQUIPMENT:	CONE
DRILL TYPE:	PHYSICAL PERFORMANCE, SPEED, AGILITY

T Drill

INTERMEDIATE **INDIVIDUAL** **NO-CONTACT**

PURPOSE

Athletes will gain a better understanding of how to quickly turn on the football field. This drill features two 90 degree turns and two complete 180 degree turns with three sections of ten yard sprints throughout.

DRILL DESCRIPTION

Athletes start at the bottom of the T and begin the drill by sprinting forward and around the middle cone. After reaching the first cone, they will come under, and go around the side cone. After performing a 180 degree turn around the side cone, they will traverse over and across the top of the T. After performing one more 180 degree turn around the other outside cone, they will come back over the middle cone and spring through the finish line past the initial bottom cone.

Tug of War

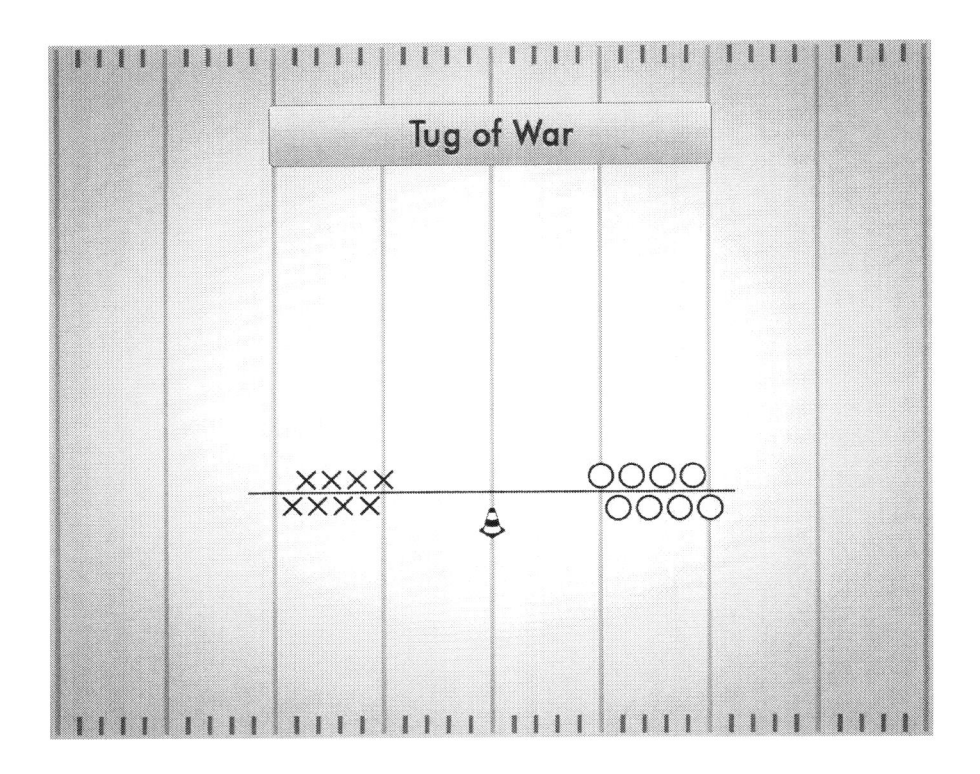

SETUP

Place a long, strong rope across the field with a cone placed in the middle of the competition.

Select two teams of players and distribute them on each side of the cone. The front player from each team will stand five yards away from the center cone.

EQUIPMENT: CONE

DRILL TYPE: PHYSICAL PERFORMANCE, TEAMWORK, COMPETITION

Tug of War

INTERMEDIATE   GROUP   NO-CONTACT

PURPOSE

This is a team building exercise that not only builds physical strength and fitness, but also creates camaraderie and a splash of fun among teammates.

DRILL DESCRIPTION

Warning: Do not allow anybody to tie the rope, or wrap the rope around any part of their body in any way! It is extremely dangerous to tie the rope or wrap it around any part of one's body as it will aggressively be ripped and pulled and can cause serious harm!

For safety purposes, have a whistle ready to be blown at the first sign of any danger. Instruct all players to drop the rope immediately upon the first sound of the whistle, regardless of whether or not the competition has been won or has come to a conclusion.

Upon starting the competition, both sides will tug on their rope and attempt to pull the other team over the center line. The first team to step across the center line loses and the competition has been won.

Break Down Drill

SETUP

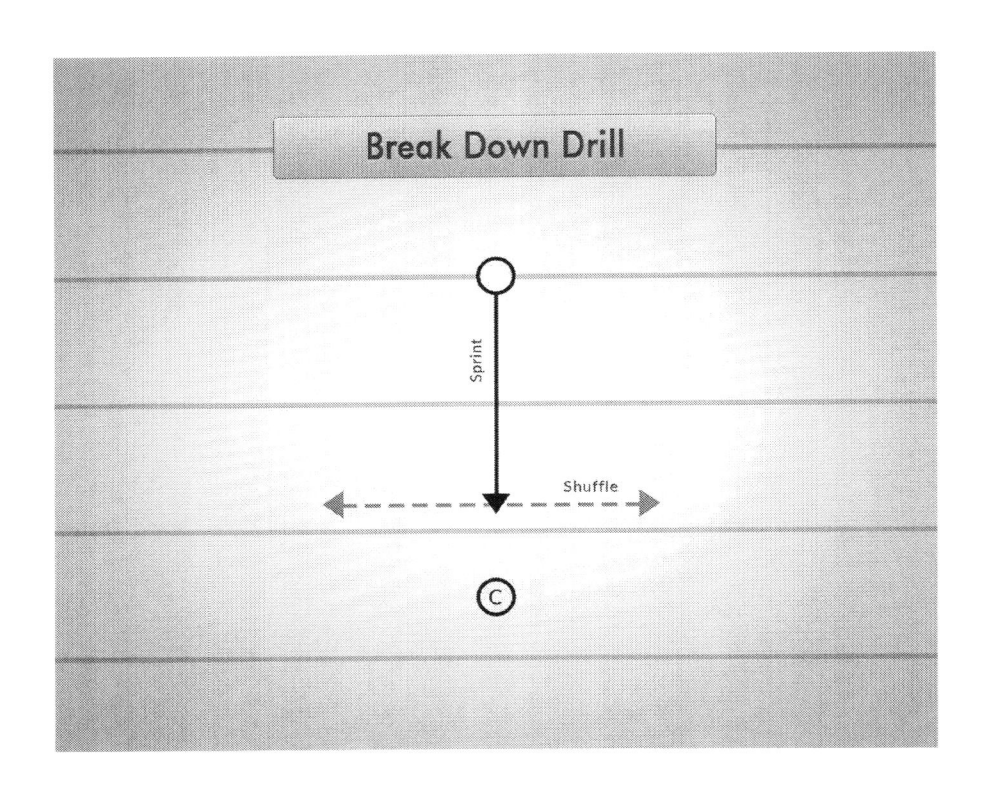

Player(s) simply stand roughly 12 yards in front of a coach.

TECHNIQUES:	**FOOTWORK**
EQUIPMENT:	**NONE**
DRILL TYPE:	**PHYSICAL PERFORMANCE, SKILL, SPEED, AGILITY**

Break Down Drill

EASY   GROUP   NO-CONTACT

PURPOSE

A lot of times, the wisest option for a defender charging towards a ball carrier is to break down and shuffle sideways in order to maintain his position in front of the ball carrier so that he does not miss the tackle. This drill works on the fitness and footwork involved in this situation.

DRILL DESCRIPTION

Coaches signal for the player(s) to spring forward towards the coach while keeping their head up and eyes on the coach. After a few yards, the coach points to one side or the other. Players then break down from their sprint and begin shuffling to the side signaled by the coach.

After a few steps of shuffles, the coach then points in the other direction, and players reverse the direction of their shuffle.

The coach continues for a few more changes of direction before the drill is finished and reset.

Barrel Role Drill

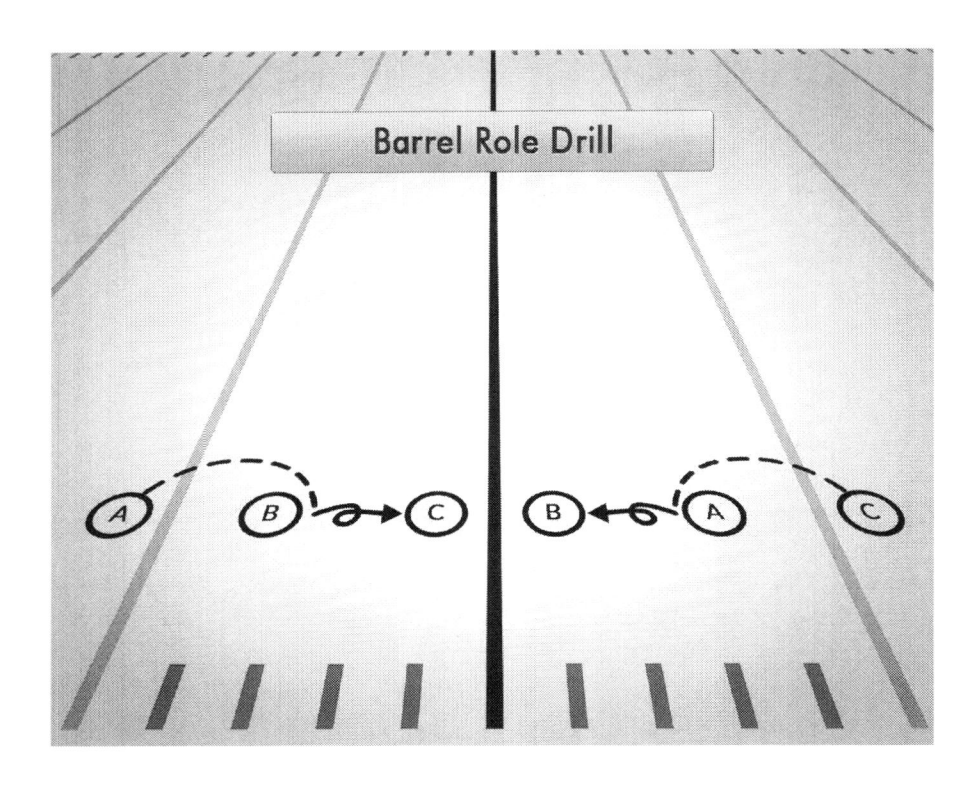

SETUP

Three players line up and lay face down in a push up position with a gap of space in between each other.

EQUIPMENT:	NONE
DRILL TYPE:	PHYSICAL PERFORMANCE, TEAMWORK

Barrel Role Drill

EASY | **GROUP** | **CONTACT**

PURPOSE

This drill does not have a direct football skill associated with it, however, it does have three purposes for players on a football team. 1) This drill teaches teamwork and cooperation. If one player fails to execute his job at the proper time in coordination with his teammates, the group will fail as a whole. This drill helps builds teamwork at the beginning of a season.   2) At younger levels, this drill also gives players a feeling and a sense for how their pads absorb contact, as they will continually throw their bodies at the ground.   3) Constant repetitions of this drill build condition and endurance.   This is a good conditioning drill because it requires strength, endurance, and focus throughout.

DRILL DESCRIPTION

Three players (A, B, & C) start face down in a push up position and continuously perform a rolling rotation where the outside player jumps in between the two other players.

Step 1: Player A jumps out of his pushup position and over Player B. As soon as he lands, he rolls towards and underneath Player C.

Step 2: Player C then jumps out of his pushup position and over the rolling Player A.   As soon as he lands, he begins rolling towards Player B.

Player B is now in Player A's starting position from Step 1, and this rotation continues until the coaches stop the drill.

Criss Cross Drill

SETUP

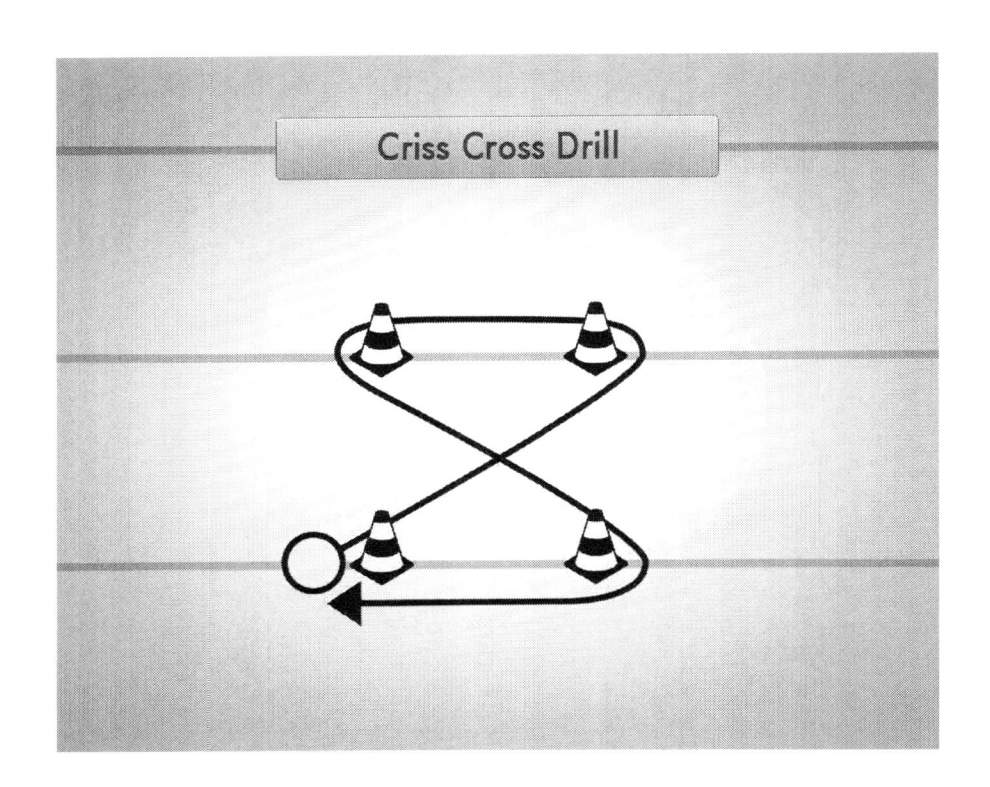

Place four cones in a 5 yard by 5 yard square.

EQUIPMENT:	CONE
DRILL TYPE:	PHYSICAL PERFORMANCE, AGILITY

Criss Cross Drill

INTERMEDIATE   INDIVIDUAL   NO-CONTACT

PURPOSE

Work on the ability for players to quickly decelerate and accelerate in and out of turns.

DRILL DESCRIPTION

Players will cross the course diagonally two times throughout this drill while maintaining a full forward run throughout the entirety of the rep.

Start the drill by diagonally crossing to the opposite cone, then turn around and run across the top of the drill, before diagonally crossing again and turning around to complete the drill by sprinting through the bottom side.

Alternate the side of the starting cone so that the number of turns to each side is evened out.

Tornado Twist

SETUP

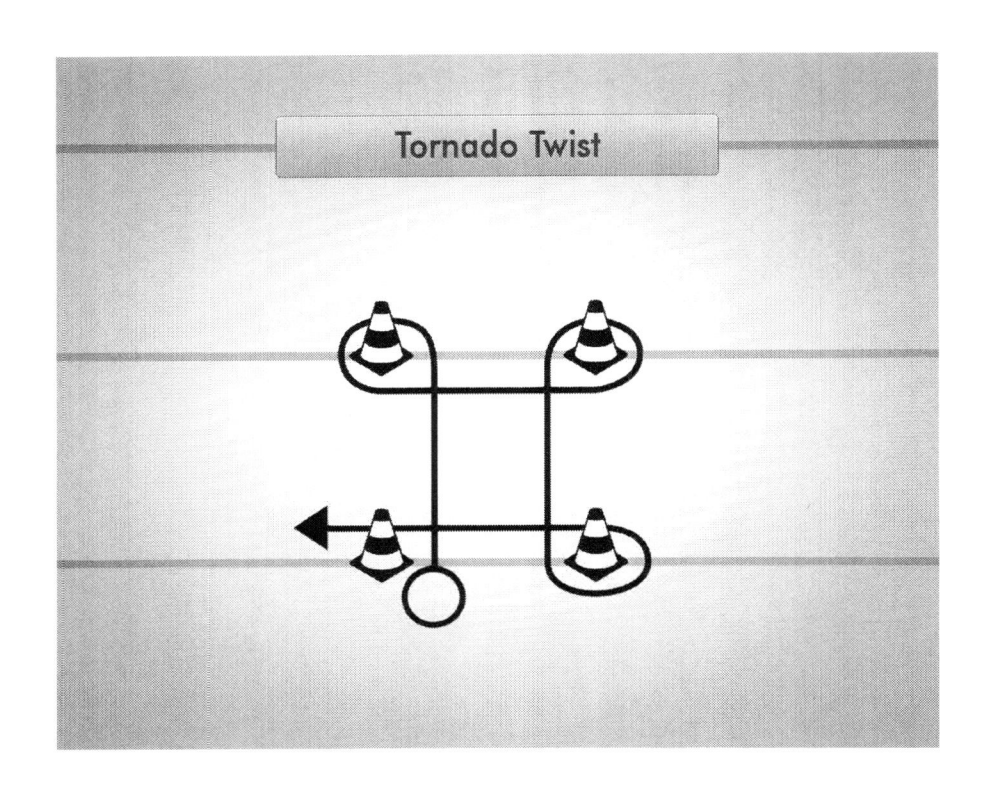

Place four cones in a 5 yard by 5 yard square.

EQUIPMENT: CONE

DRILL TYPE: PHYSICAL PERFORMANCE, AGILITY

Tornado Twist

INTERMEDIATE **INDIVIDUAL** **NO-CONTACT**

PURPOSE

Build agility and speed up the ability to swiftly turn around.

DRILL DESCRIPTION

Start on the inside of the square. Each cone will require a 360 degree turn across the inside before moving on to the next turn. This drill requires three full 360 degree turns to really focus on work on player agility and turning ability.

Alternate the side of the starting cone so that the number of turns to each side is evened out.

Arrowhead Drill

SETUP

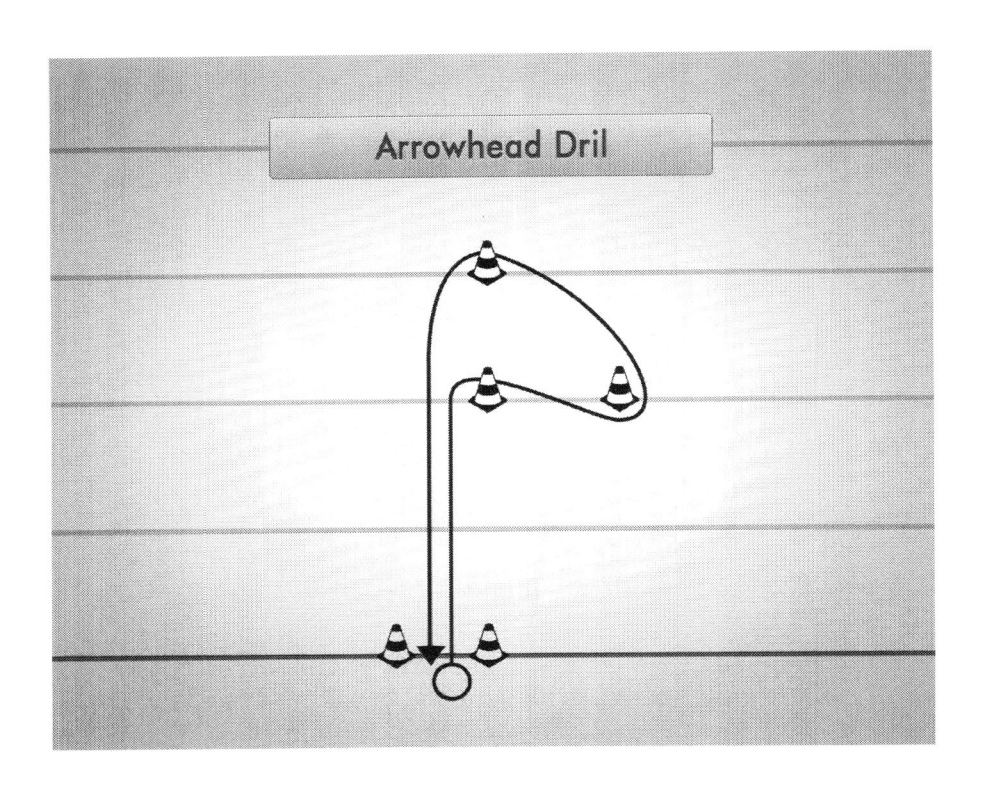

Mark the starting line which will also operate as the finish line. Place other cones 10 and 15 yards away from the starting line in a straight line, with an additional cone five yards to the side of the middle, 10 yard cone.

EQUIPMENT: **CONE**

DRILL TYPE: **PHYSICAL PERFORMANCE, EVALUATION, AGILITY**

Arrowhead Drill

EASY | INDIVIDUAL | NO-CONTACT

PURPOSE

This drill can be used as an evaluation drill to see how quickly athletes can make their way throughout turns on the field.

DRILL DESCRIPTION

Names for the shape of the route that athletes run in this drill, the Arrowhead Drill forces athletes to maneuver around two sharp turns and run for over 40 yards throughout the drill.

Players should remain close to the cones throughout their turns, without knocking them over. The sharper and quicker that players curl around the cones will allow them to complete the drill with a faster time.

Rendezvous Relay

SETUP

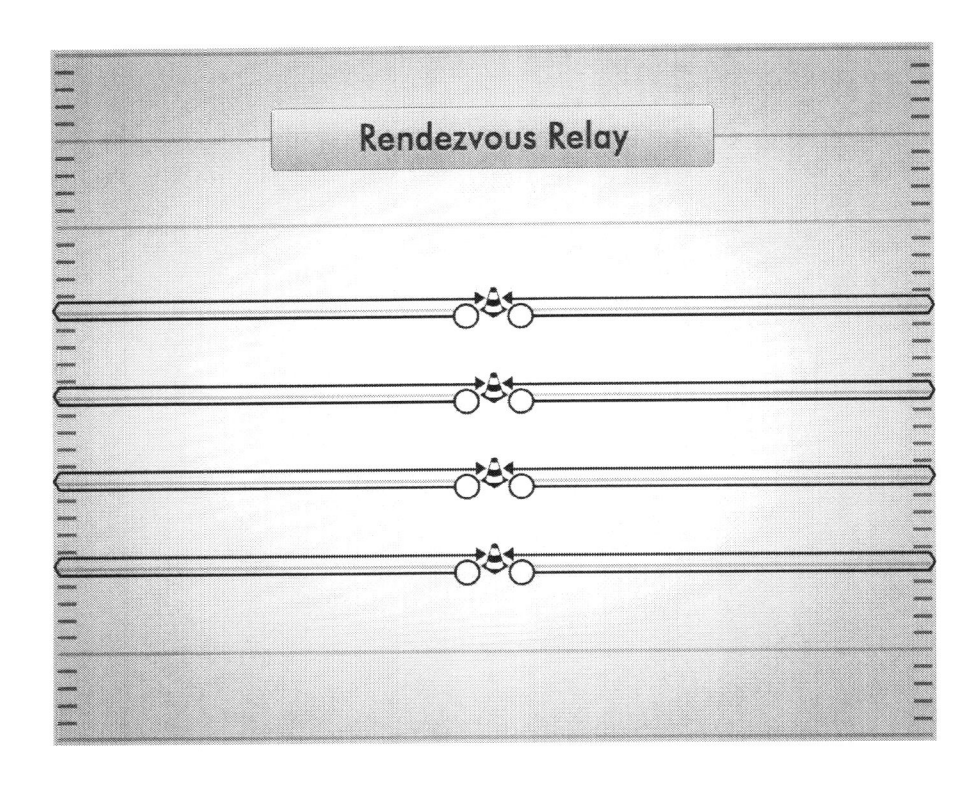

Players partner up and run this relay together as a partnership team. Cones are placed in the center of the field for each partnership to indicate the starting point.

EQUIPMENT: CONE

DRILL TYPE: PHYSICAL PERFORMANCE, CONDITIONING, COMPETITION

Rendezvous Relay

INTERMEDIATE   **PARTNER**   **NO-CONTACT**

PURPOSE

The Rendezvous Relay can turn the conditioning portion of practice into a fun competitive game. It is easier for players to push themselves harder if there is some form of tangible competition that they can aim for. This drill provides that competitive outlet for conditioning time.

DRILL DESCRIPTION

For each leg, one of the partners starts from the center cone and sprints to the sideline, touching it with their hand, then turns around and finishes their leg by running back to the center cone and tapping their partner's hand. As soon as partners tap hands, the other partner may begin his portion of the drill by running to the opposite sideline and returning to the center. After each player in the partnership has touched the sideline and returned, they have completed one entire leg.

Coaches can determine the length of this drill by specifying the number of legs that players must run. For example, the quickest version of this drill is making the partnership run one leg. However, to utilize this drill as a competitive conditioning drill, this drill can require as many as four or more legs per partnership.

Players can not leave from the center cone until their partner touches their hand. If contact is not made, then that team is disqualified from the competition.

Desperado Dash

SETUP

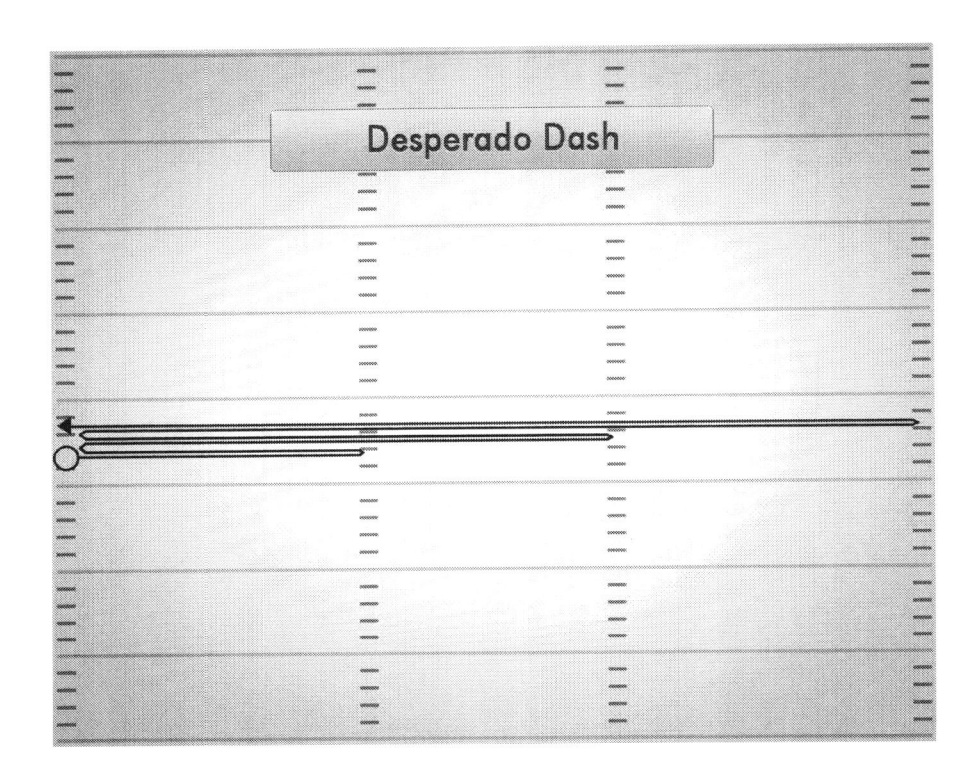

Prepare players for this drill by having all participants spread out on one of the sidelines.

EQUIPMENT: NONE

DRILL TYPE: PHYSICAL PERFORMANCE, CONDITIONING

Desperado Dash

EASY | **INDIVIDUAL** | **NO-CONTACT**

PURPOSE

This is a hardcore conditioning drill where players will run a long distance with many changes of direction. Finish off the practice with this conditioning drill to drain every last bit of energy and get every last bit of muscle fatigue and cardio out of players so that they will have the edge when desperate times come in real games.

DRILL DESCRIPTION

Players start on one sideline and will have three different landmarks to run for throughout the drill. Each time they reach a landmark, they will bend down and touch it with their hand before they return back to the initial sideline.

The three landmarks are the three sets of hashes on a football field. The first leg is the close hash, the second leg is the far hash, and the third leg is the far sideline. Upon returning from each of these landmarks, the drill has concluded.

Snake Drill

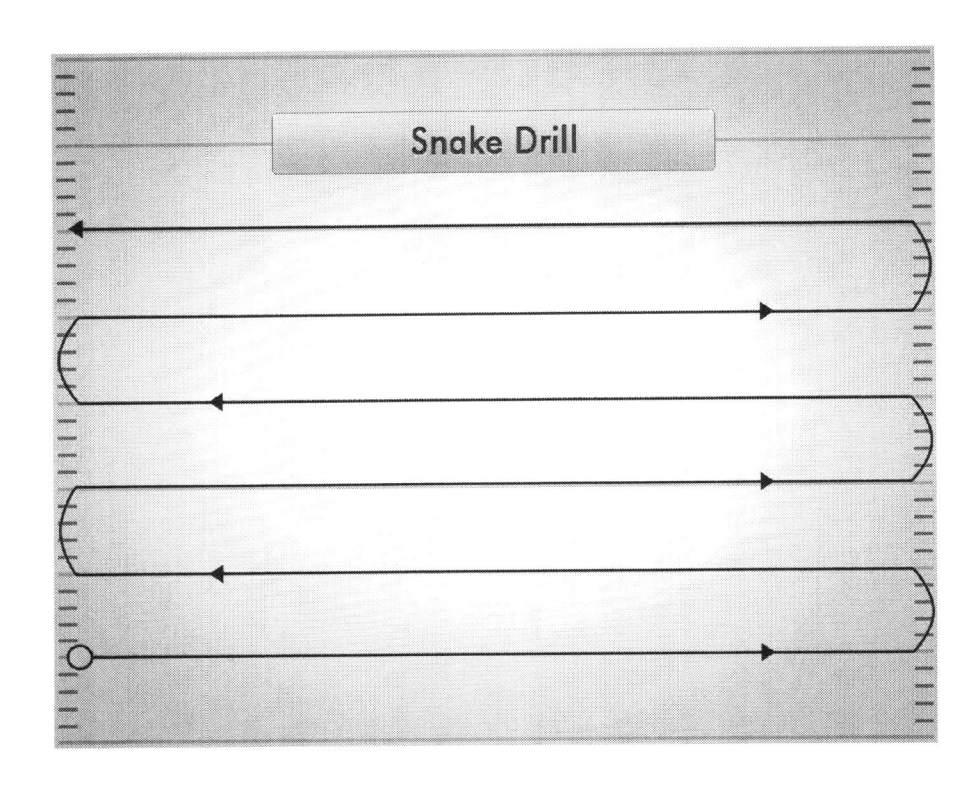

SETUP

Players begin the drill at the intersection of the sideline and the first yard line.

EQUIPMENT: NONE

DRILL TYPE: PHYSICAL PERFORMANCE, CONDITIONING

Snake Drill

EASY | **INDIVIDUAL** | **NO-CONTACT**

PURPOSE

This is a conditioning drill with the purpose of equipping players with better endurance.

DRILL DESCRIPTION

Players trace the yard lines of the football field as they snake around from sideline to sideline until they have snaked through the entire field.

To add even more conditioning to this drill, coaches can utilize their whistles to stop players and guide them through up-downs in place, until they release them to continue snaking the field.

Goalpost Relay

SETUP

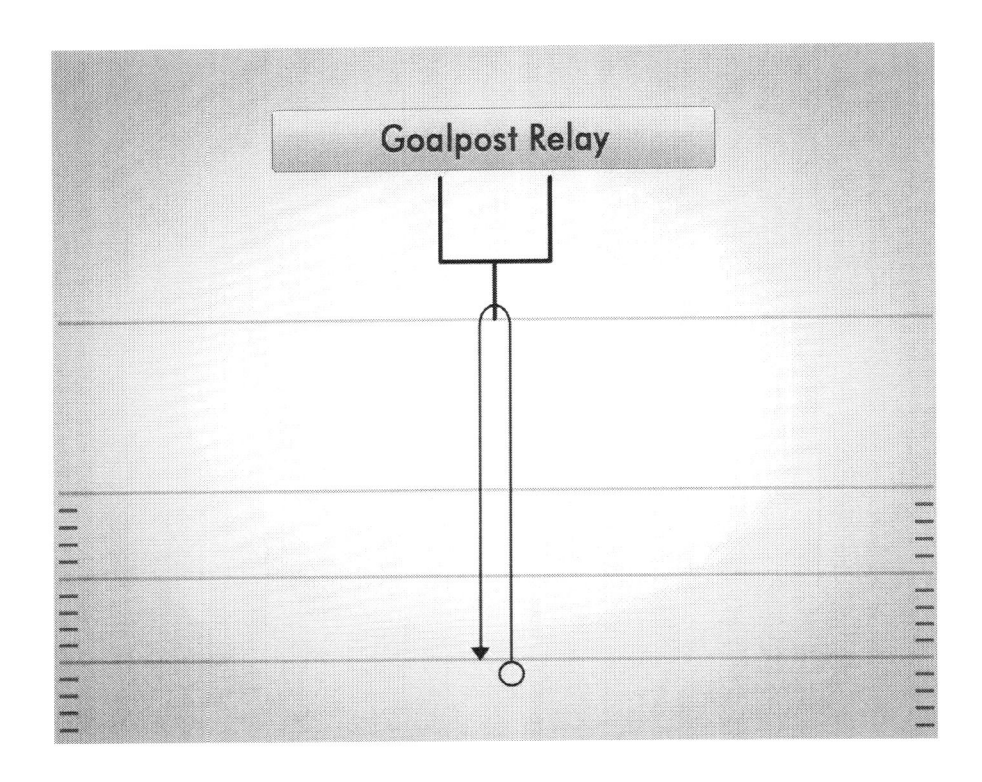

Players grab a partner and position themselves on the starting line. The starting line can be determined by the yard line that provides the desired conditioning effect for the drill.

EQUIPMENT: NONE

DRILL TYPE: PHYSICAL
PERFORMANCE, CONDITIONING, TEAMWORK, COMPETITION

Goalpost Relay

INTERMEDIATE   PARTNER   NO-CONTACT

PURPOSE

A competitive way to incorporate conditioning and teamwork into the practice.

DRILL DESCRIPTION

One of the two players in each partnership begins the drill by running towards the goalpost. The entire team runs this at once, so there will be a competition to jockey for position to get the inside track around the goalpost.

After running around the goalpost, the player then returns to the starting line and most touch his partner's hand to release his partner for his leg of the relay. Players are not allowed to leave the starting line until they have been tagged by their partner. Leaving too early results in automatic disqualification, and the player must return back to the starting line before running around the goalpost.

Coaches assign the number of legs that each player is required to run in order to get the desired conditioning effect.

W Drill

Sprint
---- Back Peddle

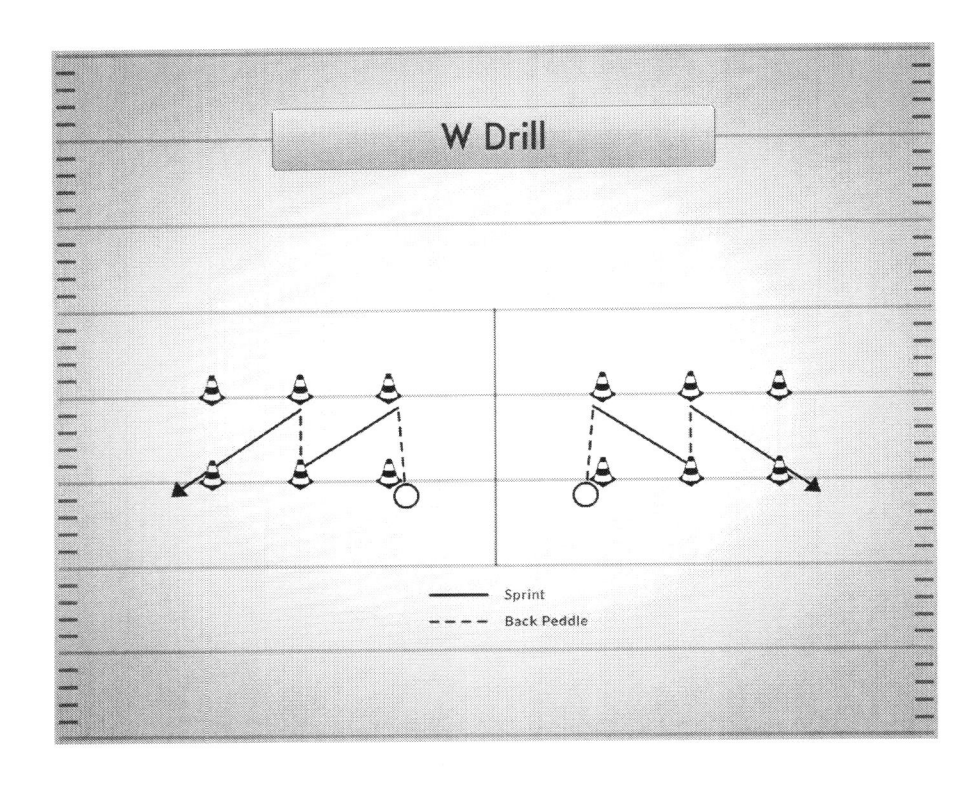

SETUP

Place two sets of three cones with a distance of five yards in between each cone to make a rectangle with a height of five yards and a width of ten yards.

TECHNIQUES: FOOTWORK

EQUIPMENT: CONE

DRILL TYPE: PHYSICAL PERFORMANCE, AGILITY

W Drill

EASY   **INDIVIDUAL**   **NO-CONTACT**

PURPOSE

Build quickness while transitioning from a back peddle into a forward sprint. This agility drill is particularly beneficial for defensive players so that they can make quick reactions and plays on the ball.

DRILL DESCRIPTION

Players back peddle directly backward for five yards, before they plant their foot into the ground and launch forward at a 45 degree angle to the front middle cone. After they have arrived to the front middle cone, they transition into a straight back peddle to the back center cone. One more transition forward at a 45 degree angle and sprinting through the final front cone will finish the "W" path and the drill is complete.

Alternate the starting direction so that players get an even amount of work cutting to each angle.

Short Box Drill

— Sprint
- - - Back Peddle

SETUP

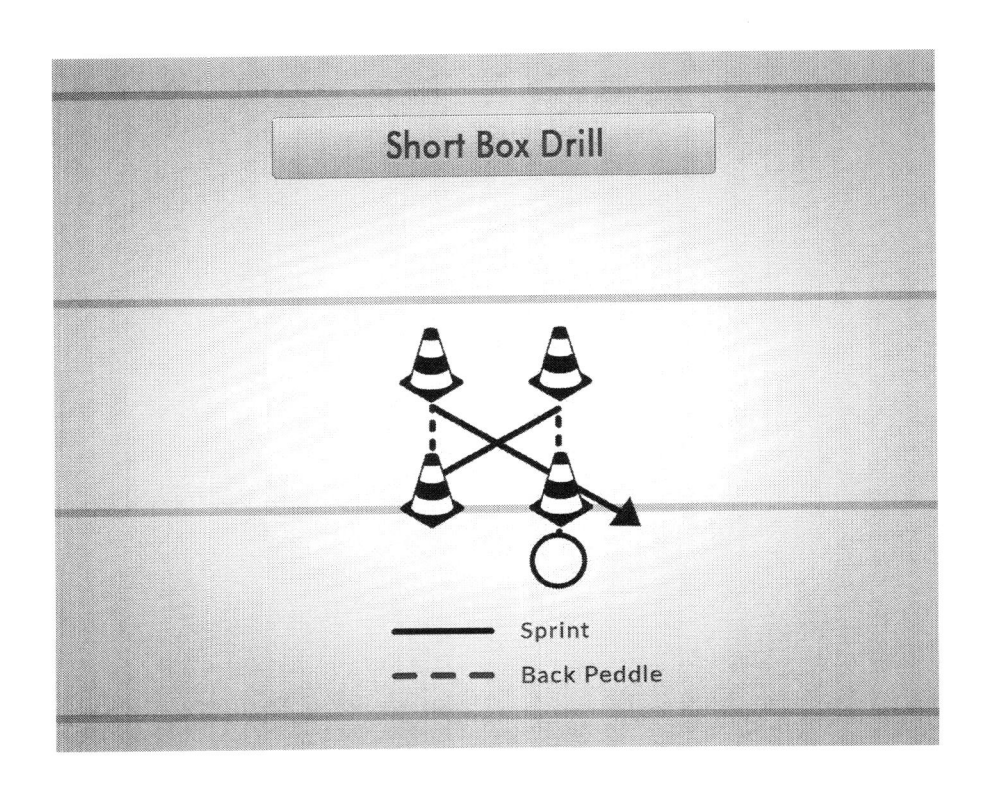

Place four cones in a three yard by 3 yard square.

TECHNIQUES: FOOTWORK

EQUIPMENT: CONE

DRILL TYPE: PHYSICAL PERFORMANCE, AGILITY

Short Box Drill

EASY | INDIVIDUAL | NO-CONTACT

PURPOSE

Quickly alternating between forward and backward movements is very important in the defensive backfield and allows defenders to quickly make adjustments while guarding against the offensive attack.

DRILL DESCRIPTION

Players make quick sharp transitions by alternating between a back peddle and a 45 degree angle cut forward. Players reach each cone one time before finishing through the starting cone.

Race Drill

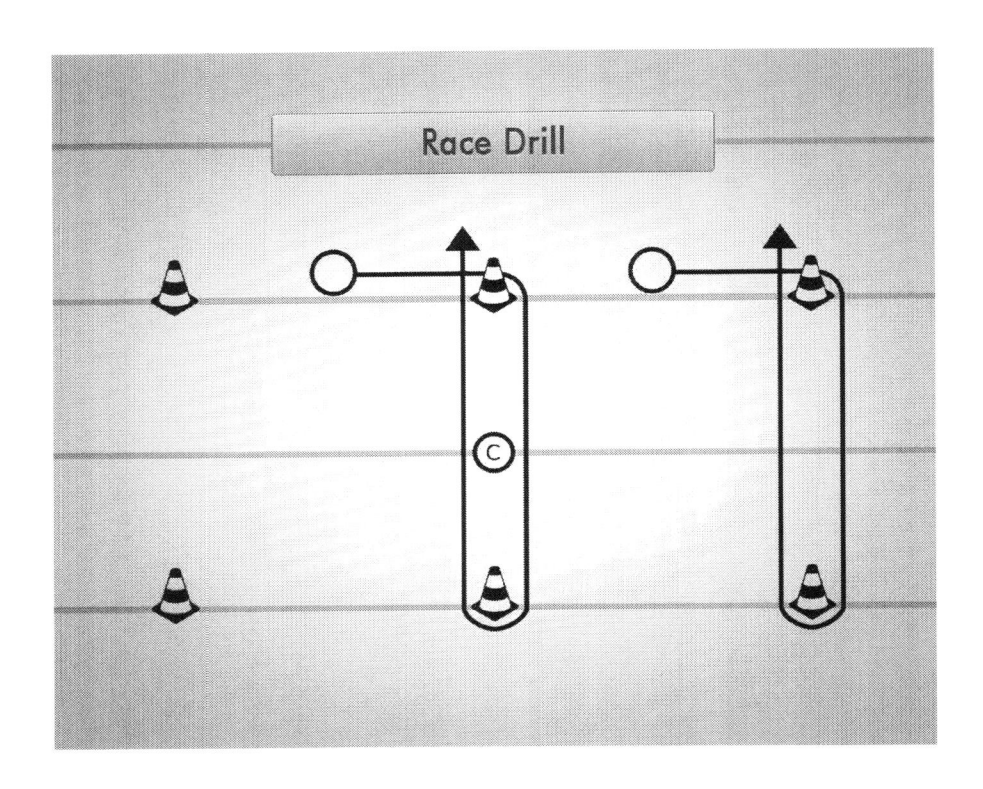

SETUP

Place three cones in s straight line with ten yards of space between each cone. Position two players in the middle of the gaps of each of these cones. Then place three more cones in the same pattern ten yards in front of the initial three cones. This will make a rectangle that is ten yards tall and twenty yards wide.

EQUIPMENT: CONE

DRILL TYPE: PHYSICAL PERFORMANCE, SPEED, AGILITY, COMPETITION

Race Drill

INTERMEDIATE   **PARTNER**   **NO-CONTACT**

PURPOSE

Create a sense of competition between teammates while training through an agility drill. The competitive nature of the race will stir up the competitive spirit in each of the players and cause them to push themselves as hard as they can.

Not only does this drill build player's ability to quickly maneuver around turns, but it also forces them to utilize a quick reaction time to get a better jump off of the starting block than their opponent.

DRILL DESCRIPTION

Players begin the drill with their feet shoulder width apart facing the coach. The coach starts the drill by saying "Ready!" and then pointing either to the right or to the left.

As soon as the coach point, the players take off in that direction and make a 90 degree cut around the first cone to that side. Players then race to the cone ten yards downfield before rounding it with a 180 degree turn and sprint back through the starting line to finish the race.

It is a fun racing drill that requires players to have a quick reaction off the start, turn twice, and run for a total of 25 yards in a race back to the finish line. Seeing their opponent out of the corner of their eyes will push them to make each turn faster and faster to catch up, or stay ahead of their competition.

Huddle Sprints

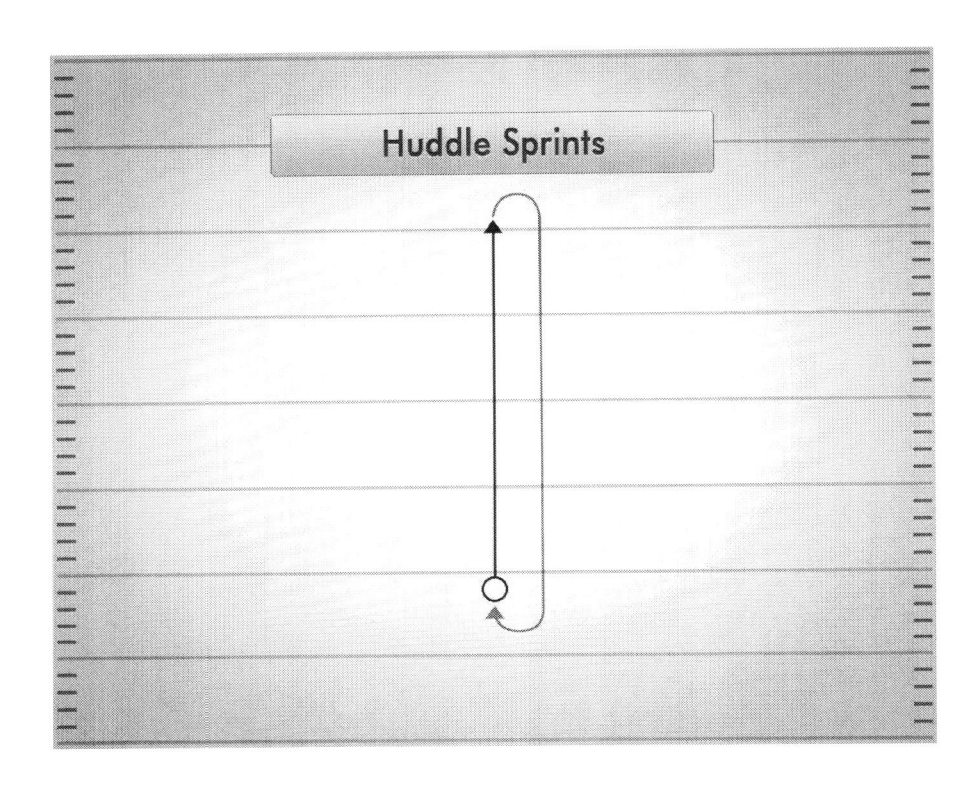

SETUP

Players line up with 20 yards of space cleared out in front of them.

EQUIPMENT:	TIMER
DRILL TYPE:	PHYSICAL PERFORMANCE, CONDITIONING

Huddle Sprints

INTERMEDIATE   INDIVIDUAL   NO-CONTACT

PURPOSE

This conditioning drill simulates the condition of a series of plays in a live football game.

The course of a play in a game consists of a sprint during the play, a jog back to the huddle, and a few seconds of rest while in the huddle. This pattern continues throughout the length of a drive, and the Huddle Sprints Drill mimics this behavior.

DRILL DESCRIPTION

Players spring forward 20 yards to simulate the action of a play. After the sprint, players then jog back to the starting line to simulate the run back to the huddle. Upon arriving to the starting line, they rest for 15 seconds to simulate the wait in a huddle.

Finally, players begin the rotation again and continue this pattern 10 or 20 more times throughout the duration of the drill.

This is a very effective conditioning drill because it very closely mimics the same anaerobic and aerobic conditions of a live football game.

Ball Drop Drill

SETUP

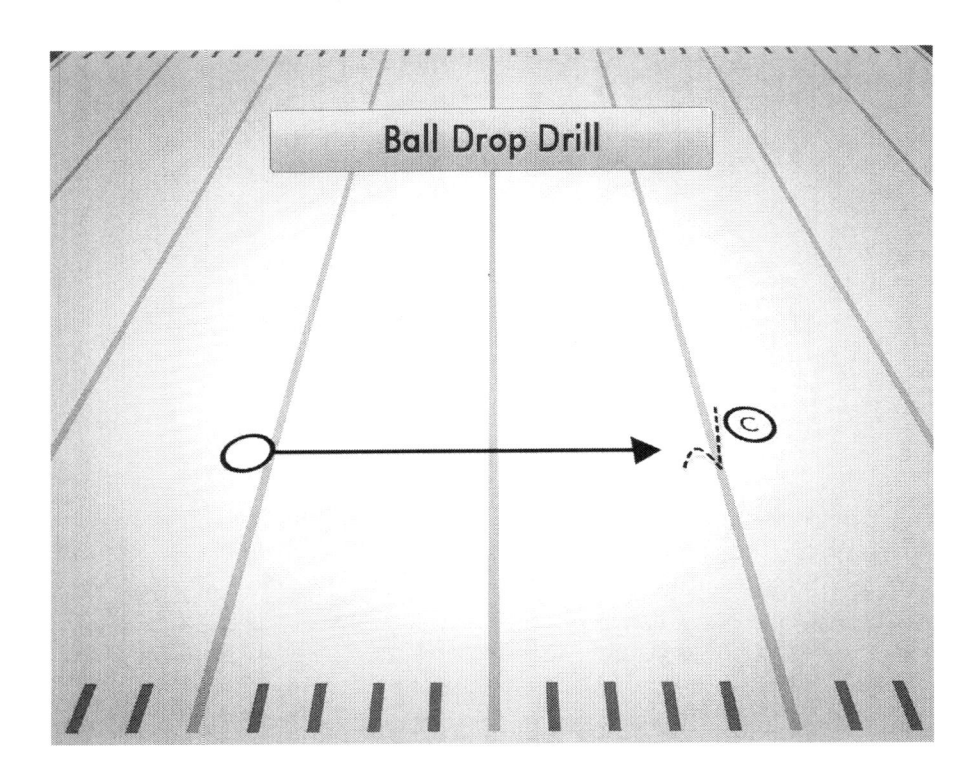

The Ball Drop Drill requires a tennis ball.

The coach stands roughly ten yards away from the player, depending on player speed.

EQUIPMENT:

DRILL TYPE: **PHYSICAL PERFORMANCE,   SPEED**

Ball Drop Drill

EASY   **INDIVIDUAL**   **NO-CONTACT**

PURPOSE

Reaction times are one of the most underrated attributes of a football player. However, quickly reacting to changes throughout the course of a play can make a major impact on the outcome.

The Ball Drop Drill develops a players ability to not only quickly react to an event, but also to blast to full speed from a stationary start.

DRILL DESCRIPTION

Holding the tennis ball out to the side of his body at shoulder height, the coach starts the drill by dropping the tennis ball straight down.

As soon as the tennis ball is released, the player bursts forward to catch the ball before it bounces for the second time. If the player is able to catch the ball before the second bounce, then you can gradually separate the distance between the player and coach to make it more and more difficult.

A quick explosion off of the line and an even quicker reaction time is necessary for players to have success with this drill.

Four Quarters Conditioning Drill

SETUP

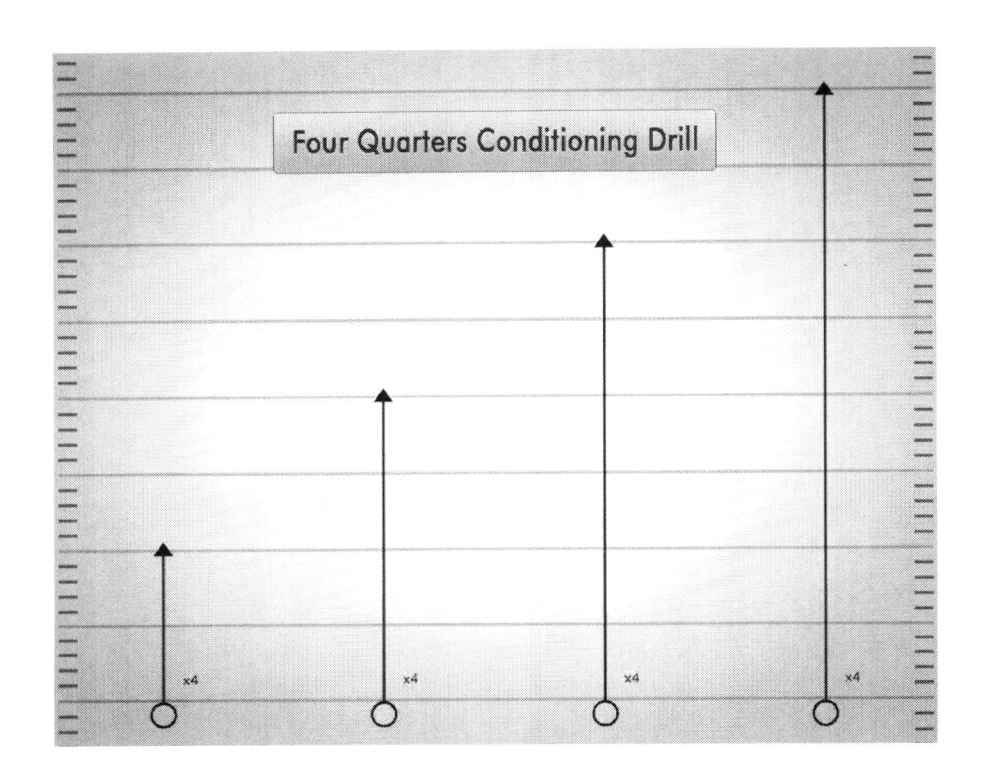

Players line up on the starting line with the field clear in front of them.

EQUIPMENT: NONE

DRILL TYPE: PHYSICAL PERFORMANCE, CONDITIONING

Four Quarters Conditioning Drill

INTERMEDIATE **INDIVIDUAL** **NO-CONTACT**

PURPOSE

This conditioning drill not only provides great endurance, but it also conditions the mental side of the game by building the mindset for players to keep fighting for all four quarters of a football game.

Split into four segments, this drill provides the mental challenge of fighting through four entire quarters, with each quarter getting more and more difficult.

DRILL DESCRIPTION

The drill is split into four quarters as follows:

1st Quarter: 4 sprints of 10 yards (10 seconds rest) 2nd Quarter: 4 sprints of 20 yards (20 seconds rest) 3rd Quarter: 4 sprints of 30 yards (30 seconds rest) 4th Quarter: 4 sprints of 40 yards (40 seconds rest)

Allow one to two minutes of rest in between each quarter before moving on.

If you really want to throw your players for a loop, add on an "overtime" and make them run one additional sprint for 100 yards to cap off the practice.

Fumble and Tumble Drill

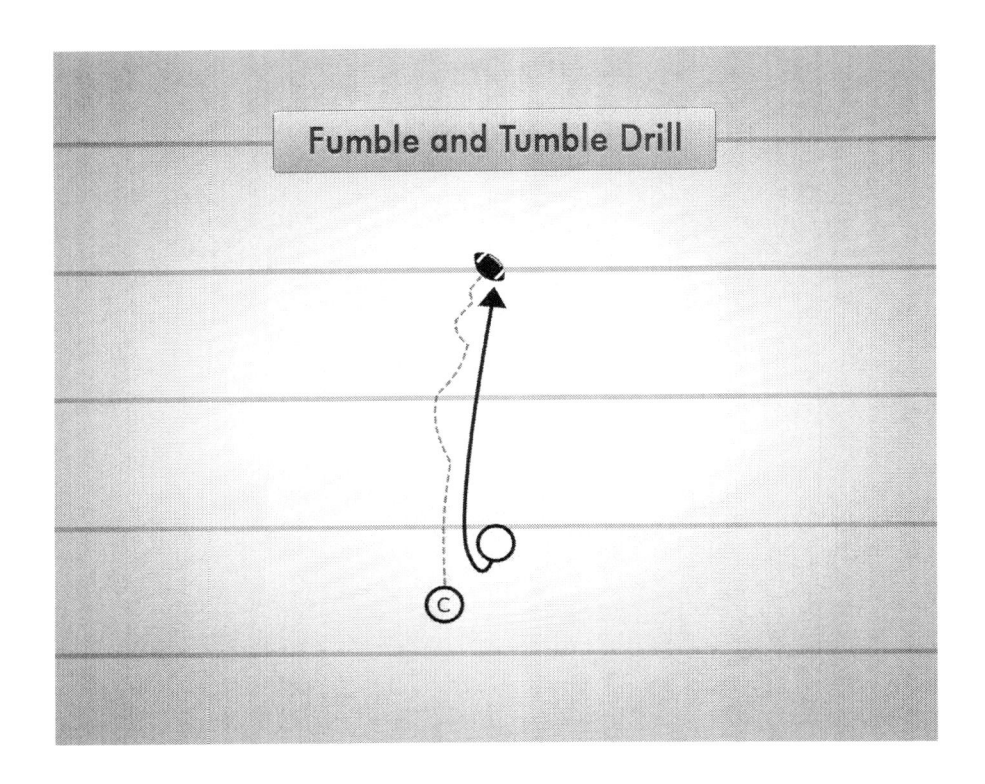

SETUP

Player lays face down in a pushup position on the ground pointing his head away from the drill. A coach with a football stands 2 yards away from the player.

EQUIPMENT: NONE

DRILL TYPE: PHYSICAL PERFORMANCE, SPEED, COORDINATION

Fumble and Tumble Drill

EASY   **INDIVIDUAL**   **NO-CONTACT**

PURPOSE

Whenever the football is on the ground in the middle of a play, it presents an absolutely critical opportunity in the game for one of the teams to recover the ball and gain possession.

The Fumble and Tumble Drill teaches players to quickly turn and recover a bouncing football while also working on their speed and quickness ability.

DRILL DESCRIPTION

A coach standing in view of the player rolls the football behind the player with enough power for the ball to roll at least ten yards down the field. As the coach begins to roll the ball, he says "Ball!" to the player which instructs him to go.

When the player sees the coach roll the football and hears him say "Ball!" the player pops up off of the ground and turns around to run after the football. As the player tracks down the bouncing football, he dives on top of the football to secure it on the ground.

Popcorn Drill

SETUP

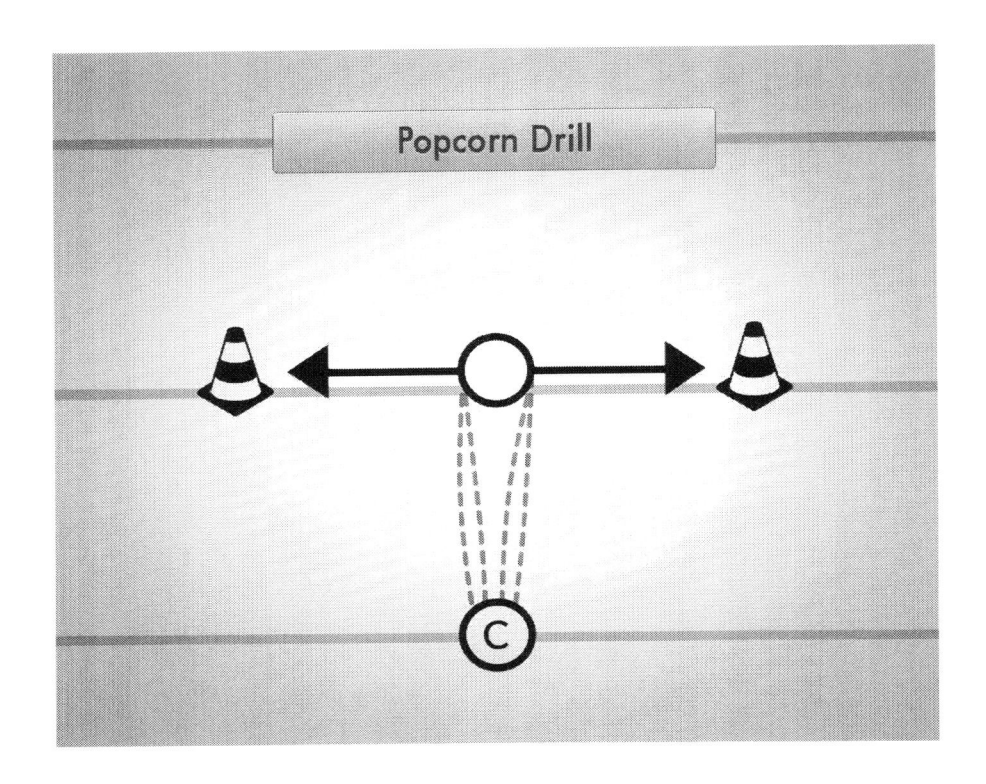

Place two cones ten yards apart and position a player in the middle of the cones. A coach stands five yards in front of the player and holds onto two footballs.

TECHNIQUES:	CATCHING, BALL CARRYING
EQUIPMENT:	CONE
DRILL TYPE:	PHYSICAL PERFORMANCE, SKILL, AGILITY, COORDINATION

Popcorn Drill

ADVANCED PARTNER NO-CONTACT

PURPOSE

The Popcorn drill doubles as both an agility drill as well as a ball handling and eye/hand coordination drill.

Players require intense focus and dual task management as they work on managing two separate footballs as well as quickly changing direction throughout the drill.

DRILL DESCRIPTION

The player begins the drill by shuffling laterally towards one of the cones while keeping his body facing towards the coach.

The coach tosses one of the two footballs to the player.

As soon as the player catches the ball, he stops his shuffle and begins shuffling in the opposite direction towards the other cone. As he changes his direction, the player immediately tosses the football back to the coach.

This begins the rapid-fire nature of this drill. As soon as the player tosses the first football back into the air, the coach then throws the second football back to him.

Throughout this drill, both footballs will simultaneously be in the air as they are thrown back and forth. Each time the player catches a ball, he must change the direction of his shuffle.

Somersault Drill

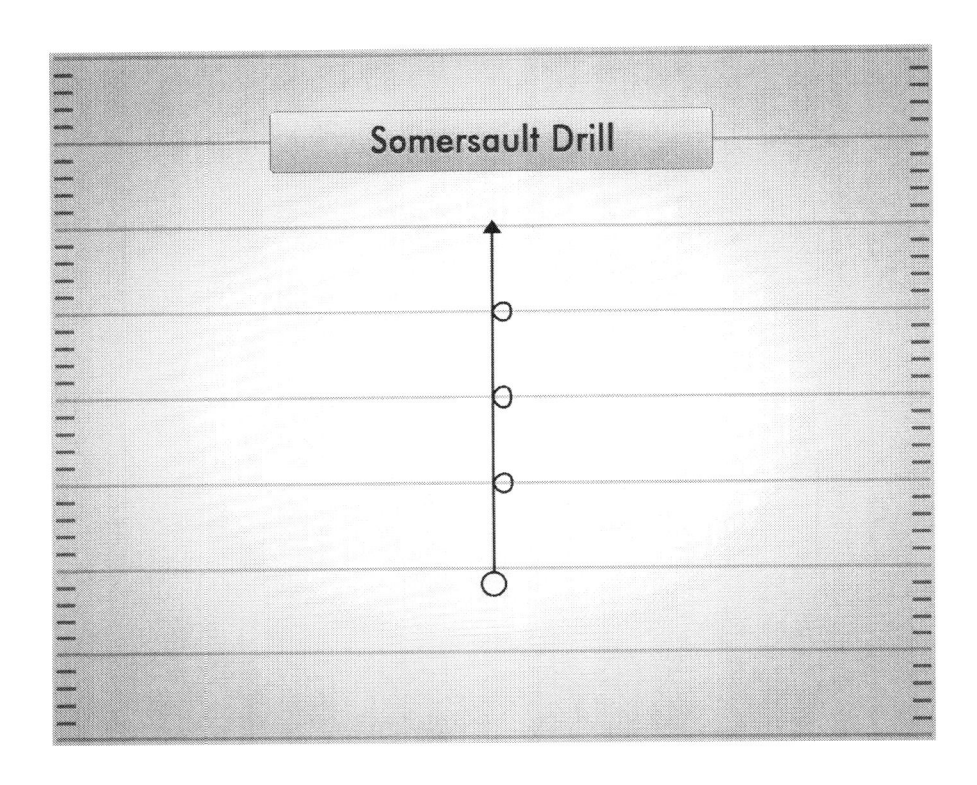

SETUP

Clear out 20 yards of space for the drill participants to run down the field.

EQUIPMENT: NONE

DRILL TYPE: PHYSICAL PERFORMANCE, CONDITIONING

Somersault Drill

EASY | **INDIVIDUAL** | **NO-CONTACT**

PURPOSE

The somersault drill is used to get players accustomed to contact with the ground while controlling their body in a low position throughout the course of this conditioning drill.

DRILL DESCRIPTION

Players begin running forward and execute a full somersault every five yards.

The somersaults teach players to control their body and how to get low to the ground while maintaining precision in the way they manipulate their body. Each time they pop off of the ground, players should quickly recover and accelerate with powerful steps upon regaining their footing.

After the third somersault, players sprint through the final 5 yards to complete one repetition of the drill.

Jump & Go Drill

SETUP

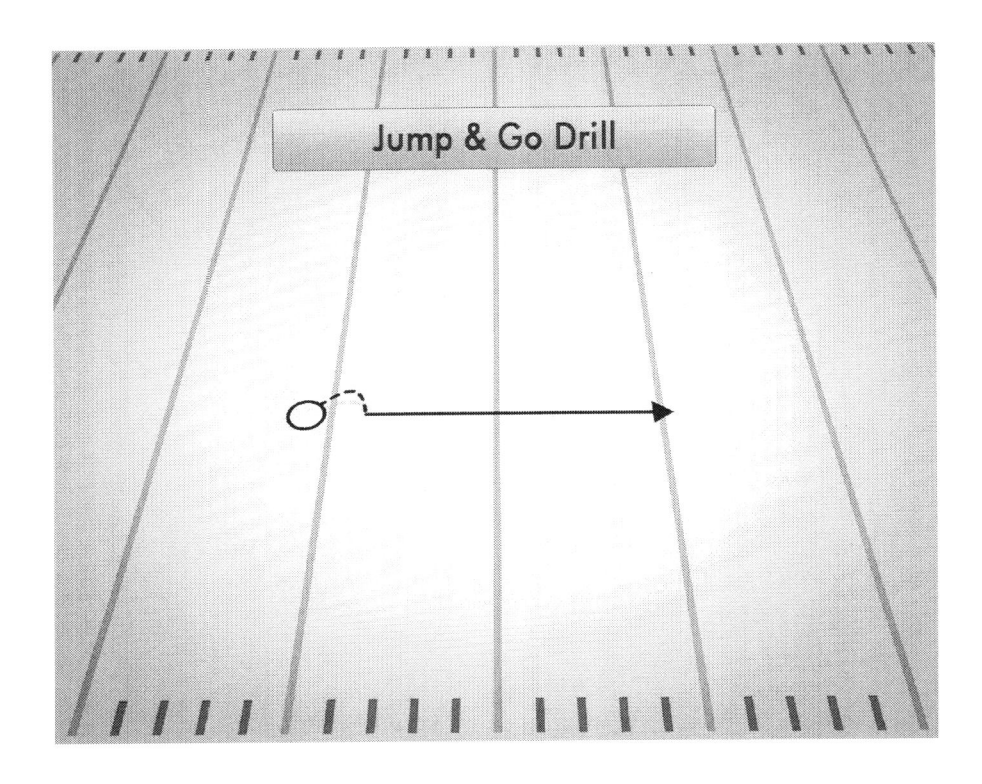

Clear ten yards of space for players to run.

EQUIPMENT: NONE

DRILL TYPE: PHYSICAL PERFORMANCE, SPEED, AGILITY

Jump & Go Drill

EASY   INDIVIDUAL   NO-CONTACT

PURPOSE

Players develop explosive power and quickness in first steps off of the line of scrimmage.

DRILL DESCRIPTION

Players begin the drill by jumping into the air vertically as high as they can.

As soon as they land, they hit the ground running as fast as the can for ten yards.

This simple drill can be repeated multiple times in one setting while players try to get a higher jump and a quicker burst each repetition.

Agility Tackle Drill

SETUP

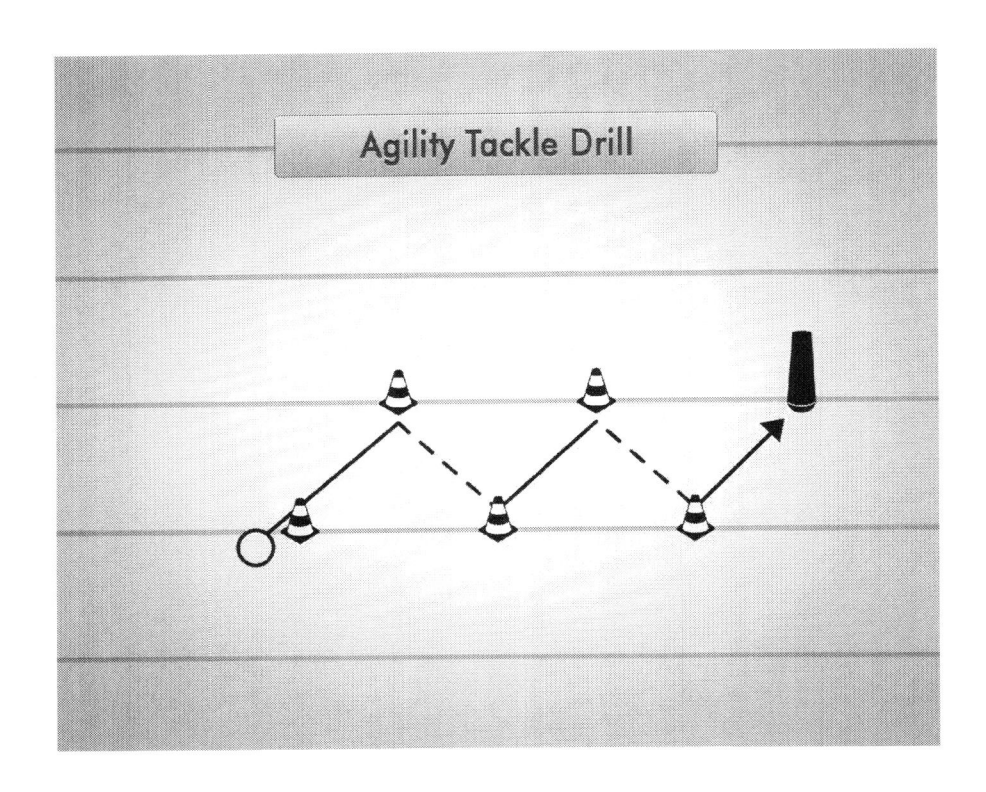

Place five cones in a diagonal zigzag formation, with each set of cones five yards away from each other.

Place a tackle dummy in the final position at the end of the zigzag.

TECHNIQUES:	TACKLING
EQUIPMENT:	CONE, TACKLE DUMMY
DRILL TYPE:	PHYSICAL PERFORMANCE, AGILITY

Agility Tackle Drill

EASY | INDIVIDUAL | CONTACT

PURPOSE

Defensive players merge their agility work with the goal of a proper form tackle to finish off the drill.

DRILL DESCRIPTION

Players sprint forward to the first cone, and then quickly change direction into a back peddle, as they move backward to the next cone.

Continue the sprint/back peddle rotation until the last cone, where players sprint forward and tackle the tackle dummy.

Weave Tackle Drill

SETUP

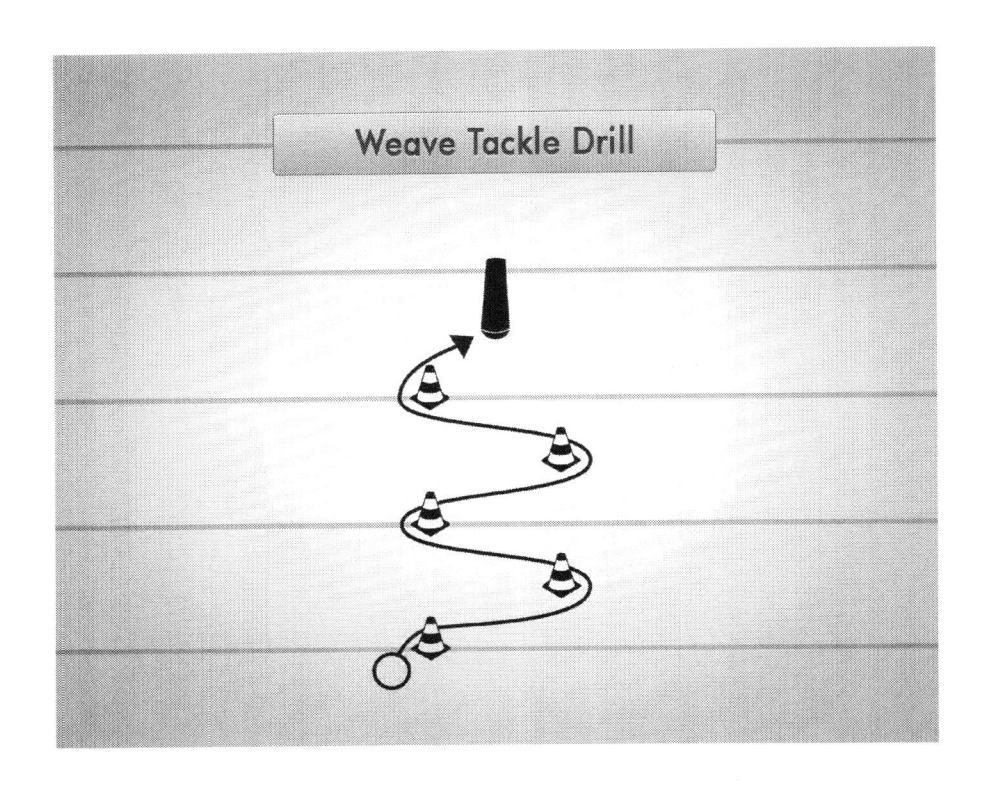

Place five cones in a zigzag formation with five yards of space in between each cone.

Position a tackle dummy at the end of the zigzag formation.

TECHNIQUES: TACKLING

EQUIPMENT: CONE, TACKLE DUMMY

DRILL TYPE: PHYSICAL PERFORMANCE, AGILITY

Weave Tackle Drill

EASY | INDIVIDUAL | CONTACT

PURPOSE

Defensive players gain agility work while incorporating the technique of a tackle on a tackle dummy at the end of the drill.

DRILL DESCRIPTION

Players sprint through the drill by quickly turning and cutting around each of the cones in the drill.

Upon cutting around the last cone, players accelerate into a tackle to finish off the drill.

Remind players to stay in a low and controlled position as they make their way throughout the drill, so that they can make a controlled tackle on the dummy.

Fumble Agility Drill

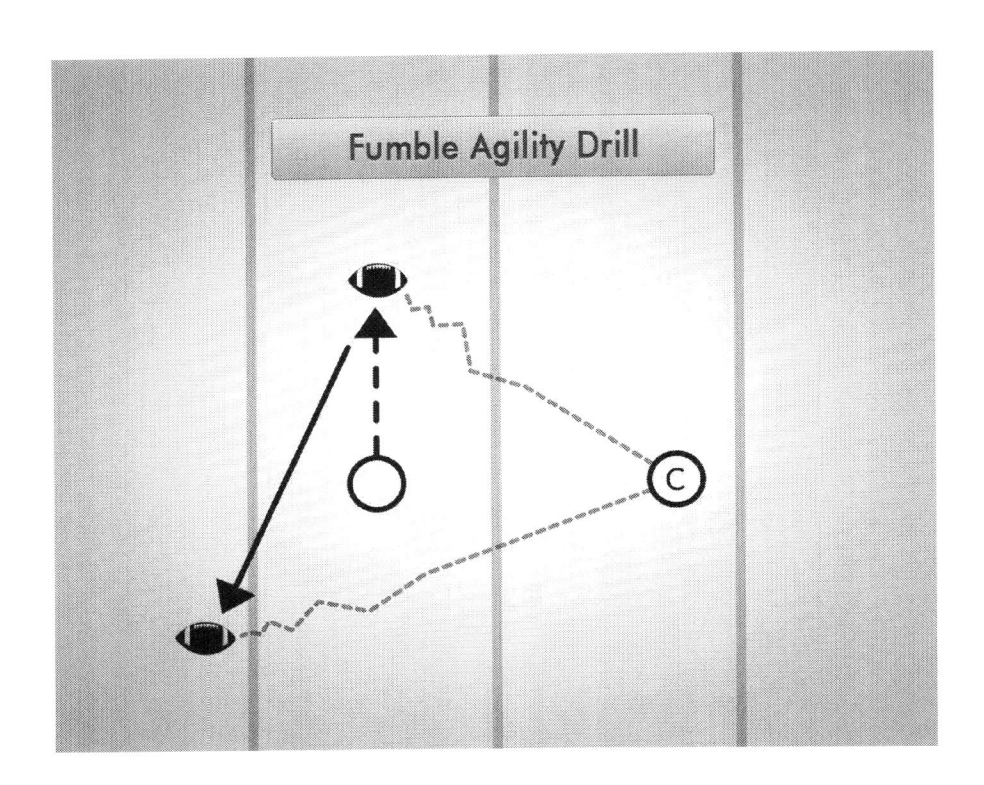

SETUP

A player and a coach face each other, about three yards apart. The coach holds two footballs.

TECHNIQUES: FOOTWORK

EQUIPMENT: NONE

DRILL TYPE: PHYSICAL PERFORMANCE, AGILITY, COORDINATION

Fumble Agility Drill

INTERMEDIATE   INDIVIDUAL   NO-CONTACT

PURPOSE

Work on the ability for players to quickly react to the football, develop smooth agility skills, and efficient recovery skills in picking up a fumbled football.

DRILL DESCRIPTION

A player steps up to the drill in an athletic stance facing the coach. The coach roles the first football about five yards to the side of the player.

The player must quickly shuffle to get in front of and pick up the football.

As soon as the player picks up the first football, the coach then roles the second football faster and further than the first football.

The player scoops up the first football, tosses it back to the coach, and then turns and sprints to scoop up and recover the second football.

The next player rotates in, and players repeatedly cycle through the drill.

Drills
Skill Drills

Pocket Presence Drill

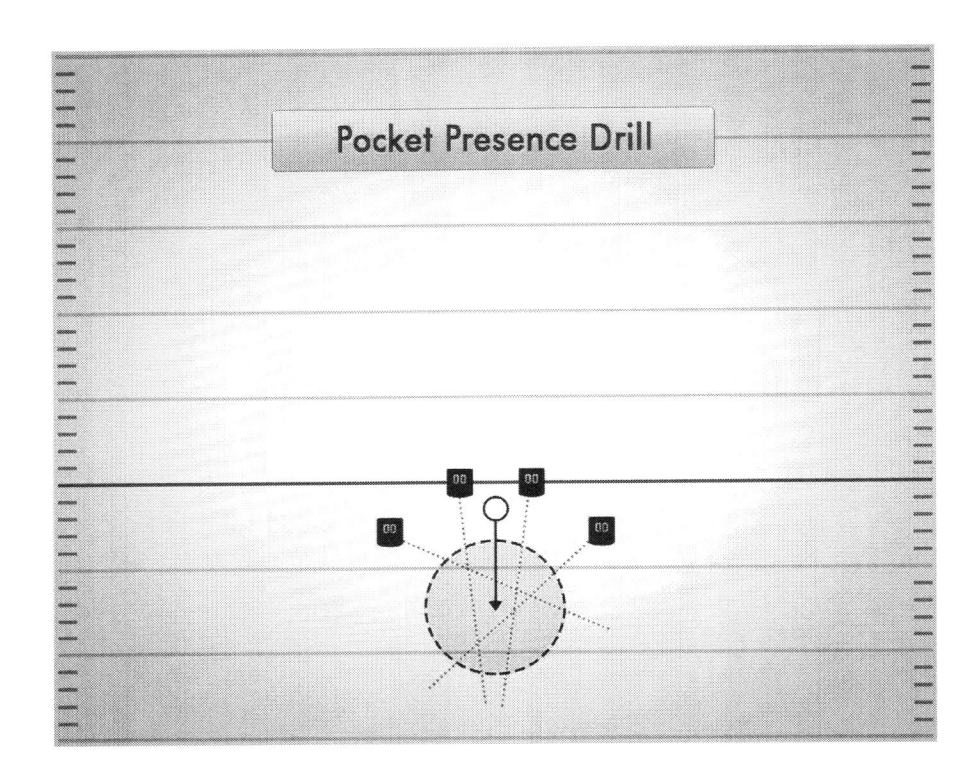

SETUP

Grab a few blocking pads or other equipment that you can safely toss at your quarterback. Select coaches and/or players to be positioned around the front of the pocket and prepared to toss their pad at the quarterback.

TECHNIQUES:	PASSING
EQUIPMENT:	BLOCKING PAD
DRILL TYPE:	SKILL

Pocket Presence Drill

INTERMEDIATE   INDIVIDUAL   NO-CONTACT

PURPOSE

Build the quarterback's awareness, comfort level, and mobility in the pocket. There is a learning curve for quarterbacks when it comes to building the confidence to stand tall in the pocket and being aware of their surroundings all while keeping their eyes downfield. This drill will give your Quarterbacks the opportunity to learn how to swiftly maneuver in the pocket.

DRILL DESCRIPTION

A quarterback starts the drill by implementing either a three-step, five-step, or seven-step drop in order to place himself within the middle of the pocket. While the quarterback keeps his feet moving, blocking pads or other soft/safe items are tossed in his direction in order to force him to move from side to side, as well as, forward and backward. As each item is tossed, the Quarterback swiftly keeps his feet under him in an athletic stance while keeping his eyes downfield.

This drill develops the Quarterback's sense of space in the pocket while ingraining the habit of keeping his eyes downfield so that he can make the proper reads in the defensive secondary and move in such a way that provides him enough space in the pocket for when it comes time to throw the ball downfield.

Elway Drill

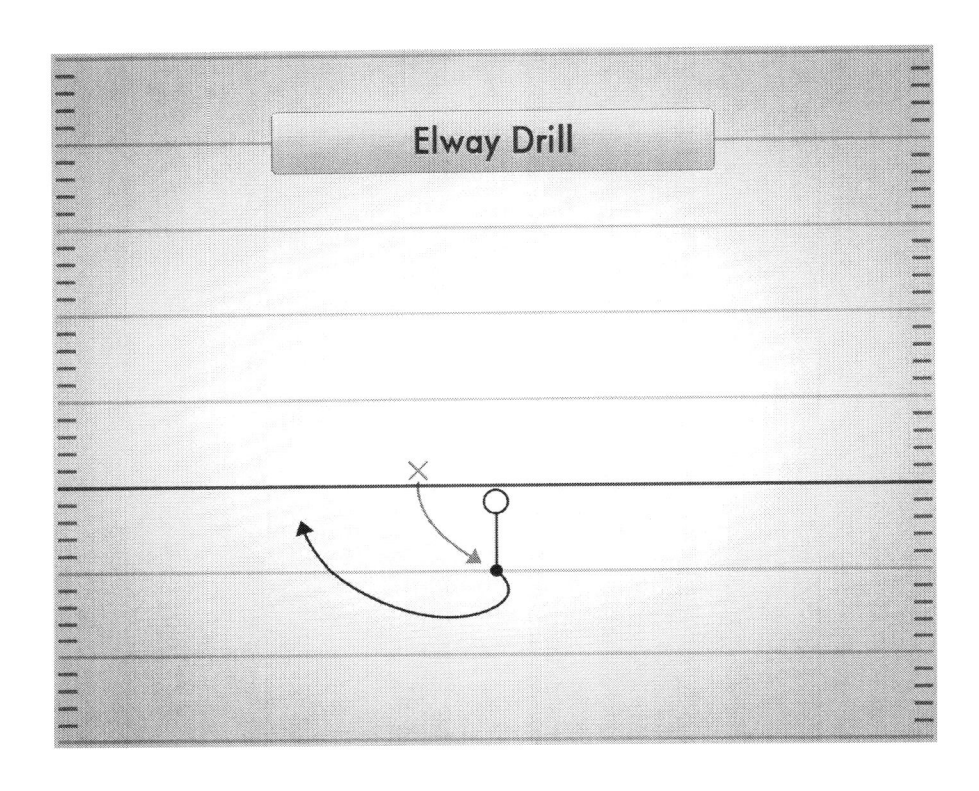

SETUP

Determine a starting location and set your Quarterback up in his typical formation alignment, whether it be under center or in the shotgun.

TECHNIQUES:	PASSING, FOOTWORK
EQUIPMENT:	NONE
DRILL TYPE:	SKILL

Elway Drill

INTERMEDIATE | INDIVIDUAL | NO-CONTACT

PURPOSE

Teach Quarterbacks the skill of the "Elway Drill" as a technique to escape the pocket when pressured from their blindside.

DRILL DESCRIPTION

This drill is named after the famous way that John Elway would spin around and escape the pocket when attacked from his blind side.

Have Quarterbacks go through their normal 3-step, 5-step, and/or 7-step drop, and set up in the pocket in order to simulate a normal passing play. Optionally, simulate a blitz towards the Quarterback's blind side.

After setting up in the pocket, the Quarterback should feel the (real or imagined) pressure from his blind side and should proceed to escape it using the "Elway Drill" technique. The proper technique is for the Quarterback to dip his back shoulder while extending his back foot straight back as if he is beginning to run completely backward. After turning his back completely away from the line of scrimmage, he should then continue and turn all the way around to turn it into a role out to the sideline.

This maneuver must be perfectly timed, because if the Quarterback waits too long, he is going to get blasted in the back by the defender, but if he leaves too early, the defender will have time to readjust and recover. Essentially the Quarterback is operating like a bullfighter who waits until the last second to get out of the way a bull, in an effort to keep himself, and the play, alive.

Flush the Pocket Drill

SETUP

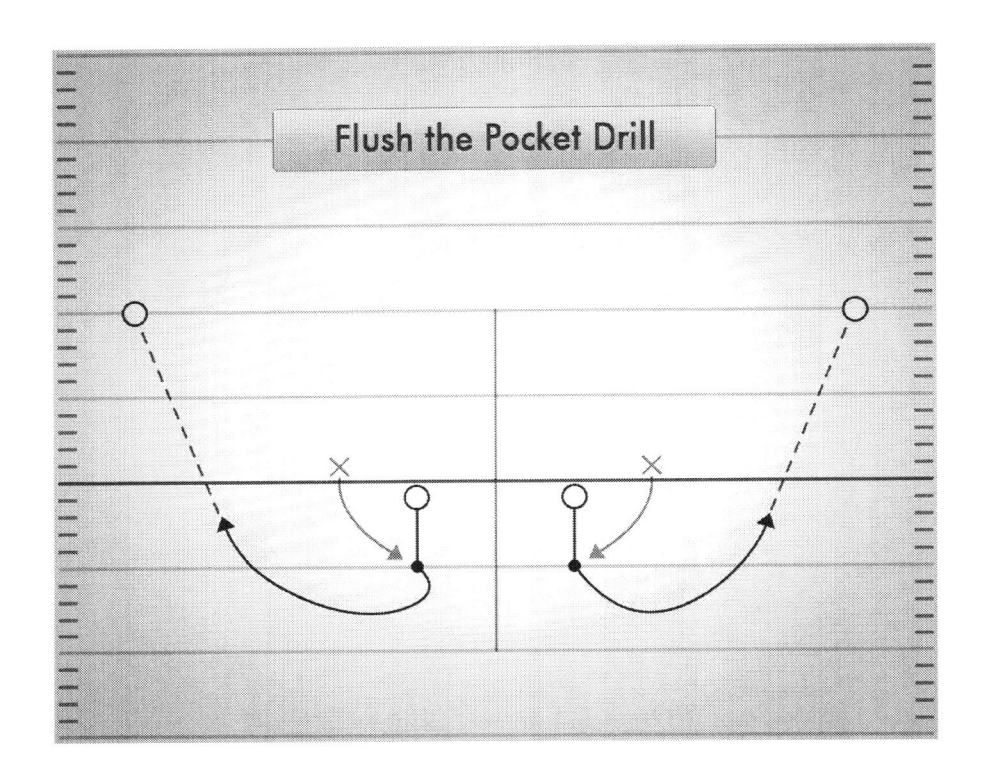

Determine a starting location and set your Quarterback up in his typical formation alignment, whether it be under center or in the shotgun.   Place one player, 10 yards deep by the sideline to receive the ball.

TECHNIQUES: **PASSING, FOOTWORK**

EQUIPMENT: **NONE**

DRILL TYPE: **SKILL**

Flush the Pocket Drill

INTERMEDIATE   GROUP   NO-CONTACT

PURPOSE

Teach Quarterbacks the footwork involved with rolling out of the pocket. Additionally, develop the Quarterback's skill of throwing the ball while on the run.

DRILL DESCRIPTION

The Quarterback performs their typical 3-step, 5-step, and/or 7-step drop and set up in the pocket. When given a command, the Quarterbacks flushes out of the pocket by either rolling out to their frontside or doing an "Elway Drill" out to their backside.

Upon rolling out, the Quarterback should gain depth by rolling about 3 yards back deeper as he begins his rollout. Once he has achieved good depth, the Quarterback finds his target and directs his body directly at his target. One thing that will make for errant throws while throwing on the run is if the Quarterback's body is facing towards the sideline instead of downfield. That is why it is absolutely critical that the Quarterback get enough depth that he can turn his body around and downfield toward his target. Upon identifying his target, the Quarterback throws the ball downfield to the target.

If there is a rotation of Quarterbacks in line for the drill the Quarterback replaces the receiver after he throws the ball, and the receiver then gets in line to perform the drill himself in order to continually keep the rotation going.

Handoff Drill

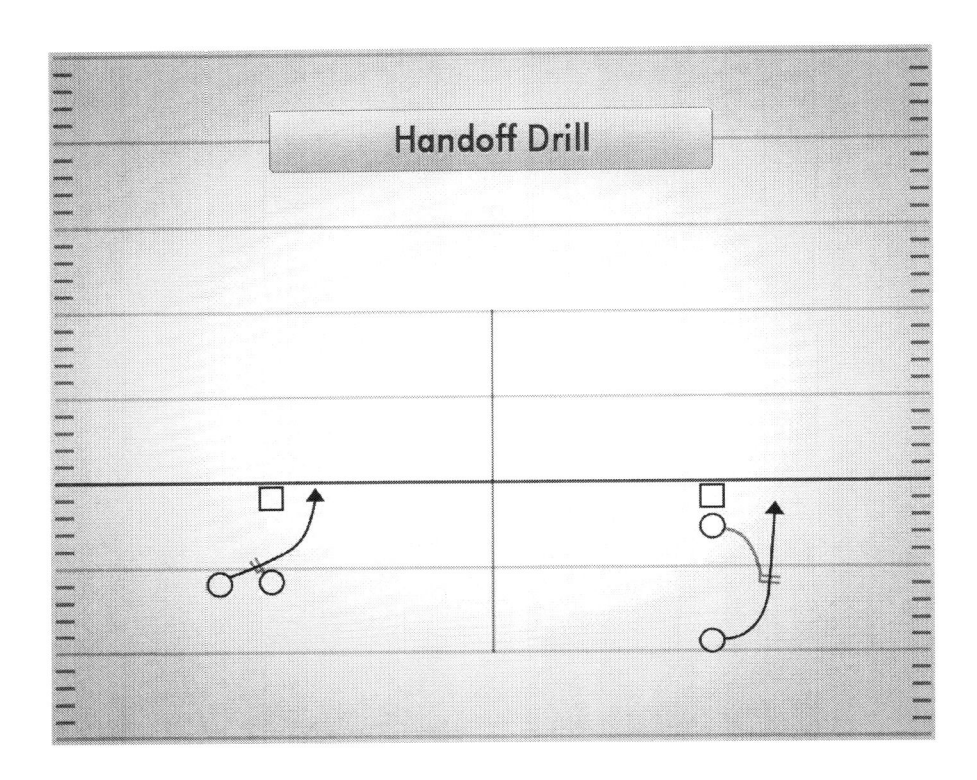

SETUP

Line up your quarterback and your running backs within the proper pre-snap backfield alignment and formation for your most common running plays.

TECHNIQUES: BALL CARRYING

EQUIPMENT: NONE

DRILL TYPE: SKILL, COORDINATION, TEAMWORK

Handoff Drill

EASY   **PARTNER**   **NO-CONTACT**

PURPOSE

Reinforce proper ball safety while handling the ball during the exchange between the quarterback and running back. The chemistry between the players in the backfield should be so firm that there is never a fumble in the backfield during the course of a handoff. Constant repetitions of the Handoff Drill while reinforcing the proper technique to minimize turnovers and maximize run play performance.

DRILL DESCRIPTION

Call a particular running play and have the quarterback and running back perform the entire play from beginning to end. Start the first few reps at walking speed in order to focus on the precise technique for the handoff, and then gradually increase the speed until your players are at full speed. By starting with the initial snap count and running the ball downfield, it will allow your players to get a sense of the timing in order to successfully execute handoffs at game speed.

There are many elements to a clean handoff; namely, spacing, timing, running back pocket location, and quarterback ball position. Your quarterback should have a firm grasp on the ball as he reaches it towards the running back. The running back, in turn, should have proper spacing from his teammate and give a large pocket with his arms in order to provide an accessible location to receive the ball. Once the quarterback places the ball in the running back's belly, the running back should clamp his forearms and hands down on the ball and secure it as he departs with the ball from the Quarterback and heads downfield.

Jump Cut Drill

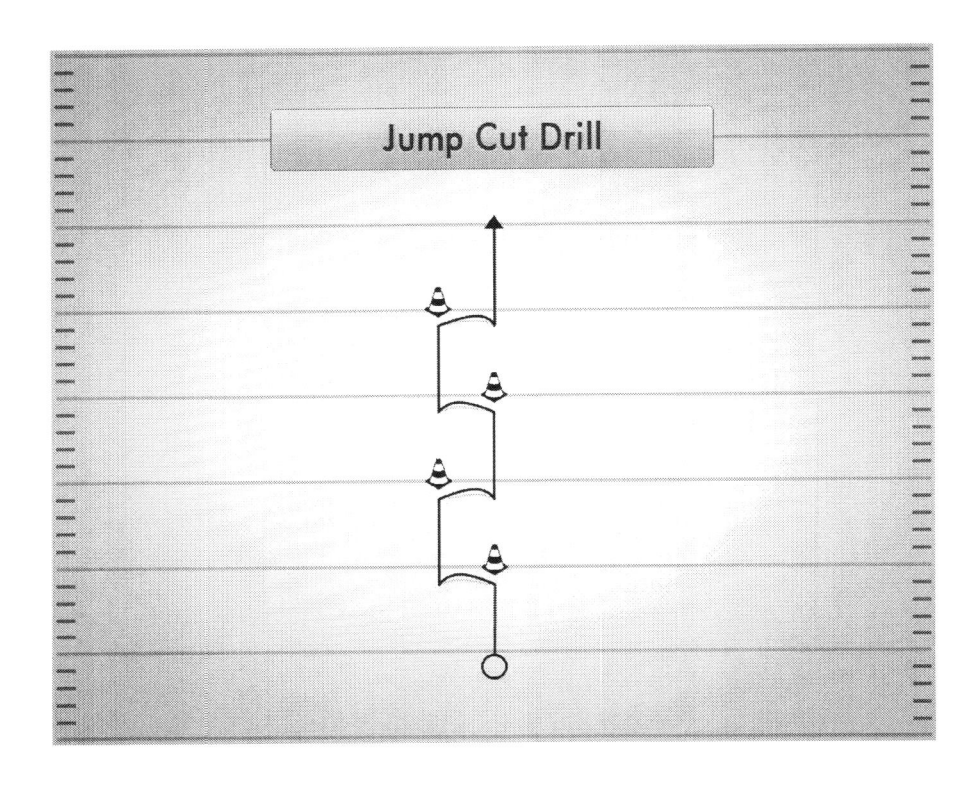

SETUP

Setup this drill by placing four cones in a staggered line every five yards down field. Each participant should carry a football throughout the drill.

TECHNIQUES:	**BALL CARRYING**
EQUIPMENT:	**CONE**
DRILL TYPE:	**SKILL, SPEED, AGILITY**

Jump Cut Drill

INTERMEDIATE   **INDIVIDUAL**   **NO-CONTACT**

PURPOSE

Primarily for Running Backs, this drill provides your ball carriers with a method to swiftly change direction as they navigate blocks and avoid tacklers while running the ball downfield. Ingraining the jump cut technique can come in very handy for Running Backs when they are looking for holes to shoot through in the offensive line.

DRILL DESCRIPTION

Running Backs line up and begin this drill by running directly towards the first cone. Prior to arriving at the cone, they employ a jump cut to jump to the side and around the cone. As soon as they land, they explode forward to the next cone. A jump cut is performed at each cone until the player sprints through the end of the course.

A jump cut is a quick horizontal jump that allows the player to quickly reposition themselves on the field. The jump should not be high up in the air, because the runner would then be defenseless against contact. Instead, it is a very low, very quick jump that allows the runner to quickly shoot from one gap to another.

This technique can be very valuable when a running back is looking for a hole to run through in the backfield of a run play. For example, if they are attempting to run through the 4-hole, in between the offensive guard and tackle, but that hole closes up while the 2-hole opens up, between the center and the guard, a quick jump cut can quickly allow the running back to switch holes while still retaining their forward momentum to get downfield.

DB Back Peddle Drill

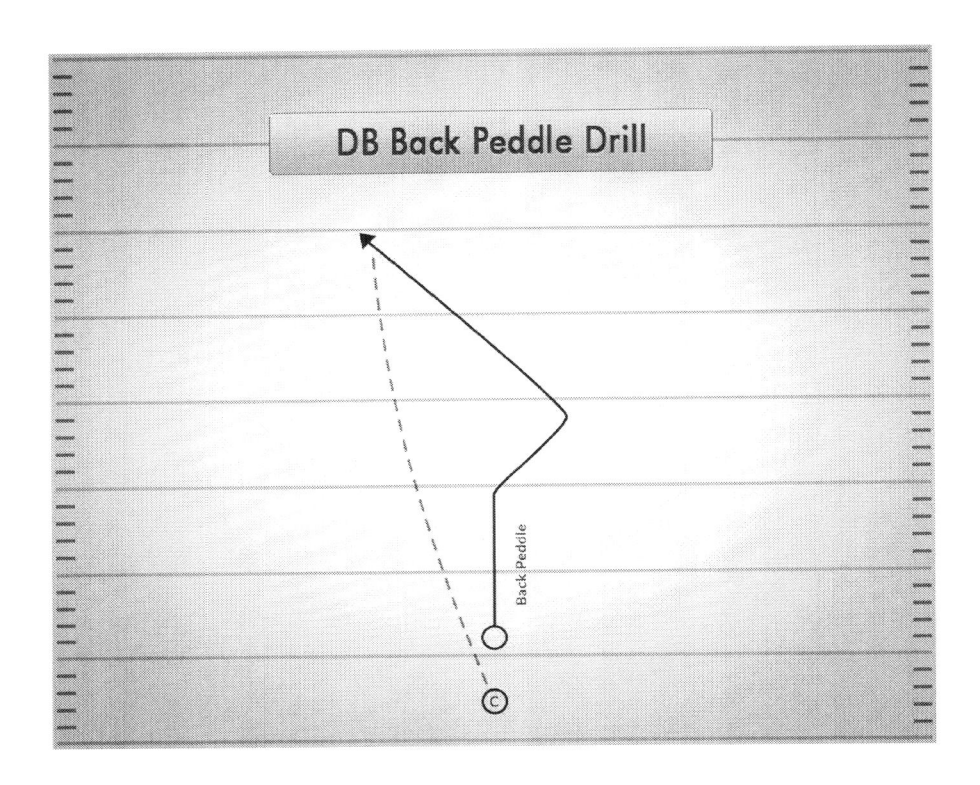

SETUP

Position a coach and a player face to face a few yards apart. Ensure that there is at least 25 yards of open space behind the player in order to avoid any collisions. The coach should have a football in his hands.

TECHNIQUES:	PASS DEFENDING, FOOTWORK
EQUIPMENT:	NONE
DRILL TYPE:	SKILL

DB Back Peddle Drill

EASY | **INDIVIDUAL** | **NO-CONTACT**

PURPOSE

Build a defender's ability to back peddle into a pass defending position, as well as, increasing their ability to quickly react and navigate in the defensive backfield.

DRILL DESCRIPTION

Initiate the drill by sending the defender straight backward in a back peddle. After a few yards, the coach should point by extending the football with his hands, either to the back right, or the back left. The player should then react and turn his body into a run at a 45 degree angle towards the direction that the coach pointed while still looking back at the coach. After a few more yards the coach points in another direction. At this juncture, the defender turns and run in that direction while keeping his eyes on the coach.

It is very important that the defender always keep his eyes on the coach and never turn his back to the coach. When turning on the second turn, he must open up his hips so that he remains facing the coach. This is because, in game situations, if the defender turns his back to the receiver he is guarding, he will get lost in coverage and would allow the receiver to make a move away from the defender while his back is turned.

After the player has gone downfield, the coach throws the ball up into the air and the player goes up and intercepts the ball by jumping up high with his hands in the air.

Break on the Ball Drill

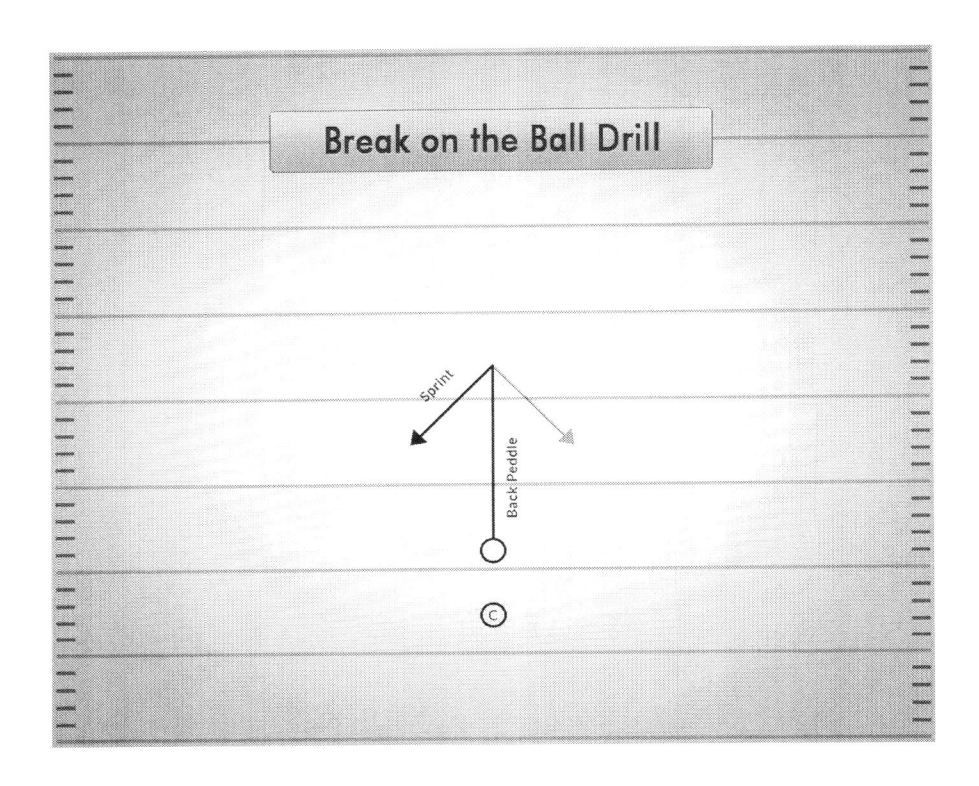

SETUP

A coach and a player begin the drill by facing each other and standing a few yards apart. Ensure that the player has ample room behind them in order to give them space to back peddle into the field and avoid any collisions.

TECHNIQUES:	PASS DEFENDING
EQUIPMENT:	NONE
DRILL TYPE:	SKILL, AGILITY

Break on the Ball Drill

EASY | INDIVIDUAL | NO-CONTACT

PURPOSE

Teaches defenders to break on the ball by quickly transitioning from a back peddle into a sprint down on the ball. This drill is particularly beneficial for defensive backs who are back peddling into coverage but quickly need to react to a throw underneath them in order to make a play on the ball.

DRILL DESCRIPTION

The coach begins the drill by sending the player backward into a back peddle downfield. After a few seconds, the coach points down and to either the right or left side to indicate to the players to transition out of their back peddle and break down in the direction the coach points. The length of time that the coach keeps the player in the back peddle should vary each repetition in order to keep players on their toes so that they are forced to build their reaction speed.

The players should anticipate the signal from the coach and react as quickly as possible as they stick their back foot into the ground and quickly break on the ball in front of them.

This can either be an individual drill or a group drill. If there is a group of players doing this drill simultaneously, then they should each space out across from the coach. Since the coach will point them all in the same direction, all players will be able to break down and run at the same angle without running into each other.

Dip & Rip Drill

SETUP

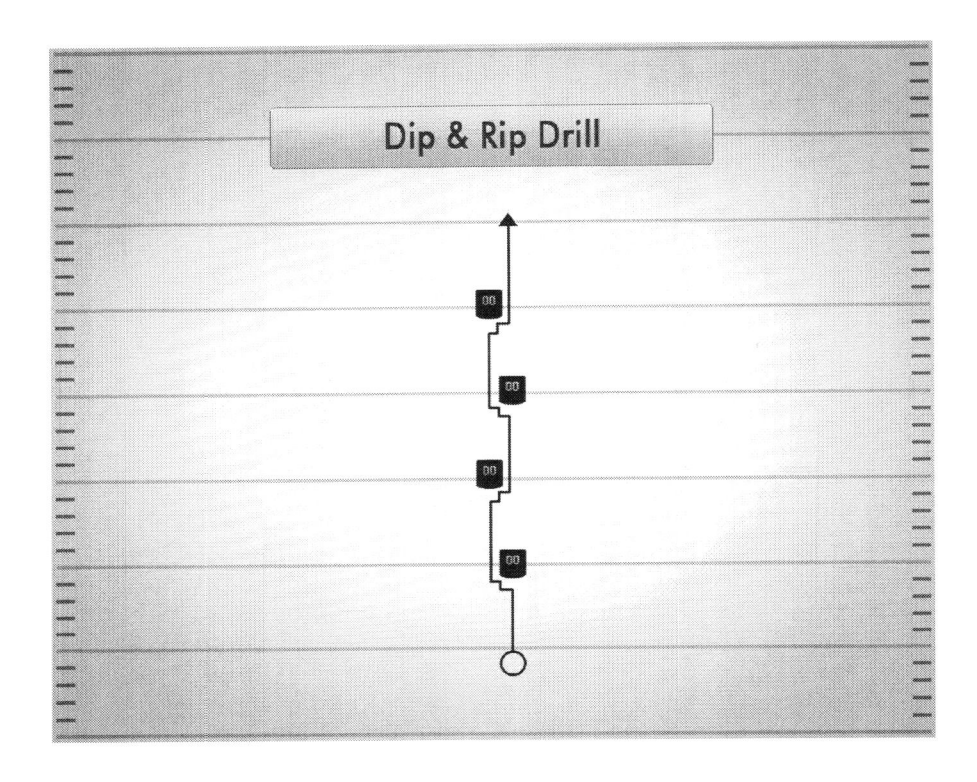

Assign two to four people to hold blocking pads and evenly space them out in a staggered line upfield from the starting line.

EQUIPMENT: BLOCKING PAD

DRILL TYPE: SKILL, COORDINATION

Dip & Rip Drill

INTERMEDIATE   **GROUP**   **NO-CONTACT**

PURPOSE

The purpose of the Dip & Rip Drill is to teach defenders how to avoid blocks as they make their way up the field. The Dip & Rip is a particular technique a defender uses to rip through blocks and get to the ball carrier. This drill helps to develop that skill so that the defenders will have this technique in their toolset for game time.

DRILL DESCRIPTION

A defensive player will traverse this drill at about 75% speed when running upfield in order to focus less on speed and more on building the muscle memory for the Dip & Rip technique.

As the defensive player approaches a blocker, he will need to prepare to implement the three stages of the Dip & Rip. 1) Dip shoulder down and across to the middle of your body. 2) Rip arm through your body and in front of the blocker. 3) Sidestep to the side that you are dipping and ripping to.

By implementing this technique, a defender makes it hard for the blocker to make a clean block. Dipping your shoulder down and ripping your arm through gives the blocker very little room to initiate the blocking contact. If timed properly the blocker will only be able to contact the side of the player's shoulder resulting in a slight shove to the side instead of a major blow back to the chest.

The defensive player repeatedly practices this maneuver by making his way up the field and dipping a ripping through each of the blocking pads in the drill.

Tip Drill

SETUP

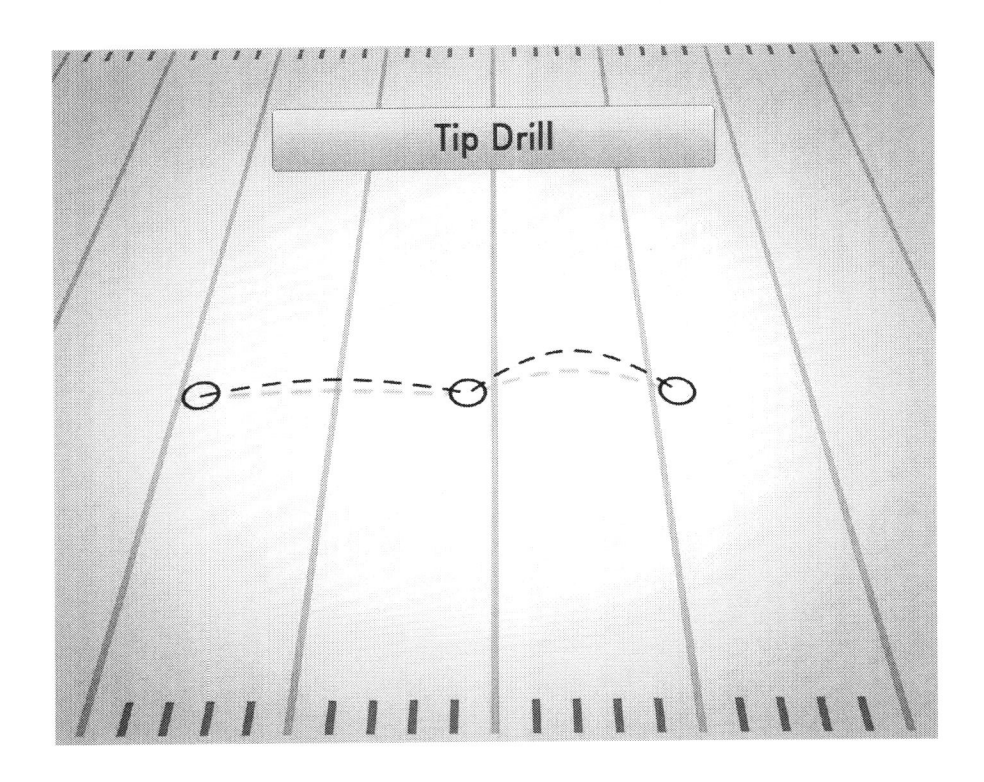

Determine who is responsible for the three roles in this drill. There should be a thrower on one end of the drill, a tipper in the middle of the drill, and a catcher on the other end of the drill. Participants should be aligned together with the tipper directly in the middle of the thrower and the catcher.

TECHNIQUES:	CATCHING, PASS DEFENDING
EQUIPMENT:	NONE
DRILL TYPE:	SKILL, COORDINATION, TEAMWORK

Tip Drill

INTERMEDIATE   **GROUP**   **NO-CONTACT**

PURPOSE

Build the ability for players to react quickly to different types of tips when the ball gets tipped up in the air. This is an amazing opportunity for a defense to come up with an interception when the ball gets tipped up in the middle of the play. Developing your players' ability to react to a tip and catch the ball will allow your team to be prepared to create turnovers while on defense.

DRILL DESCRIPTION

The person throwing the ball aims his throw above the head of the tipper in order to allow the tipper to easily tip the ball up into the air. The tipper uses both of his hands, almost like a volleyball set, to tip the ball up into the air behind them towards the catcher.

The catcher prepares to quickly react to where the ball gets tipped and go catch the ball wherever it goes, even if a dive is needed.

Due to the fact that no single tip will be identical, this drill prepares your players to react to all different types of scenarios and trajectories in order to go catch the ball and secure the interception.

Gauntlet Drill

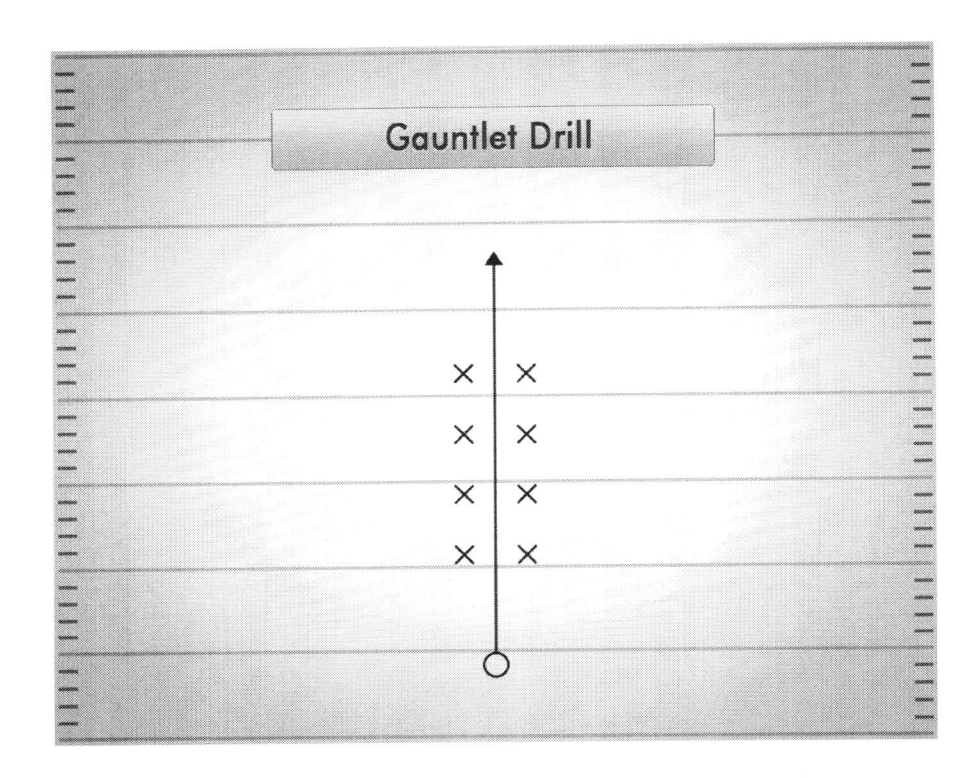

SETUP

Select one ball carrier and devote the rest of your players to form the "gauntlet" by lining up in a way that provides a narrow path for your ball carrier to run through. There should be the same amount of people on each side of the gauntlet.

TECHNIQUES:	BALL CARRYING
EQUIPMENT:	NONE
DRILL TYPE:	SKILL, COORDINATION

Gauntlet Drill

INTERMEDIATE   GROUP   CONTACT

PURPOSE

Build ball security by focusing the ball carrier on protecting the football amidst a barrage of contact and attempts to strip the football.

DRILL DESCRIPTION

The ball carrier proceeds to run half speed through the gauntlet. His focus is to cover up the football and hold on as tight as possible so that he does not fumble the football in the gauntlet. Proper ball carrying technique is to hold the ball up high and tight to the runner's chest while bringing his off hand up and over the ball so that he is protecting it with both of his arms and both of his hands.

The people forming the gauntlet reach out their arms in an effort to knock the ball out of the hands of the ball carrier. They try to punch the ball directly, as well as, try to grab and pull on the arms to provide a variety of ways to force a fumble so that the runner can experience and defend against all sorts of attacks on the ball.

It is important that the ball carrier only runs half speed, because if he runs too fast, you could risk injuring one of the hands or arms of the players forming the gauntlet. The focus of this drill is not on speed, but is instead on the ball protection.

Mano-e-Mano

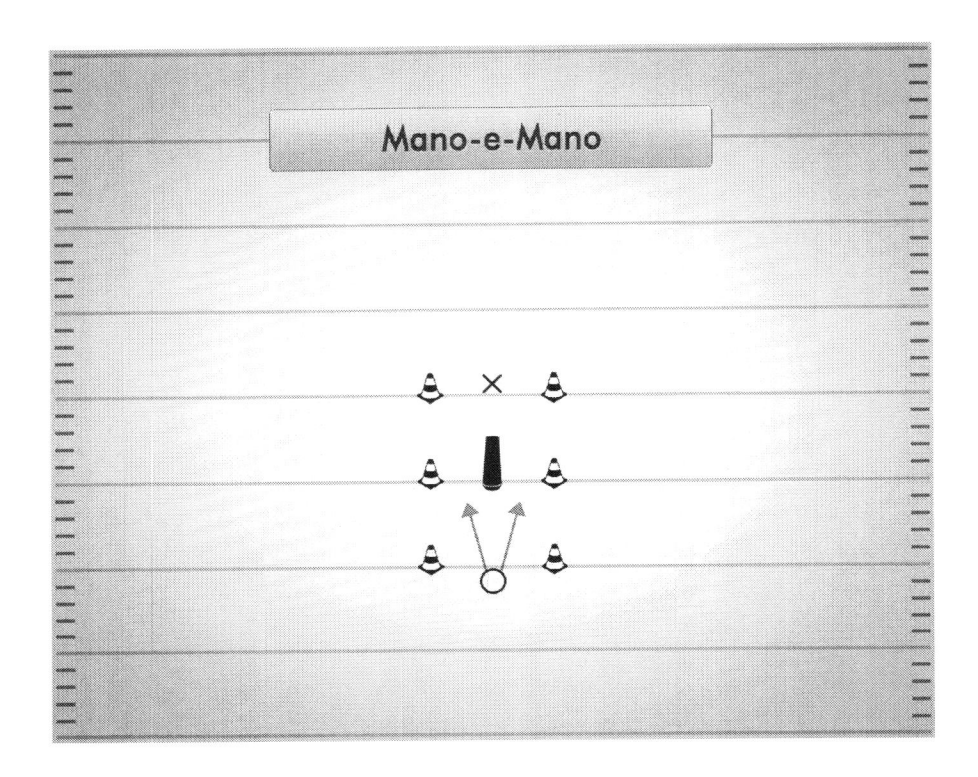

SETUP

Setup a boundary to condense the drill to six yards wide by 10 yards long. Place a tackle dummy directly in the middle of the drill. A defender should be positioned on one end of the drill opposite of the ball carrier on the other side of the drill.

TECHNIQUES:	BALL CARRYING, TACKLING
EQUIPMENT:	CONE, TACKLE DUMMY
DRILL TYPE:	SKILL

Mano-e-Mano Drill

EASY   PARTNER   CONTACT

PURPOSE

Defenders learn how to track down and tackle the ball runner when there is an obstruction in between the players. The offensive player, on the other hand, learns how to utilize an obstruction to create space and get around a defender.

DRILL DESCRIPTION

Start the drill with a command to the players to start running towards each other. The goal of the defender is to tackle the offensive player despite the presence of the tackle dummy in the middle of the drill. The goal of the ball carrier is to get around the defender and score a touchdown.

The narrow boundaries and the tackle dummy add an element to this drill that gives it a different situation than purely an open field tackling drill. Either player is allowed to knock down the tackle dummy if they feel the need to.

The offensive player can use his creativity to get around the defender any way he sees fit as long as he stays within the sideline boundaries. Keeping the boundaries narrow ensures that players have to deal with the presence of the tackle dummy and the runner can not simply try to outrun the defender to the side.

Open Field Tackle Drill

SETUP

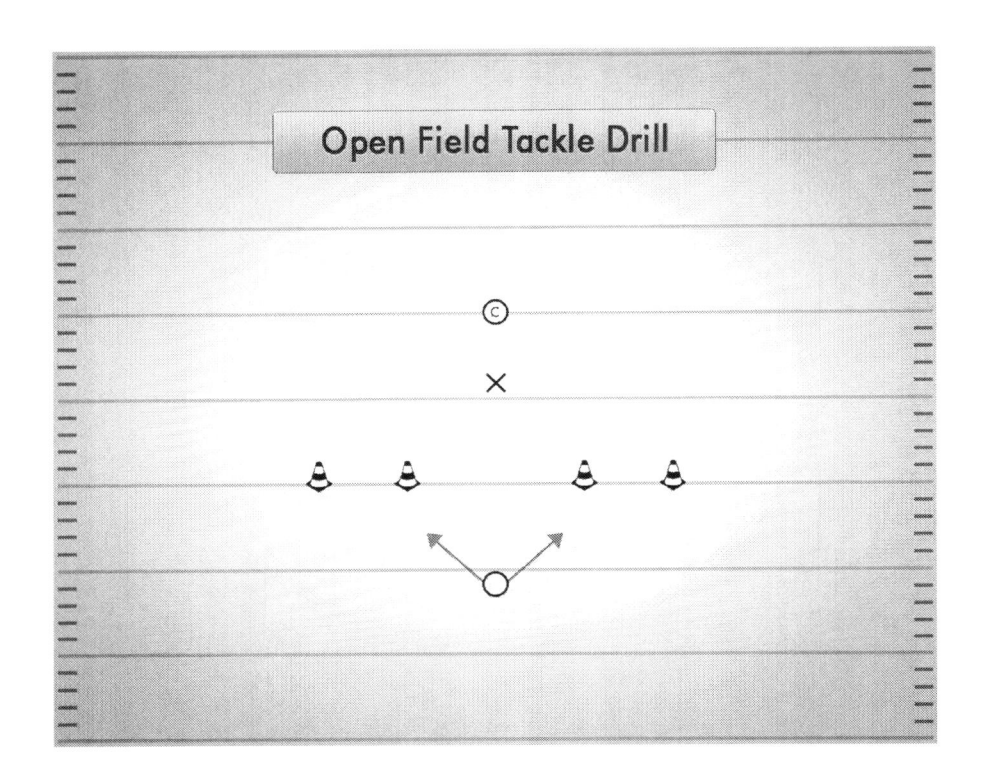

Position a defender and a ball carrier ten yards apart from each other. A coach will stand behind the defender so that the defender can not see him.

In between each player, set up two sets of cones, one on each side of the drill. Each set of cones should have two cones that are five yards apart. These sets will act as the gaps that players run through.

TECHNIQUES:	BALL CARRYING, TACKLING
EQUIPMENT:	CONE
DRILL TYPE:	SKILL, COMPETITION

Open Field Tackle Drill

EASY   PARTNER   CONTACT

PURPOSE

Making a tackle in the open field is one of the toughest tackles that a football player has to make. This drill provides defensive players a practice scenario to improve their open field tackling ability.

DRILL DESCRIPTION

To start the drill, the coach standing behind the defender will say "Ready!" to indicate that the drill is about to begin. The coach will then signal to the offensive player by clearly pointing to the right or to the left.

The offensive player must start running in that direction as soon as he gets the signal, and he is not allowed to initially do any jukes on his first step that will throw the defender off. After the drill has started, the ball carrier must run through the set of cones on the side he was assigned. He is allowed to juke once he gets close to the defender to avoid the tackle, but he must still run in between the cones.

The defensive player reacts to the ball carrier's first movement. As soon as he breaks to one direction, the defender runs and tackles the player in the open field as he tries to make it through the cones.

Gap Attack

SETUP

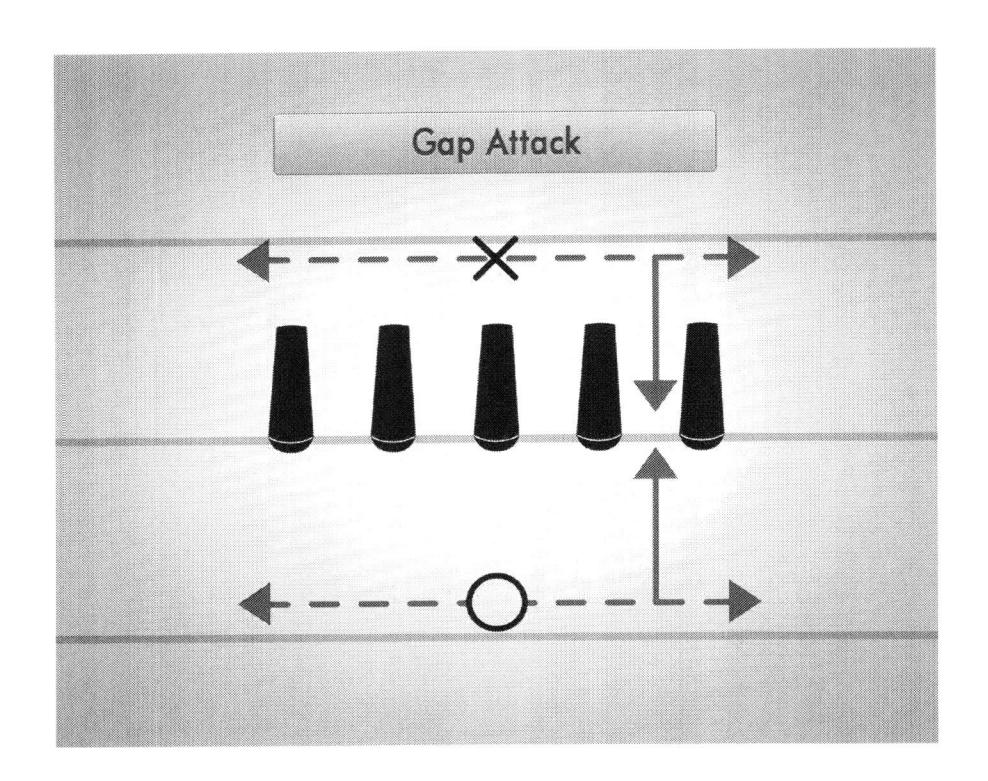

Place five tackle dummies with 1-2 yards of space in between them like an offensive line would line up in formation. One defender and one ball carrier should stand across from each other five yards behind the dummies.

TECHNIQUES: **BALL CARRYING, TACKLING**

EQUIPMENT: **TACKLE DUMMY**

DRILL TYPE: **SKILL, COMPETITION**

Gap Attack

ADVANCED | PARTNER | CONTACT

PURPOSE

The purpose of this drill is for both the defender and the ball carrier to read and attack the gaps of the offensive line. The ball carrier's purpose is to attack the open gap and get through the defense. The defender's purpose is to react and attack the same gap as the ball carrier in order to make a tackle.

DRILL DESCRIPTION

A coach gives commands in order to run the drill. Begin the drill by having both players shuffle horizontally, side-to-side, without creeping up closer to the line of scrimmage. The ball carrier, can shuffle whichever direction he wants, when he wants, as long as he stays horizontal and inside the span of the drill.

The coach will give a command to "Go!" and the ball carrier will shoot towards one of the gaps. The defender then must attack that same gap in order to make the tackle and stop the player from getting past him.

The ball carrier is allowed to change direction and shoot through any of the gaps that he chooses. The defender will want to attack forward and try to initiate contact in the gap.

Sack Attack

SETUP

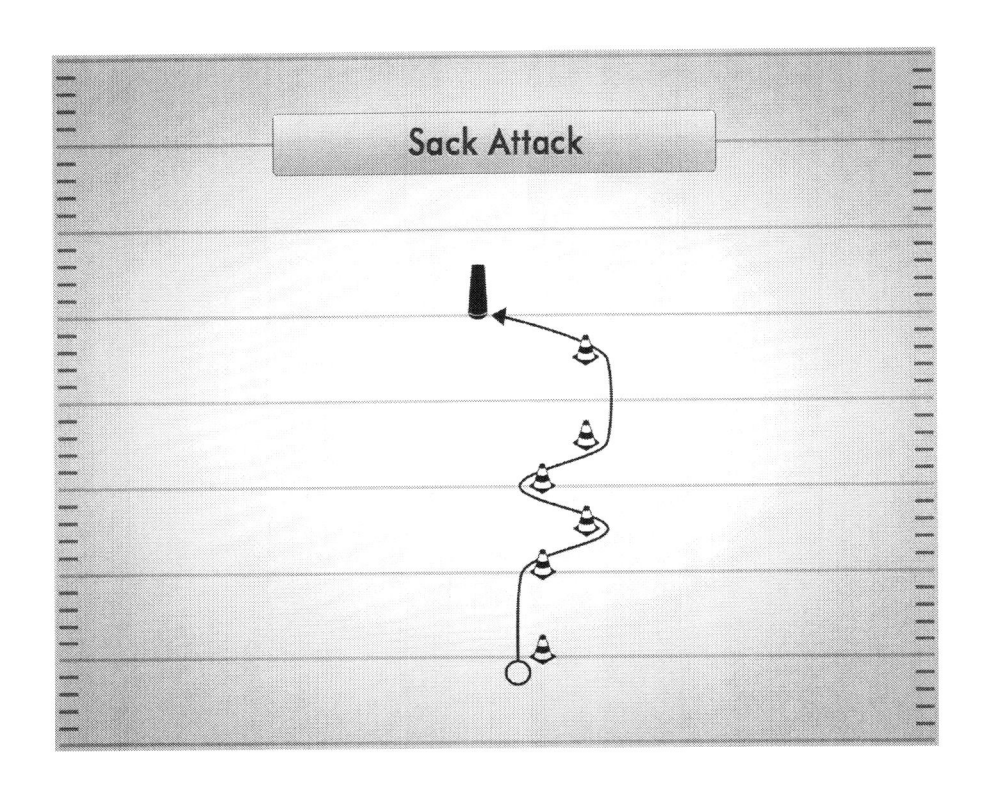

Place a series of cones in a zigzag formation about two and a half yards apart. After the series of zigzags, place another cone five yards further upfield. After the last cone, place a tackle dummy around the corner and five to seven yards inside.

TECHNIQUES:	TACKLING, FOOTWORK
EQUIPMENT:	CONE, TACKLE DUMMY
DRILL TYPE:	SKILL, AGILITY

Sack Attack

EASY | **INDIVIDUAL** | **NO-CONTACT**

PURPOSE

Work on a defensive player's footwork through an obstacle course that eventually leads to a simulated sack of the quarterback.

DRILL DESCRIPTION

Players begin in either a two or three point stance depending on the normal way their position lines up. The first portion of the obstacle course is a series of cones that the players must weave through by running and turning as quickly as possible.

After the zigzags, players will need to fly around a corner in order to attack and sack the quarterback. Players complete the drill by tackling the tackle dummy at the end of the obstacle course.

Bull Rush Drill

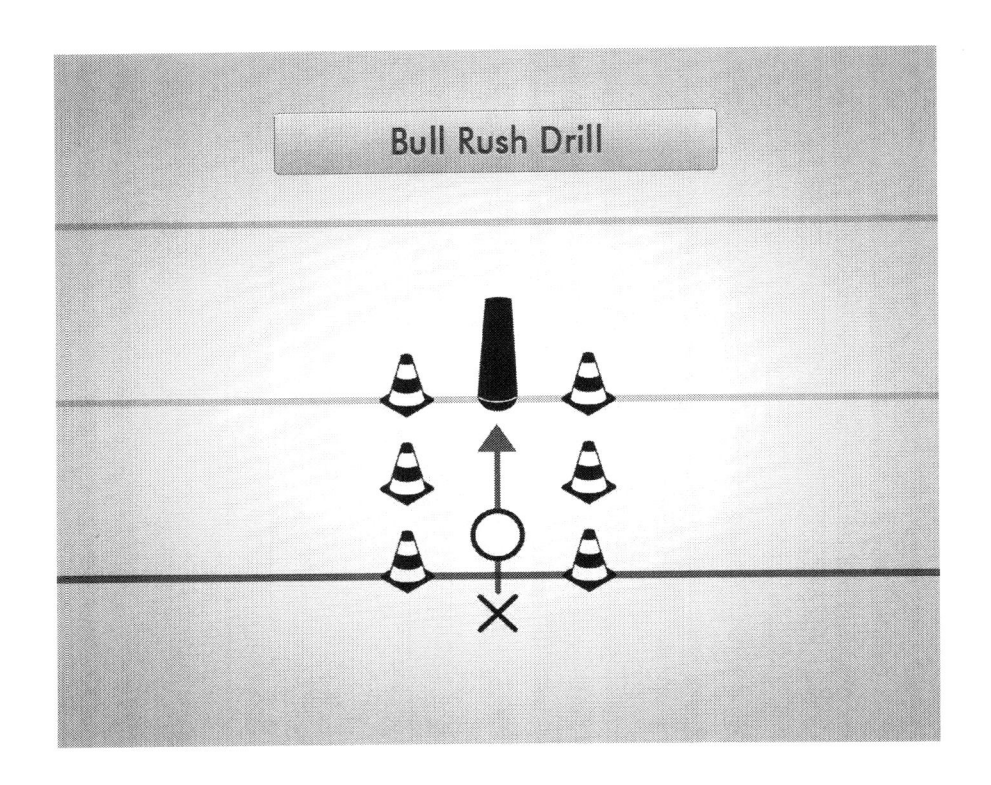

SETUP

Position a defensive lineman face to face against an offensive lineman. Place a tackle dummy five yards behind the line of scrimmage and contain the drill by setting up a series of cones that creates a boundary for the drill to make it five yards wide.

TECHNIQUES: BLOCKING, TACKLING

EQUIPMENT: TACKLE DUMMY

DRILL TYPE: SKILL, COMPETITION

Bull Rush Drill

INTERMEDIATE   PARTNER   CONTACT

PURPOSE

Simulate a battle in the interior line to work on pass rush ability and pass protection ability.

DRILL DESCRIPTION

Unlike the Around the Corner Drill, which simulates a blitz around the edge of the offensive line, this drill simulates a blitz up in the middle of the offensive line.

Upon the start of a drill, the defensive lineman will begin bull rushing the offensive lineman by pushing them back into the quarterback, resembled by the tackle dummy. The offensive lineman will utilize proper pass blocking techniques to stay low and in front of his opponent to keep him from getting into the backfield and tackling the dummy.

There are three ways that this drill can end. The first way to end the drill is after five seconds have elapsed. If time runs out, then the offensive lineman wins. The second way to end the drill is if the defensive lineman steps outside the bounds of the cones. The defender is allowed to try to get around his opponent on the way to the tackle dummy, be he must stay within the narrow bounds to the drill, because the purpose is to simulate a rush up the middle interior of the offensive line. The third way to end the drill is if the defender is successfully able to knock the tackle dummy over by either completing a tackle or pushing the offensive lineman into the dummy.

Around the Corner Drill

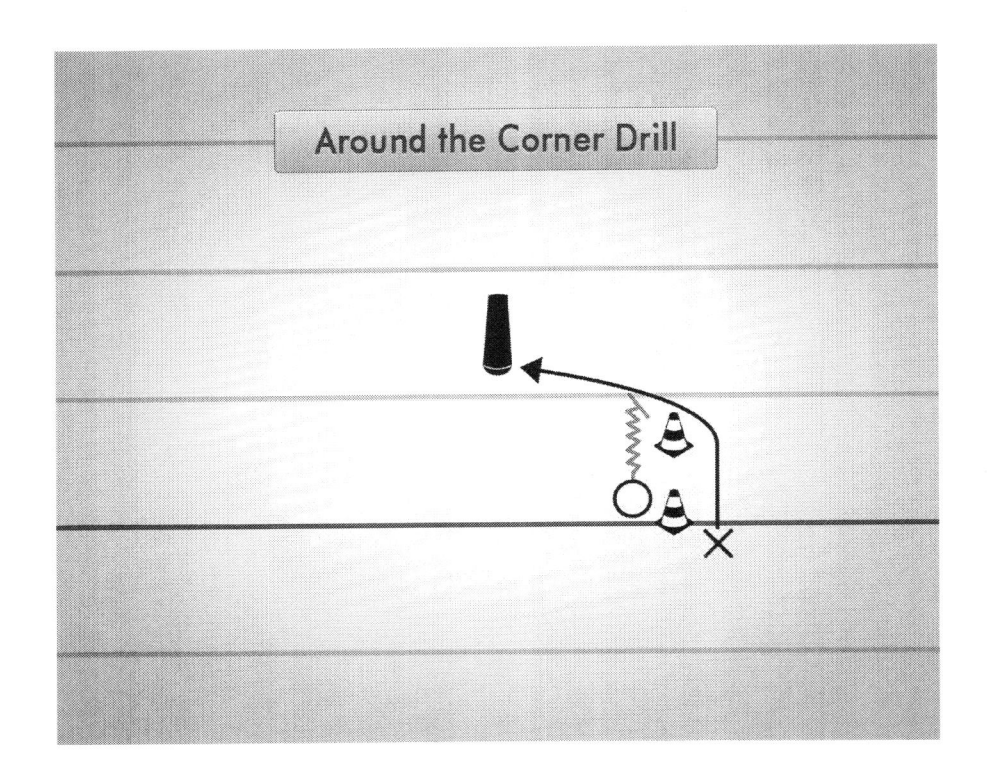

SETUP

Place one cone on the line of scrimmage and another cone three yards behind the cone on the line of scrimmage. Place a tackle dummy to represent the quarterback roughly six yards inside of the cones and six yards behind the line of scrimmage. The offensive tackle lines up inside the cones on the LOS and the defender lines up outside the cones on the LOS.

TECHNIQUES: BLOCKING, TACKLING

EQUIPMENT: CONE, TACKLE DUMMY

DRILL TYPE: SKILL, COMPETITION

Around the Corner

ADVANCED | PARTNER | CONTACT

PURPOSE

This drill simulates a pass rush off the edge of the offensive line. The offensive tackle will need to work on how to properly block an outside blitz, while the defender works on techniques to avoid the block and get to the quarterback.

DRILL DESCRIPTION

Unlike the Bull Rush Drill, which simulates a pass rush up the middle of the offensive line, this drill simulates a blitz around the edge of the offensive line.

Players should perform their pass blocking / pass rushing techniques as they would a normal play, with a few rules and restrictions. The defender must go outside of the second cone. He is allowed to blitz around the blocker, or even cut underneath the blocker, but he must at least go deep enough to go around the three yard cone. This is to simulate the obstructions of where the rest of the offensive line would be on a normal play.

Run the drill for five seconds. If the defender gets a sack on the tackle dummy, then he wins. If the blocker holds the blitz off for five seconds and protects the quarterback, then he wins.

Stiff Arm Drill

SETUP

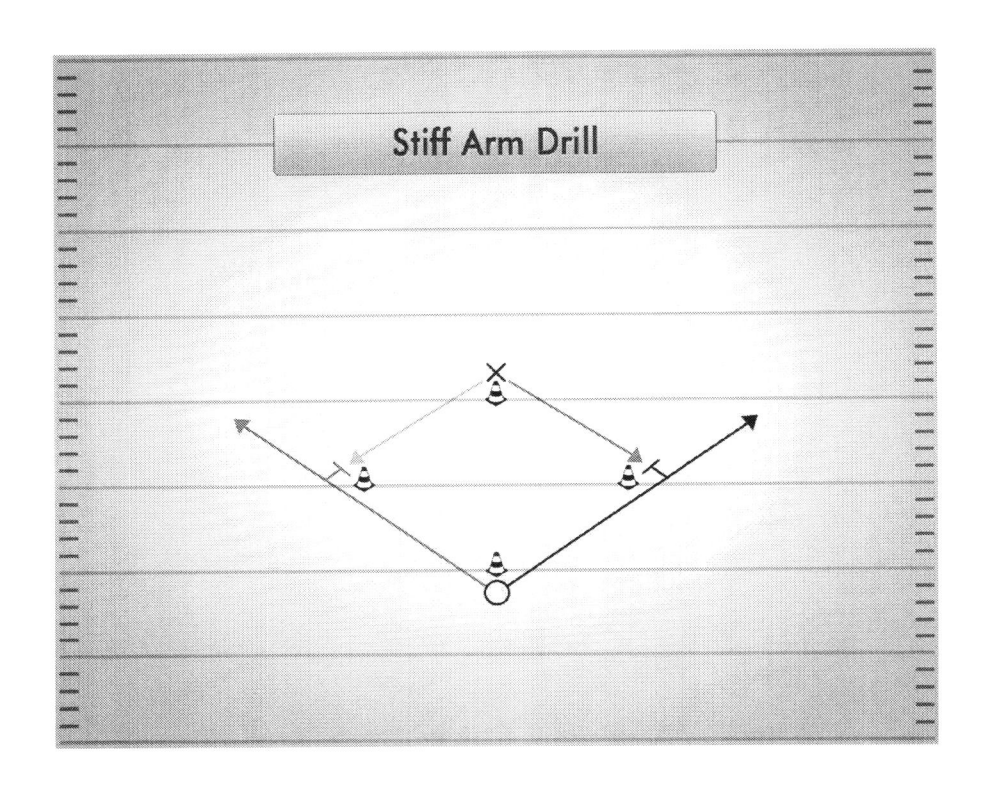

Place four cones in a diamond shape with a height of ten yards.

TECHNIQUES: BALL CARRYING

EQUIPMENT: NONE

DRILL TYPE: SKILL, COORDINATION

Stiff Arm Drill

ADVANCED PARTNER CONTACT

PURPOSE

Work on the proper placements, timing, and technique of the stiff arm, as a way to avoid tacklers while carrying the football.

DRILL DESCRIPTION

Run this drill at half speed to teach the proper technique and increase the speed only after good habits have been built. The defender approaches the ball carrier at an angle that is acceptable for a stiff arm attempt.

When initiating the stiff arm, there are three locations that the ball carrier should aim for.   1) Top of the helmet, to push down and away.   2) Side of the should pad, to push out and away.   3) Center of the breastplate, to push back and away.

Coaching a practice should first focus on placement, then focus on power, then focus on speed. There is no need to actually involve real defenders for this drill. Simply utilize other running backs and/or offensive personnel to rotate through this drill.

Spin Drill

SETUP

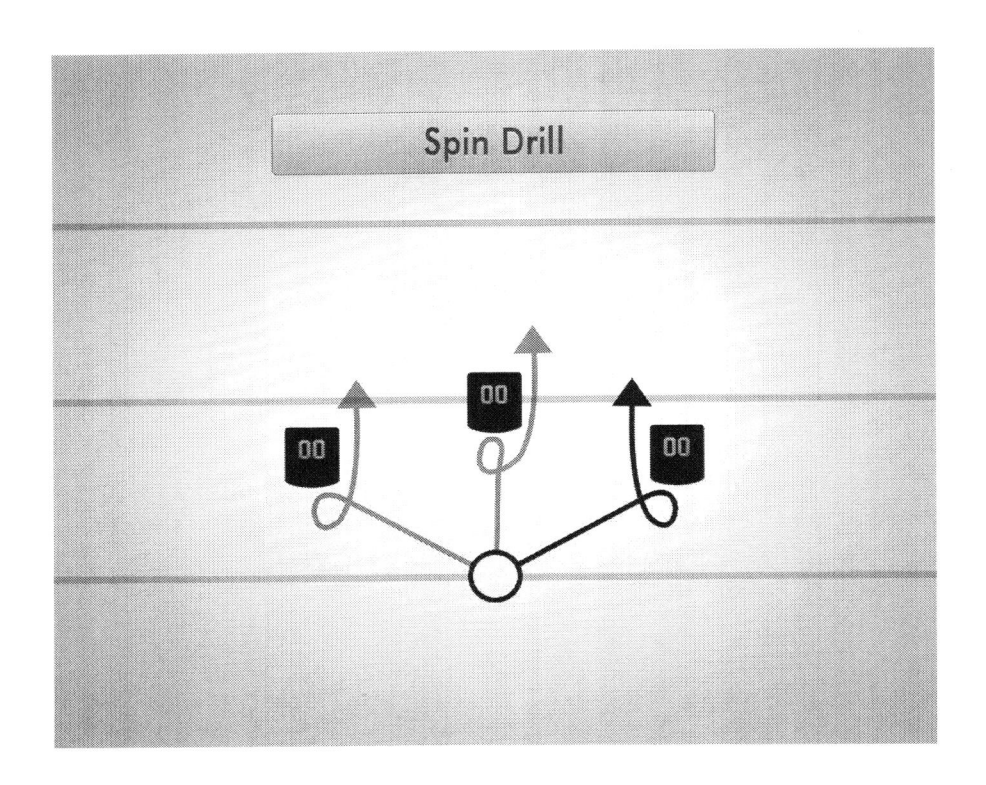

This drill requires one ball carrier and one person holding a blocking pad roughly five yards away. There are three different angles to work for this drill. Two diagonal angles, and one head-on, in front angle.

TECHNIQUES: BALL CARRYING

EQUIPMENT: BLOCKING PAD

DRILL TYPE: SKILL, COORDINATION

Spin Drill

ADVANCED | INDIVIDUAL | CONTACT

PURPOSE

Practice initiating the spin move to utilize as a ball carrying technique to avoid a tackle.

DRILL DESCRIPTION

Players run towards a blocking pad with the mindset of breaking out a spin move to break the tackle. This drill focuses on the proper technique of the spin move.

Spin moves are not usually utilized in the open field, but are instead used at the very onset of contact. If a ball carrier times the spin right at the moment of contact, before the defender can gain a grasp of the ball carrier, then the spin move has a high chance of success.

The runner must lower his shoulder into the defender as if he is trying to run him over with power, but right as soon as they make contact, the runner must spin out and to the side to throw the defender for a loop and break free past the defender.

Run this drill at different angles to practice all the different perspectives that a runner may face when using the spin move.

Overflow Drill

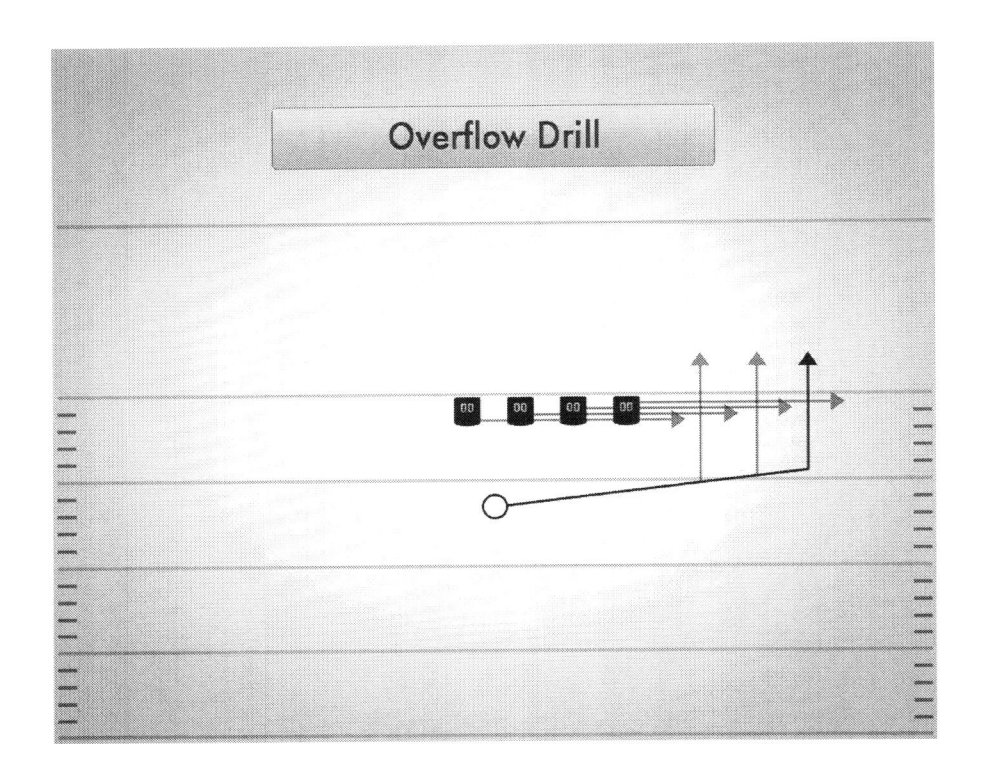

SETUP

This drill consists of one ball carrier, and four "defenders" holding onto a blocking pad. The defenders stand on the one yard line and spread out two to three yards from each other. The ball carrier starts the drill on the six yard line.

TECHNIQUES:	**BALL CARRYING**
EQUIPMENT:	**BLOCKING PAD**
DRILL TYPE:	**SKILL**

Overflow Drill

ADVANCED | GROUP | CONTACT

PURPOSE

Focusing on a goal line or short yardage situation, this drill teaches ball carriers how to cut back against the grain when the defense is overflowing to the side. Often times, the defense can do too good of a job of flowing to the outside to prevent a sweep. This drill teaches runners to use the defense's flow against them, and how to find a gap in between defenders to cut back against the flow.

DRILL DESCRIPTION

Upon the start of the drill, the ball carrier begins an angle to the corner of the drill. All the defenders begin running sideways to cut him off from running around to the outside.

This drill is set up so that the runner will not be able to actually outrun the defense, and will need to find a gap to shoot through.

The defenders can use contact to hit the ball carrier backward if he does not do a good enough job of finding a gap and gets too close to the defenders.

Multiple repetitions of this drill will increase your ball carrier's awareness and give him the toolset to respond and attack a defense that is overflowing.

Read the Block Drill

SETUP

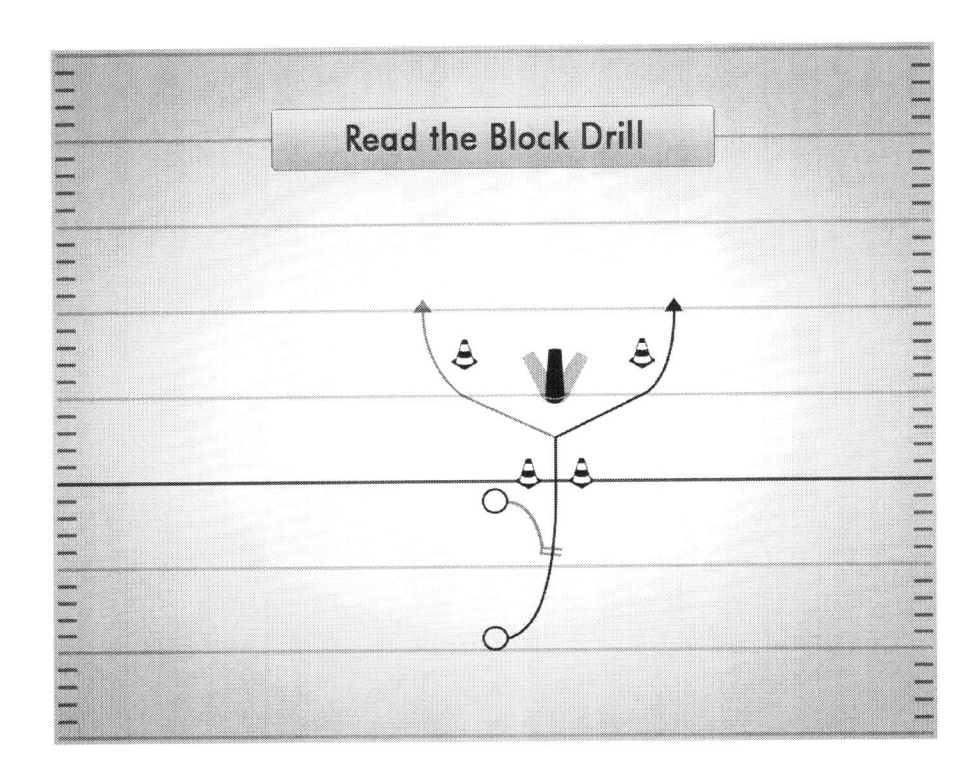

Place two cones on the line of scrimmage to mark the target hole for the running back. Place a tackle dummy five yards behind the line of scrimmage where a linebacker would stand. Two additional cones spread out ten yards are beyond the dummy. One person needs to man the dummy in order to tilt it one direction or the other. One person acts as the quarterback to handoff the ball to the running back.

TECHNIQUES: BALL CARRYING, FOOTWORK

EQUIPMENT: CONE, TACKLE DUMMY

DRILL TYPE: SKILL, SPEED, AGILITY

Read the Block Drill

ADVANCED	GROUP	NO-CONTACT

PURPOSE

All running backs need to learn how to read a block a respond instantaneously when quick changes of direction are needed. This drill teaches the awareness and change of direction needed to read block and successfully execute run plays.

DRILL DESCRIPTION

Begin the drill by executing the handoff and beginning stages of a run play in your playbook. Running backs keep their eyes up and their head on a swivel as they enter through the hole in the line of scrimmage to keep an eye on the second level.

When they break through the line of scrimmage, the person manning the tackle dummy aggressively tilts it either to the right or to the left. If it goes left, then the player cuts right, and vice-versa.

After executing the cut, the running back continues through the drill by rounding the final cone and heading upfield.

Rapid Catch Drill

SETUP

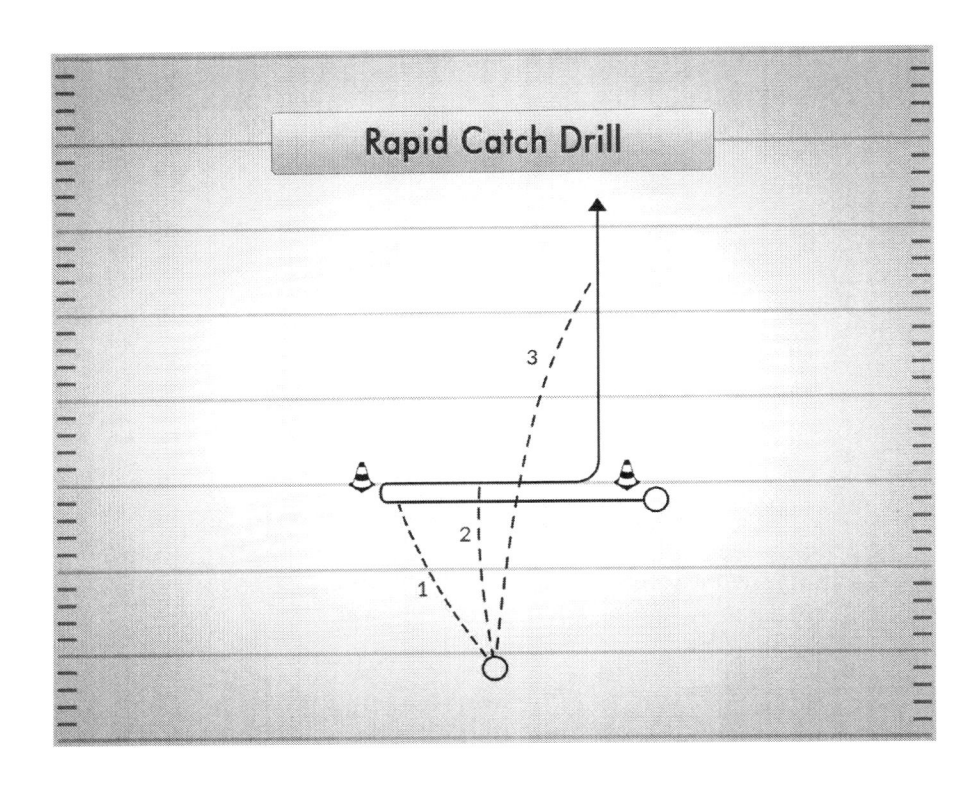

Place two cones fifteen yards apart. A quarterback or coach stands ten yards away from the cones.

TECHNIQUES:	CATCHING
EQUIPMENT:	NONE
DRILL TYPE:	SKILL

Rapid Catch Drill

ADVANCED   **INDIVIDUAL**   **NO-CONTACT**

PURPOSE

Wide receivers quickly gain practice catching the football in rapid succession through diverse and realistic situations.

DRILL DESCRIPTION

Running from right to left, the player runs across the field catching the first pass, and then tossing the ball to the side.

Continuing the drill, players do a 180 and traverse from cone to cone in the opposite direction as the catch their second pass.

After they release the second ball, they turn upfield and receive a lobbed deep pass downfield to conclude the drill.

Catch and Twist Drill

SETUP

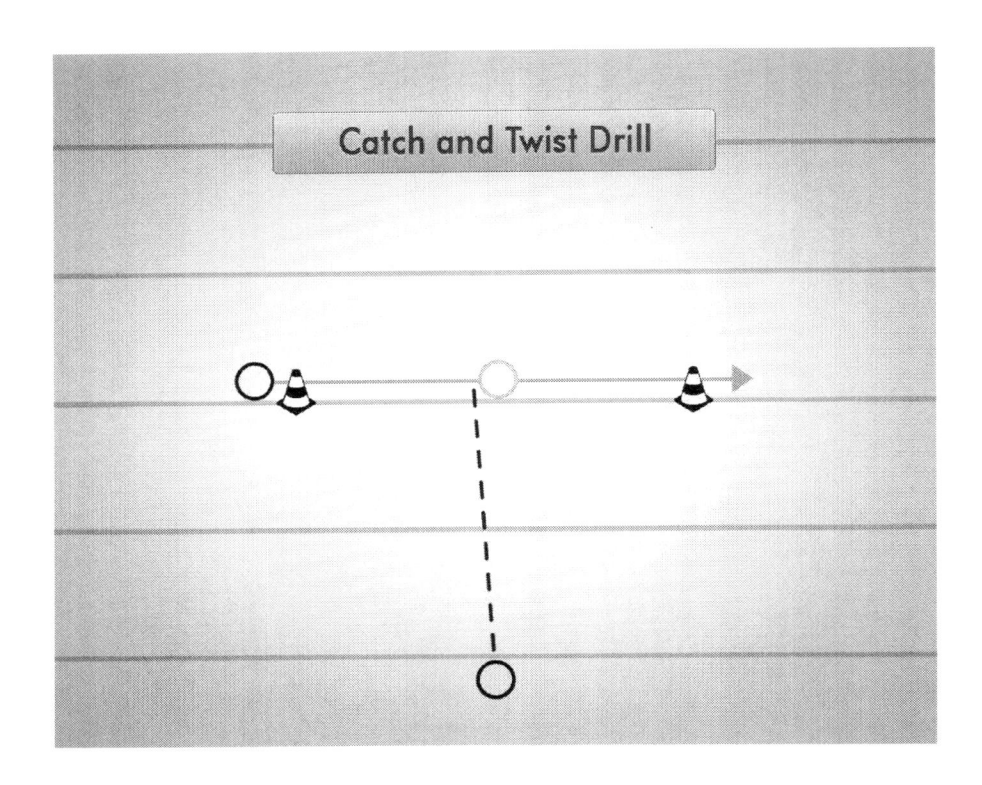

Place two cones fifteen yards apart and position a quarterback or coach ten yards away to throw the ball to the drill participants.

TECHNIQUES: CATCHING

EQUIPMENT: NONE

DRILL TYPE: SKILL

Catch and Twist Drill

ADVANCED | INDIVIDUAL | NO-CONTACT

PURPOSE

This drill teaches players how to use the proper technique when catching a ball that is thrown behind them.

DRILL DESCRIPTION

Player run half speed horizontally across the field. The thrower purposely throws a bad throw behind the receiver.

To catch the pass players should twist themselves around backward so that their momentum doesn't tear them away from the ball. As they twist backward to catch the ball, they procure the catch, and then continue the spin, making a complete 360 in order to successfully make the catch and stay on their feet.

Late Catch Drill

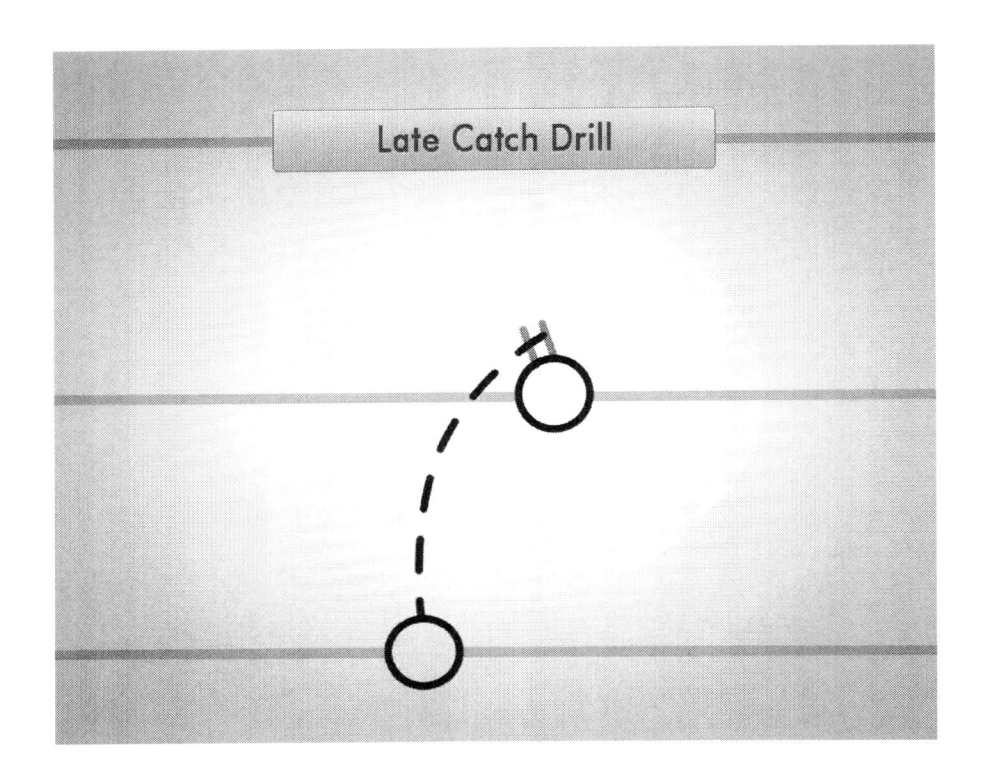

SETUP

All players grab a partner and each set of partners grabs a football for the drill. Players stand five yards downfield and two yards to the side of their partner.

TECHNIQUES:	CATCHING
EQUIPMENT:	NONE
DRILL TYPE:	SKILL, COORDINATION

Late Catch Drill

ADVANCED   PARTNER   NO-CONTACT

PURPOSE

Waiting until as late as possible to catch a ball while running a deep route can mean the difference between an incompletion and a touchdown. If the receiver extends his hands too early, it could either tip off the defense to the fact that the ball is coming, and give them time to knock the ball down, or it could slow the receiver down from running his fastest and prevent him from being able to run the ball down before it hits the ground.

This drill ingrains the habit of waiting until the last second to reach out your hands and make the catch.

DRILL DESCRIPTION

The player throwing the ball tosses it nice and easy out in front of his partner.

The player catching the ball turns their back to their partner and fires his hands in a running motion while keeping his feet planted. He continues his running motion until as late as possible, before reaching out his hands to catch the ball.

Players should push themselves further and further to get more and more comfortable waiting until as late as possible.

Push Up & Catch Drill

SETUP

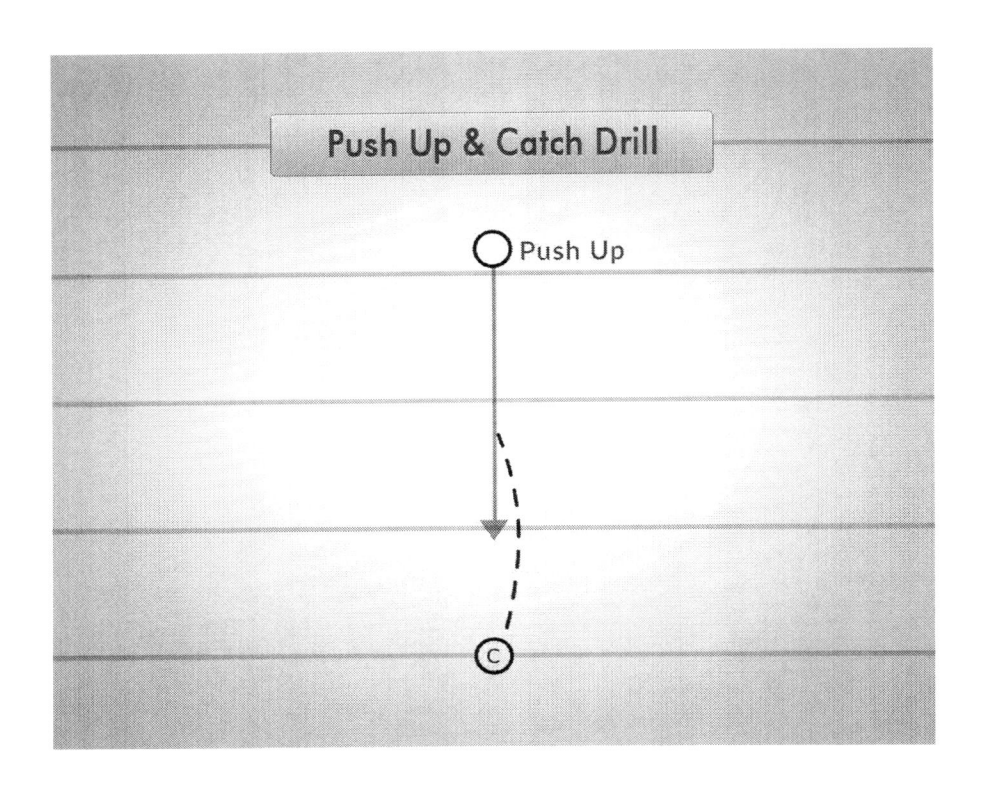

The receiver should lay face down on the ground 15 yards in front of the coach/quarterback.

TECHNIQUES:	CATCHING
EQUIPMENT:	NONE
DRILL TYPE:	SKILL

Push Up & Catch Drill

EASY INDIVIDUAL NO-CONTACT

PURPOSE

Teach the receiver to get up quickly off of the ground and still receiver a pass even if he were to trip or fall during the course of the play.

DRILL DESCRIPTION

This drill simulates a portion of an in-game scenario where the wide receiver trips or falls during the course of his route. Players should never give up in the middle of a play and this drill demonstrates to receivers what to do in that scenario.

The wide receiver pushes himself off of the ground as quickly as possible and runs straight towards the coach. The coach will throw a pass to the player who will then need to complete the catch to finish the drill.

Hook Around Drill

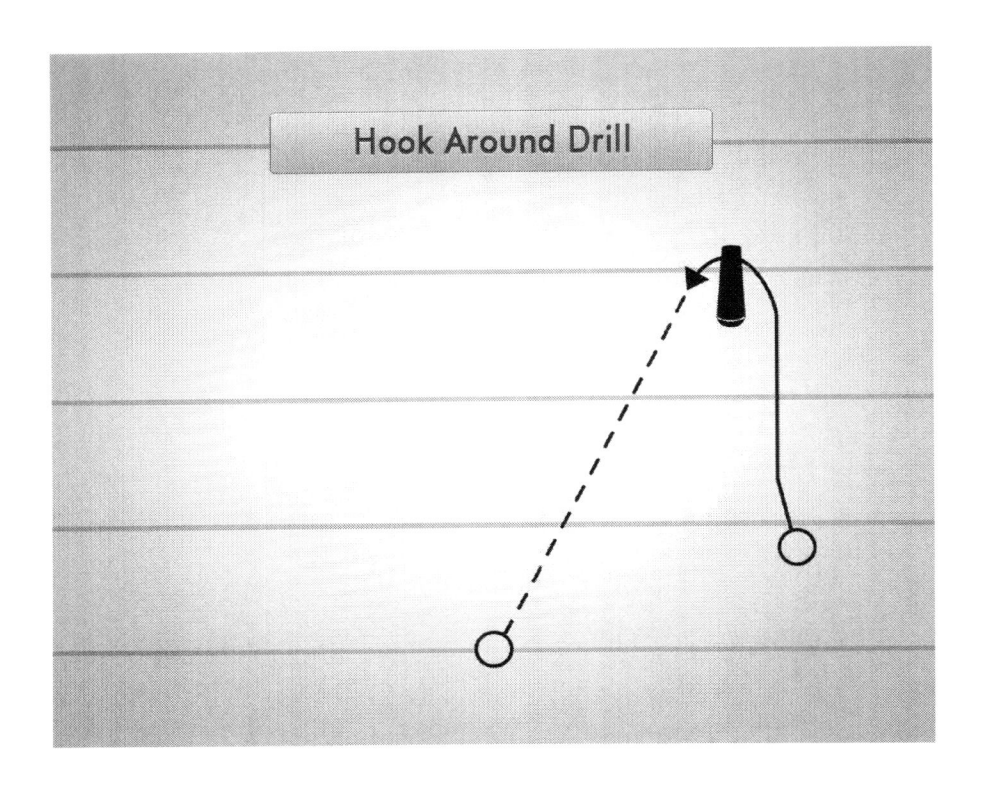

SETUP

The quarterback and receiver line up with a tackle dummy placed a step inside of the receiver and eight yards downfield.

TECHNIQUES: PASSING, CATCHING

EQUIPMENT: TACKLE DUMMY

DRILL TYPE: SKILL, TEAMWORK

Hook Around Drill

INTERMEDIATE | **GROUP** | **NO-CONTACT**

PURPOSE

The purpose of the Hook Around drill is to teach wide receivers how to hook around a defender who is hanging around in the zone of their route.

It also helps build chemistry between the quarterback and receiver as they get a feel for how far each player tends to hook around a defender when encountering this situation.

DRILL DESCRIPTION

The quarterback begins the drill by simulating a snap and beginning his drop back. The receiver runs a ten yard hook route with the presence of the tackle dummy/defender in mind.

The route should take him beyond and around the tackle dummy before hooking up beyond the dummy and to the inside.

The quarterback will deliver the ball before the receiver has completely wrapped around the dummy and the ball will be there for the receiver to catch once he has crossed around and hooked into position.

QB High Release Drill

SETUP

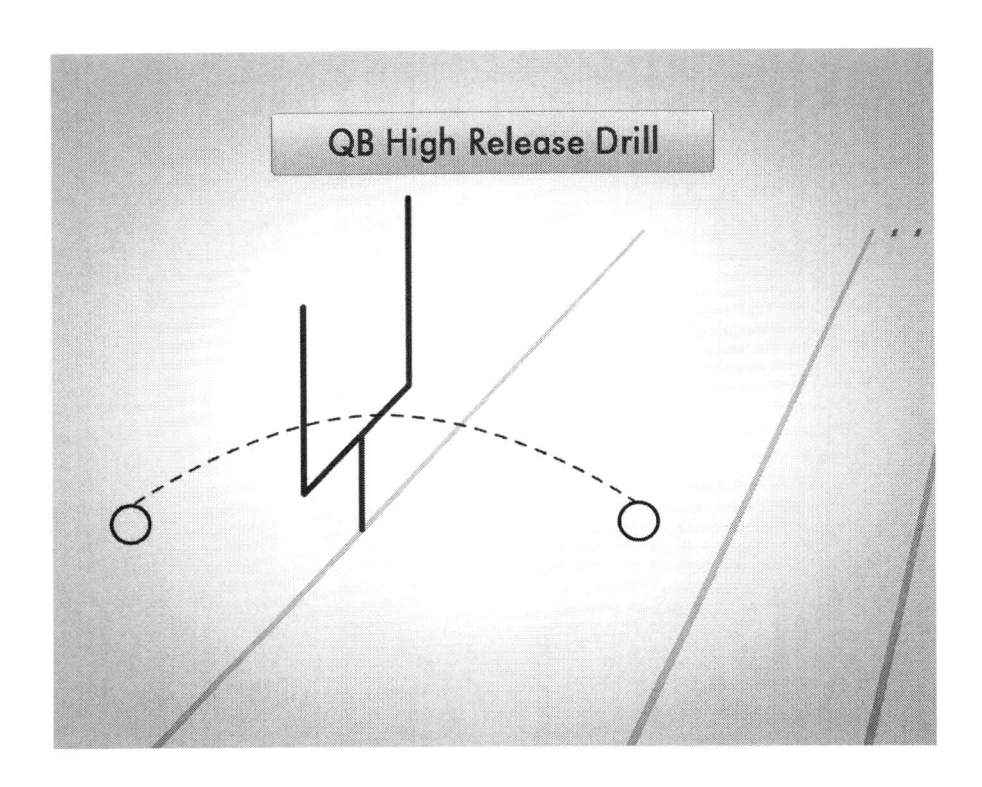

Two quarterbacks stand on either side of the goalpost, ten to twenty yards away from each other depending on age and height.

TECHNIQUES: **PASSING**

EQUIPMENT:

DRILL TYPE: **SKILL, COORDINATION**

QB High Release Drill

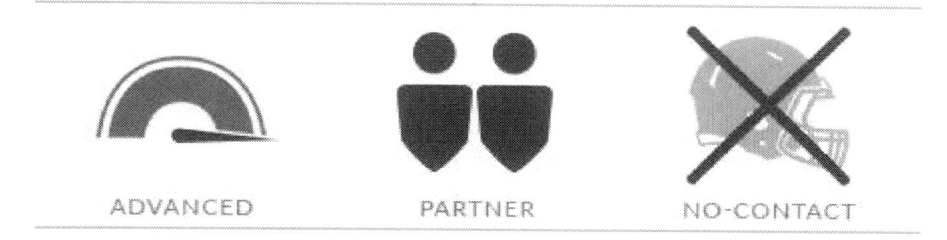

ADVANCED   PARTNER   NO-CONTACT

PURPOSE

The quickest way for a defense to stop a pass is to knock the ball down at the line of scrimmage. That is why it is essential for quarterbacks to have a high release when they throw the ball in order for the trajectory of the pass to take the ball over the swiping hands of the defensive linemen.

DRILL DESCRIPTION

Quarterbacks simply pass the ball back and forth to each other. The focus should be on their throwing motion as they try to extend their arm high and release the ball at the highest point in their motion.

Sidearm throws will often get knocked down at the line of scrimmage, so quarterbacks need to be taught to release the ball high to keep it at a safe trajectory.

This drill will clearly show quarterbacks if their release is to low, because the ball will bang off the cross beam or even go underneath it.

Passing Tree Drill

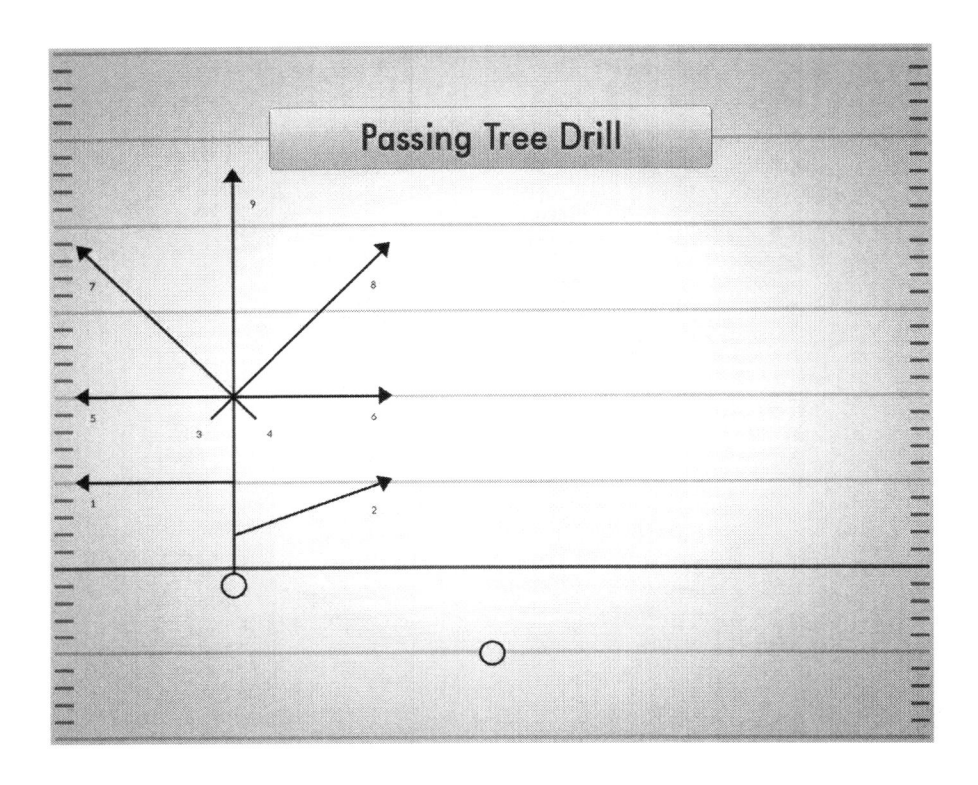

SETUP

Quarterbacks line up in the middle of the field while wide receivers line up on the line of scrimmage prepared to run all the routes in the passing tree.

TECHNIQUES:	PASSING, CATCHING
EQUIPMENT:	NONE
DRILL TYPE:	SKILL, TEAMWORK

Passing Tree Drill

INTERMEDIATE   GROUP   NO-CONTACT

PURPOSE

Players learn the number system for your team's passing tree and how to run and execute each of the routes.

DRILL DESCRIPTION

Receivers line up and individually run each route in the passing tree. Quarterbacks throw the ball to each receiver as they run the routes. Starting with the lowest number and going to the largest number, receivers each run one route once until all receivers have looped through every route in the passing tree.

Each team's passing tree numbers may vary slightly, but in general, one popular way to number the routes is to have the even numbers run to the inside of the play and the odd numbers run to the outside of the play. The bigger the number, the further the route. This allows players and coaches to quickly communicate the routes with each other in an easily understandable way.

Man-to-man Press

SETUP

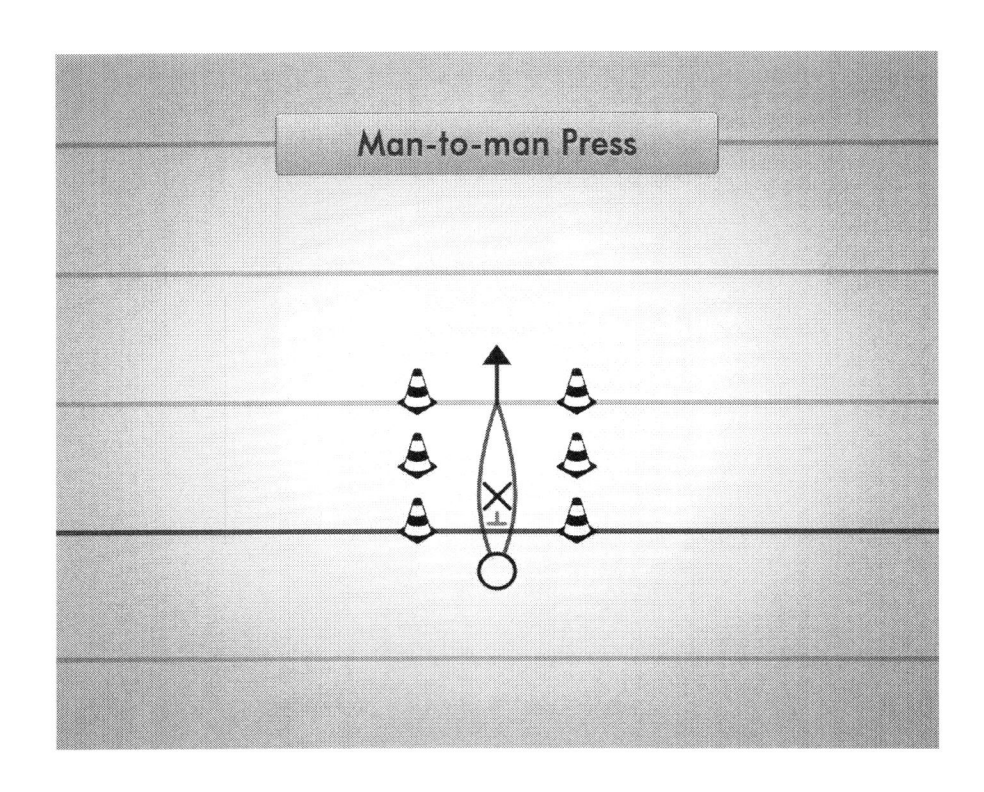

A receiver and a defensive back face off at the line of scrimmage. Place cones to contain the drill to a width of six yards, and extend them five yards up field.

TECHNIQUES:	PASS DEFENDING
EQUIPMENT:	CONE
DRILL TYPE:	SKILL, COMPETITION

Man-to-man Press Drill

ADVANCED — PARTNER — CONTACT

PURPOSE

Often times a defense will want to slow down the release of the receivers at the line of scrimmage. To do this, they will place their defensive backs in press coverage where they will meet the offense at the line of scrimmage.

The dual purposes of the Man-to-man Press drill are to teach the defensive back how to successfully execute a press coverage on a receiver, and to teach the wide receiver how to quickly fend off the coverage when being pressed by a defensive back.

DRILL DESCRIPTION

The defensive back will stand as close as possible to the line of scrimmage with his feet even and shoulder width apart. His eyes are locked in on the hips and torso of the receiver, because his target will be to maintain his position on top of the receiver and prevent him from gaining a quick release off of the line of scrimmage.

Upon starting the drill, the receiver will release off the line of scrimmage at the same time that the defensive back will fire his hands in the chest of the receiver. The receiver needs to use his arms and dip his shoulders to deflect the press coverage as he attempts to step around the defender and push upfield.

Meanwhile, the defender needs to move his feet to mirror the movement of the receiver and stay in front of him for as long as possible.

Blast Through Drill

SETUP

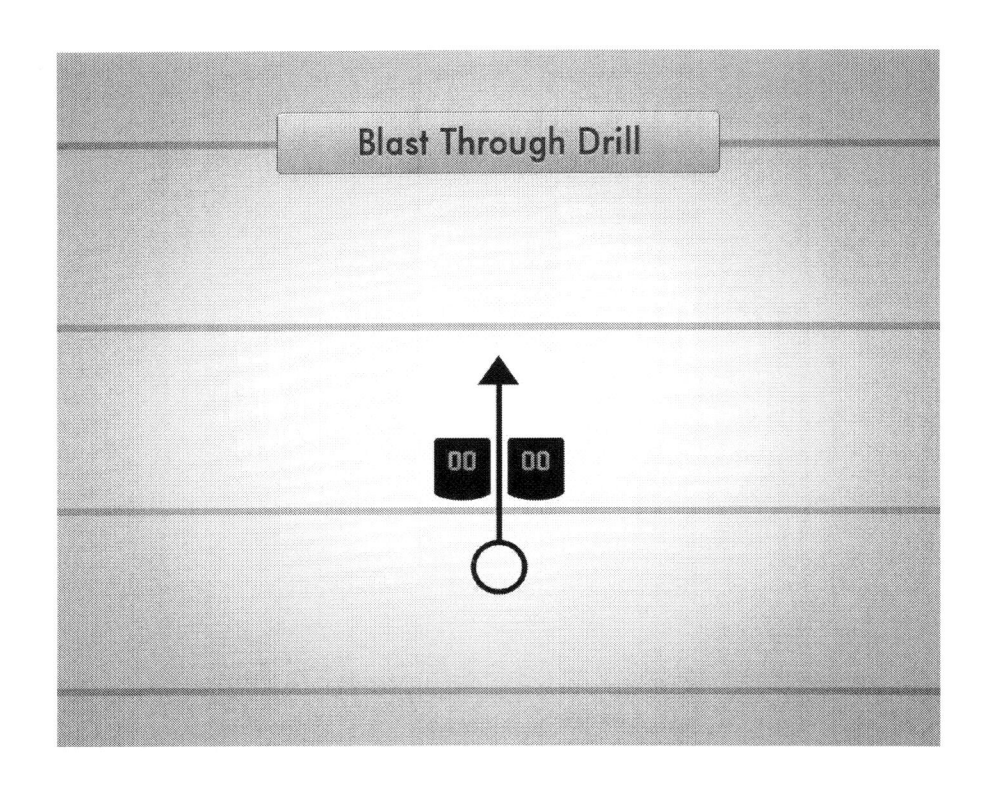

Assign two players to stand even with each other while holding blocking pads. Drill participants grab a football and while line up in front of the gap in the two blocking pads.

TECHNIQUES:	BALL CARRYING
EQUIPMENT:	BLOCKING PAD
DRILL TYPE:	SKILL

Blast Through Drill

EASY   GROUP   CONTACT

PURPOSE

Teaches players how to initiate contact by lowering their shoulders and blasting through contact. Ball carriers can use this drill to improve their ability to lower their shoulders and run through defenders. Breaking a tackle from two defenders at once can be difficult, but blasting through it can mean gaining enough yards for a first down, or maybe even a touchdown.

DRILL DESCRIPTION

As players approach the blocking pads, they lower their shoulders while keeping their head up. They need to get low to the ground and use the power of their legs to drive forward and explode through the blocking pads.

Those holding the blocking pads should get low in their stance and provide firm contact to the ball carrier. The pads should not be lurched out at the ball carrier, but instead should provide firm resistance.

Players rotate as ball carriers and blocking pad holders, as they take turns blasting their way through the blocking pads.

Block Battle Drill

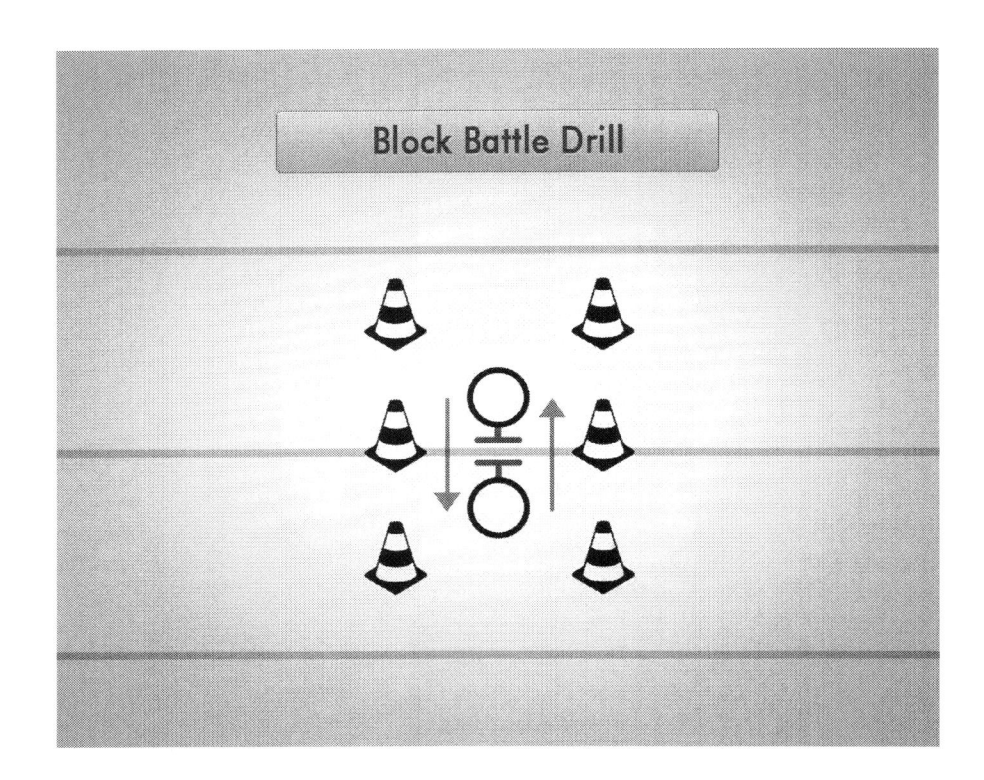

SETUP

Use cones to create a boundary for the drill that is six yards wide. A yard line through the middle will be helpful to indicate the line of scrimmage, and cones may be placed to indicate three yards of height on either side of the line of scrimmage to indicate the end of the back boundary.

TECHNIQUES: **BLOCKING**

EQUIPMENT: **CONE**

DRILL TYPE: **SKILL, COMPETITION**

Block Battle Drill

EASY   PARTNER   CONTACT

PURPOSE

Players face off with the purpose of increasing their run blocking ability and building their power to move people in the trench in the middle of a play.

DRILL DESCRIPTION

Match players up as partners with an even size and skill level. Each set of partners faces off in the block battle to push each other backward.

Players begin the drill close to each other, without a running start, to limit the vicious, high-velocity contact. Instead, this drill almost acts as a form of a one-on-one tug of war.

A player wins the drill if they can push their opponent backward beyond the back cones before time runs out. Coaches let the drill go for 5-10 seconds depending on the competition level.

Break Down Drill

SETUP

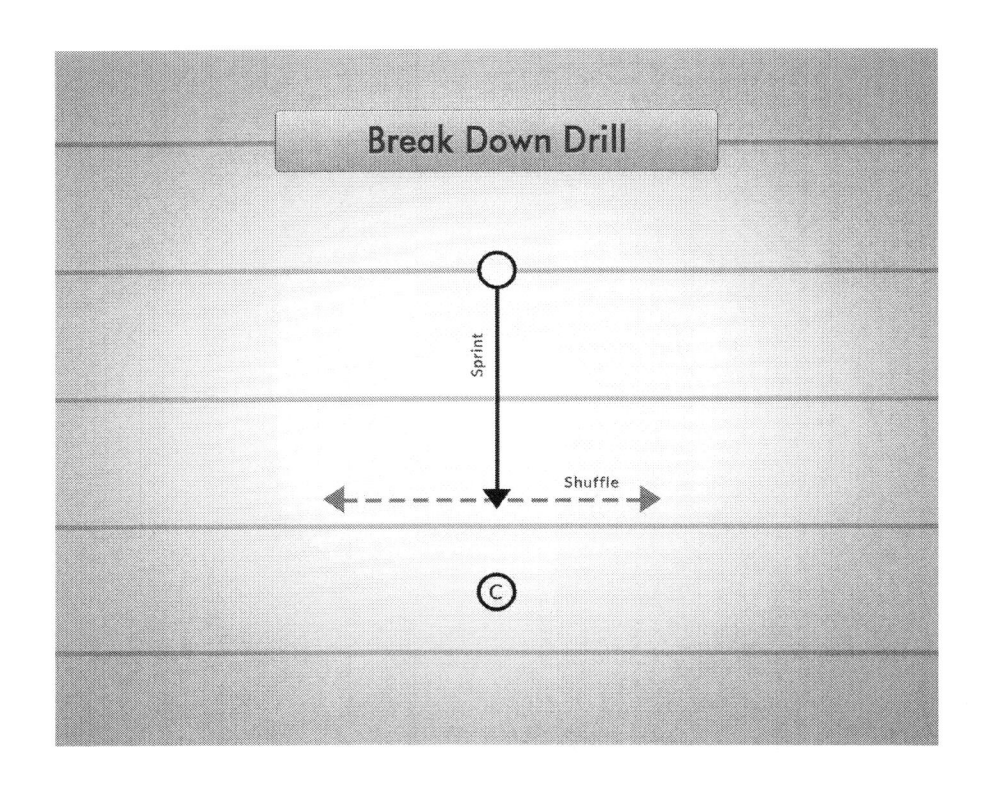

Player(s) simply stand roughly 12 yards in front of a coach.

TECHNIQUES:	FOOTWORK
EQUIPMENT:	NONE
DRILL TYPE:	PHYSICAL PERFORMANCE, SKILL, SPEED, AGILITY

Break Down Drill

EASY   GROUP   NO-CONTACT

PURPOSE

A lot of times, the wisest option for a defender charging towards a ball carrier is to break down and shuffle sideways in order to maintain his position in front of the ball carrier so that he does not miss the tackle. This drill works on the fitness and footwork involved in this situation.

DRILL DESCRIPTION

Coaches signal for the player(s) to spring forward towards the coach while keeping their head up and eyes on the coach. After a few yards, the coach points to one side or the other. Players then break down from their sprint and begin shuffling to the side signaled by the coach.

After a few steps of shuffles, the coach then points in the other direction, and players reverse the direction of their shuffle.

The coach continues for a few more changes of direction before the drill is finished and reset.

QB Center Exchange - Snap

SETUP

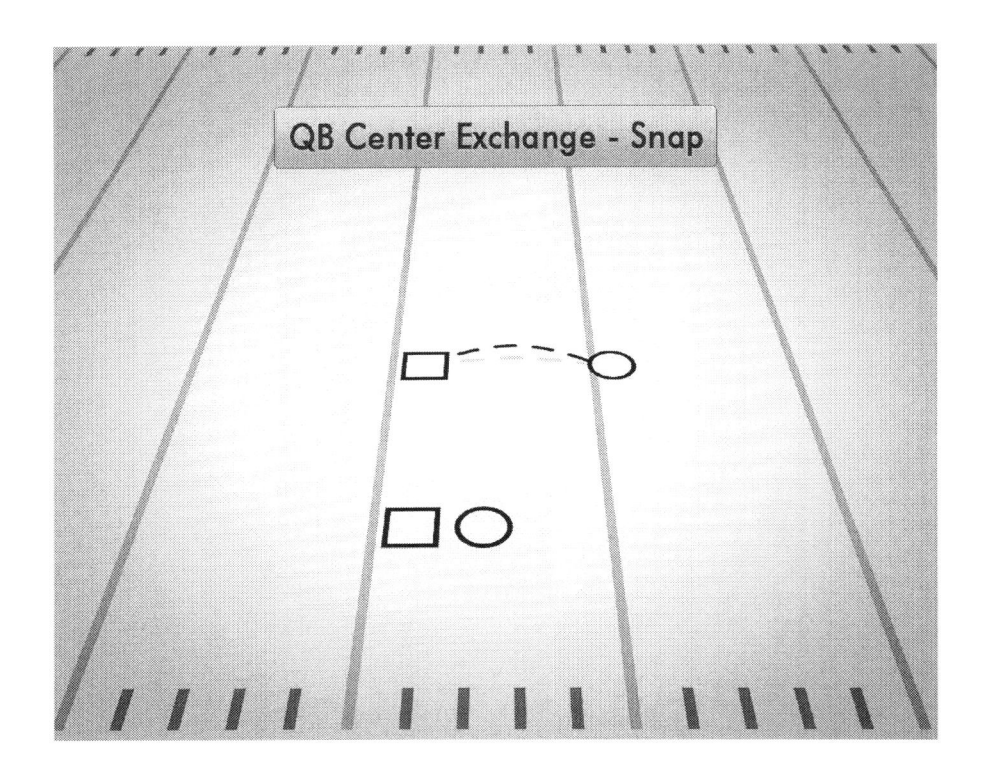

Line up your quarterbacks and centers in their typical formation alignment; either under center, in the shotgun, or both.

EQUIPMENT: NONE

DRILL TYPE: SKILL, COORDINATION, TEAMWORK

QB Center Exchange - Snap Drill

EASY   PARTNER   NO-CONTACT

PURPOSE

The start of every offensive play begins with the QB/Center exchange. Often overlooked, if this exchange does not succeed, then the entire play will be ruined, or could even end in a turnover. Ensuring that this exchange is automatic and secure is the very first foundational step in every offense.

DRILL DESCRIPTION

Simply snap the football between quarterback and center continuously for the duration of the drill. It is absolutely imperative that this task becomes second nature, because one failure in the game can result in either a complete loss of the play or the entire loss of possession.

Sideline Catch Drill

SETUP

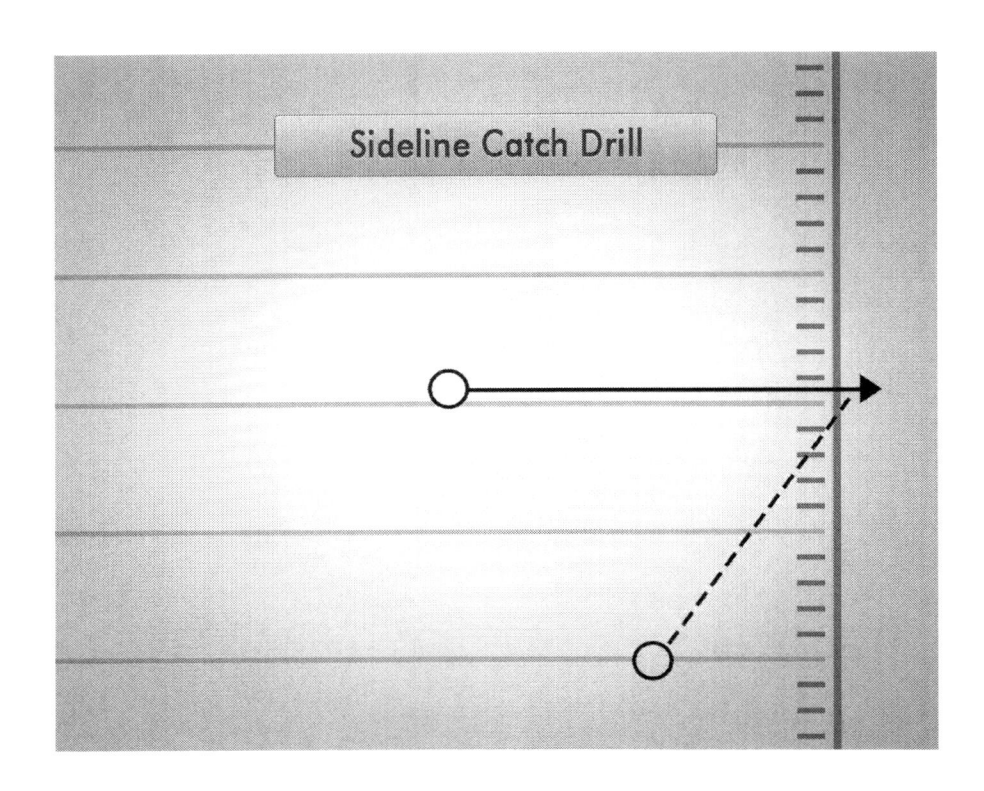

Place receivers ten yards away from the sideline and ten yards downfield from the coach/quarterback.

TECHNIQUES:	CATCHING, FOOTWORK
EQUIPMENT:	NONE
DRILL TYPE:	SKILL, COORDINATION

Sideline Catch Drill

ADVANCED | GROUP | CONTACT

PURPOSE

Increase comfort level with routes on the sideline and develop the ability to haul in the ball while keeping a foot in bounds to successfully complete the catch.

DRILL DESCRIPTION

The receiver runs towards the sideline as the coach/quarterback throws a ball that will purposefully make it difficult for the receiver to catch it while remaining in bounds. Many repetitions of this drill will teach receivers to not look down directly at the sideline, but instead, feel where it is and not step over. Outside of the professional leagues, most leagues require only one foot to remain in bounds for a catch.

As the ball is arriving, proper sideline technique is for receivers to stick their last foot in the ground, never letting it lift off the ground. The other leg can be brought up to allow the receiver to reach his upper body further, but only let that leg touch the ground again if the ball is already secure in the hands. As the receiver drifts out of bounds, the back foot can lift to the toe, but the toe must drag on the ground, never lifting off the ground. The trail of dirt on the ground will signal to the referee that the receiver did indeed stay in bounds long enough to make the catch.

Distraction Catch Drill

SETUP

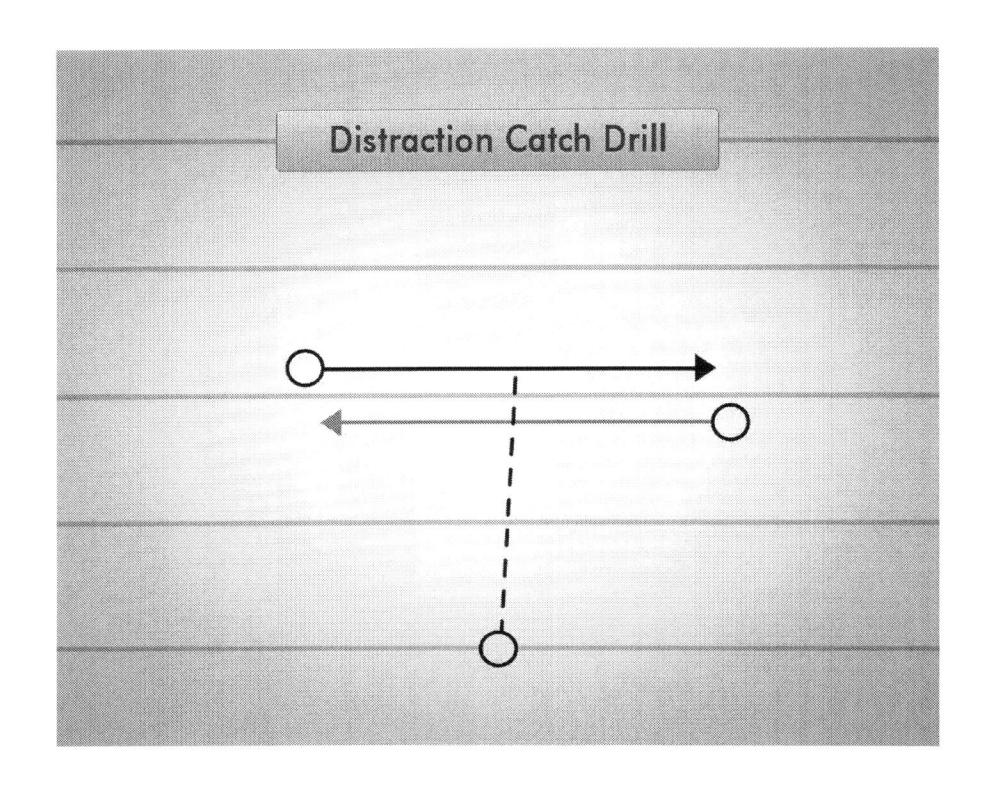

Form two lines of receivers facing each other, ten yards apart. One line, the distraction line, should be staggered a yard or two in front of the other, regular line. A coach/quarterback is placed ten yards downfield.

TECHNIQUES:	CATCHING
EQUIPMENT:	NONE
DRILL TYPE:	SKILL, COORDINATION

Distraction Catch Drill

ADVANCED   GROUP   NO-CONTACT

PURPOSE

The purpose of the Distraction Catch drill is to provide a very difficult distraction for receivers as they attempt to haul in a pass. On any single play in a game, there are 21 other players on the field. These players are bound to be distracting when a ball is in the air, so it is critical that players get experience with traffic flying in front of their face as the ball is flying towards their face.

DRILL DESCRIPTION

The coach signals for the receiver and the distraction player to run across the field at the same time. The thrower attempts to have the ball arrive in the receiver's hands right around the time that the distraction player is close to the receiver.

The distraction player waives his hands and arms in the air to provide a distraction and make it hard for the receiver to make the catch, but does not allow himself to get hit by the ball so that it can make its way through to the receiver.

The receiver then catches the ball and gets in the distraction line to take his turn as the distraction player.

Lead Blocker Drill

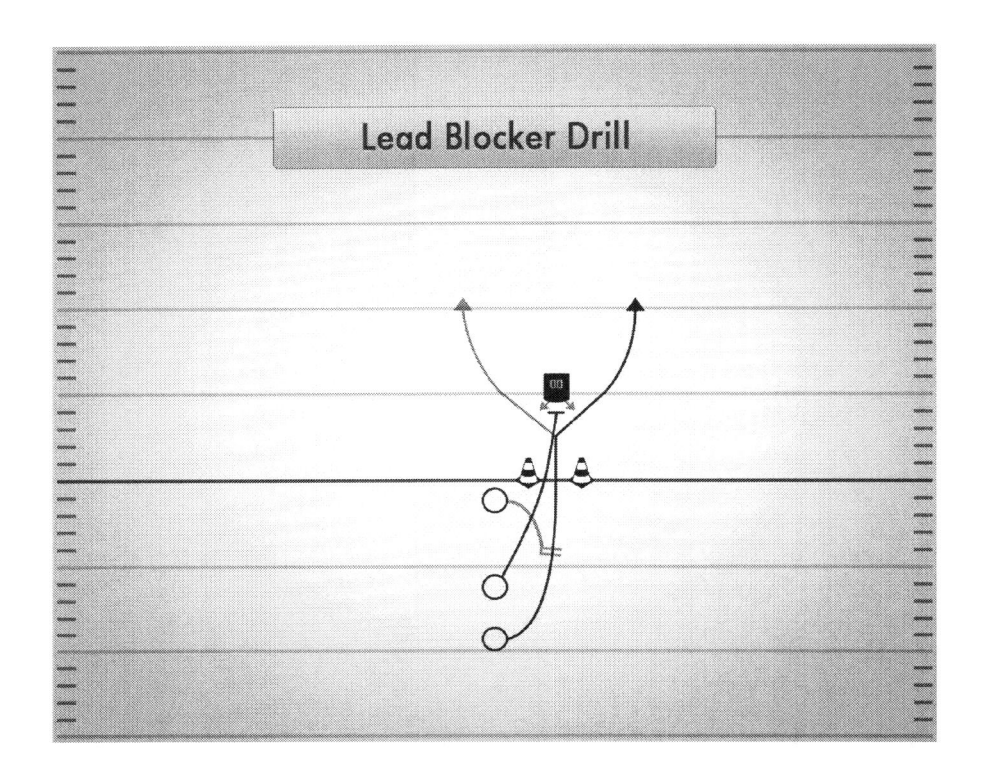

SETUP

Align the offense in a running formation with a lead blocker in position to be the lead blocker for the running back. The lead blocker can either be a fullback or a pulling guard, depending on the team's typical plays and playbook. A person holding a blocking pad stands as the linebacker, five yards past the line of scrimmage.

TECHNIQUES:	BALL CARRYING, BLOCKING
EQUIPMENT:	NONE
DRILL TYPE:	SKILL, TEAMWORK

Lead Blocker Drill

ADVANCED　　　　　GROUP　　　　　CONTACT

PURPOSE

The Lead Blocker Drill is a drill for both the lead blocker and the running back. Reactions must be incredibly quick in the middle of the defense and both players must immediately react and make moves based upon each other and the defense. This drill allows the lead blocker to practice paving the way for the running back, while the running back gets to practice making a move off of the block from the lead blocker.

DRILL DESCRIPTION

The lead blocker runs through the hole and towards the linebacker. The linebacker makes a move either to the right or to the left. When the linebacker makes his move, the lead blocker makes his block and pushes him out of the way.

The running back receives the handoff, makes his way through the hole behind the lead blocker. The running back must read the block of the lead blocker and cut off of the block and run downfield.

Tackle Lanes Drill

SETUP

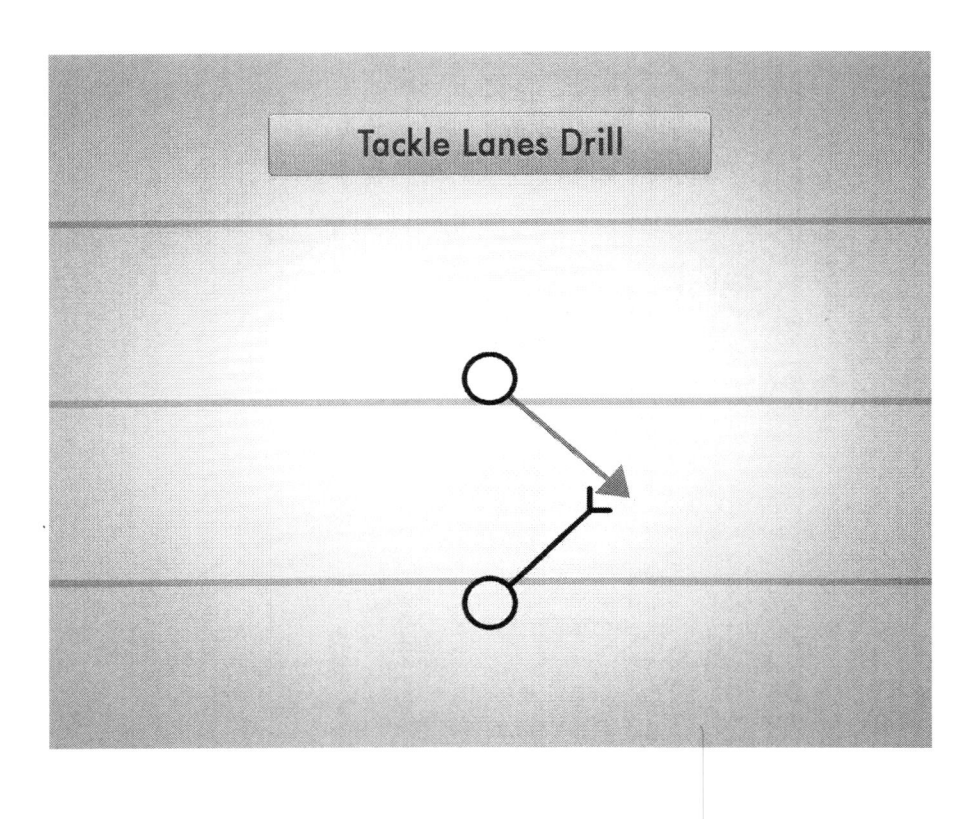

Two players line up face-to-face, five yards apart from each other.

TECHNIQUES:	TACKLING
EQUIPMENT:	NONE
DRILL TYPE:	SKILL

Tackle Lanes

EASY　　　PARTNER　　　CONTACT

PURPOSE

Teach proper tackle technique with the Tackle Lanes Drill. This drill focuses on the particular body placement and form of a textbook tackle.

This drill is also effective in pregame warmups to expose your defense to some light contact before the game begins.

DRILL DESCRIPTION

Both players run half speed at a 45 degree angle to the side. The tackler works on making a proper form tackle. The tackler gets low, keeps his head up and places his body in front of the body of the runner so as to not accidentally perform an arm tackle. An arm tackle is when only the arms of the defender make contact on the ball carrier, which is a very easy tackle to break out of.

After wrapping his arms around the tackle, the tackler drives through and pushes back for a couple of yards. Both players should remain on their feet at all times throughout the drill.

The tackler then rotates and takes his place in the other line and continues the rotation.

Get to the Sticks

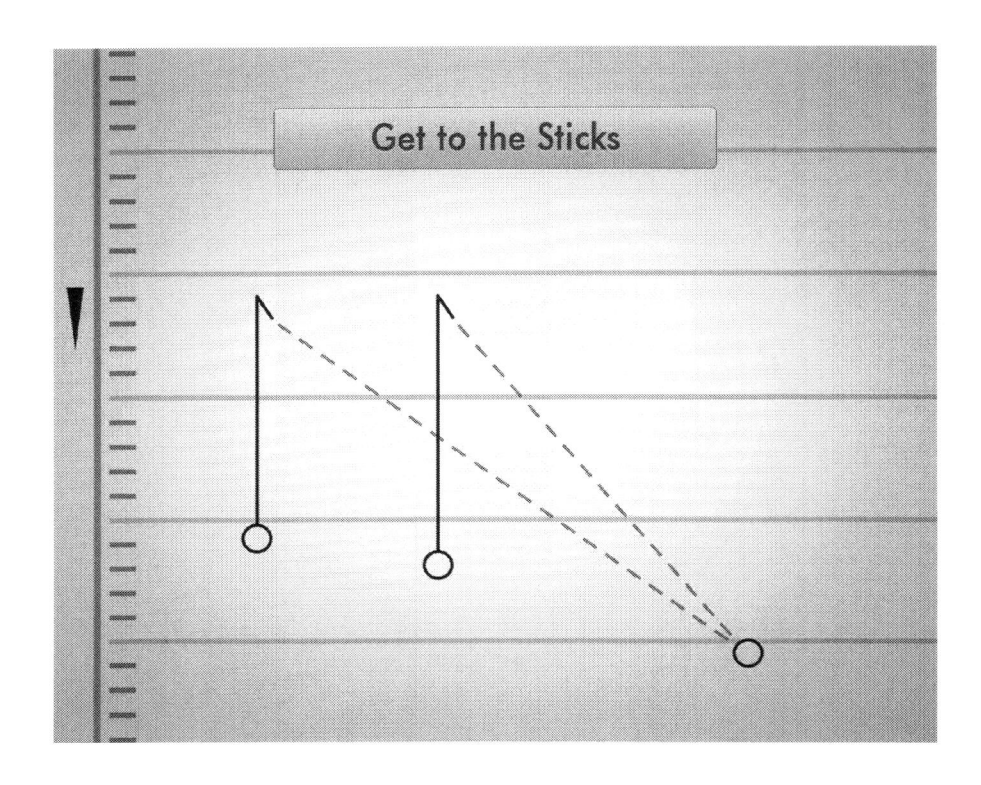

SETUP

Indicate the first down line by using yardage markers or some sort of symbolic representation of the down and distance chain.

TECHNIQUES: PASSING, CATCHING

EQUIPMENT: NONE

DRILL TYPE: SKILL, TEAMWORK

Get to the Sticks

ADVANCED   GROUP   NO-CONTACT

PURPOSE

Train your wide receivers to have awareness of the field and awareness of the situation while running their routes. On a third down play, it would be useless to gain five yards if you need seven. This drill teaches players to watch the "sticks" to know where they need to go to adjust their route to get the first down.

DRILL DESCRIPTION

Players run hook routes and modify the distance to ensure they pushed to the proper depth to ensure they gain a first down if thrown to. This usually means that receivers push upfield a yard or two further than the first down line in order to give them enough space to plant and come back for the ball without giving up space in front of the first down line.

Utilizing a quarterback for this drill also adds an element of teamwork and helps build chemistry, as the quarterback learns how far his wide receivers tend to go in a given situation.

Throughout the drill, a coach can modify the location of the first down line so that players must continually keep an awareness for where they need to go in order to "get to the sticks" and procure a first down.

Sticky Drill

SETUP

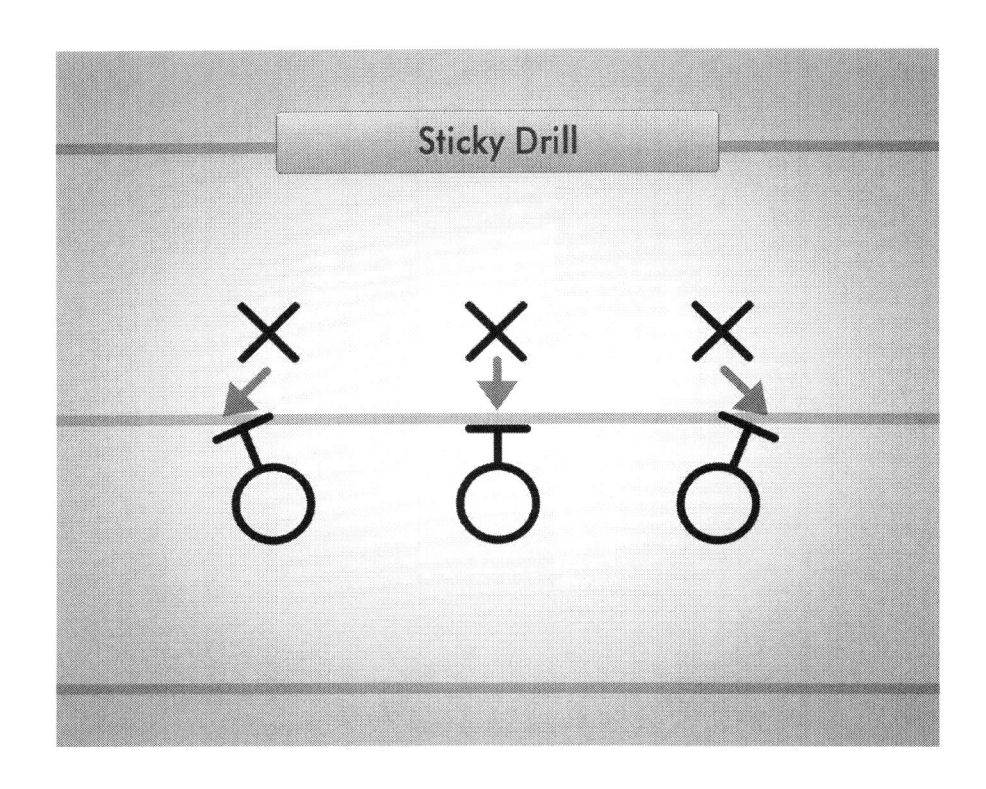

Player partner up according to size and ability in this blocking drill.

TECHNIQUES:	**BLOCKING**
EQUIPMENT:	**NONE**
DRILL TYPE:	**SKILL**

Sticky Drill

INTERMEDIATE **PARTNER** **CONTACT**

PURPOSE

Holding a defender is the easiest way to keep him from making a tackle. However, obviously, holding is illegal while blocking. This drill teaches blockers how to make themselves "sticky" and stick to defenders without getting a flag thrown for holding.

DRILL DESCRIPTION

Players line up face to face with one player acting as the defender and the other acting as the blocker. The defender starts the drill by making a move either directly forward, or at an angle to the side.

Upon the defender's first move, the blocker must shuffle his feet to remain in front of the defender, and then stick his hands into the defender's chest.

Flags are thrown for holding in one of two situations. Either when referees see a player tugging and stretching a jersey, or when the blocker wraps his arms around the defender. When blockers keep their hands inside the defender's chest, however, they are given leeway to attach onto the player without a holding flag being thrown. Therefore, the proper blocking technique is for blockers to center up on the defender and stick to them by gaining a grasp on the defender's chest plate. Only after the defender separates and extends away does the grip need to be released in time to avoid the holding call.

Remaining face to face and chest to chest is critical for a good block, and this drill teaches blockers the technique to center up and stick to defenders.

Shadow Boxing Drill

Shuffle & Strip

Run

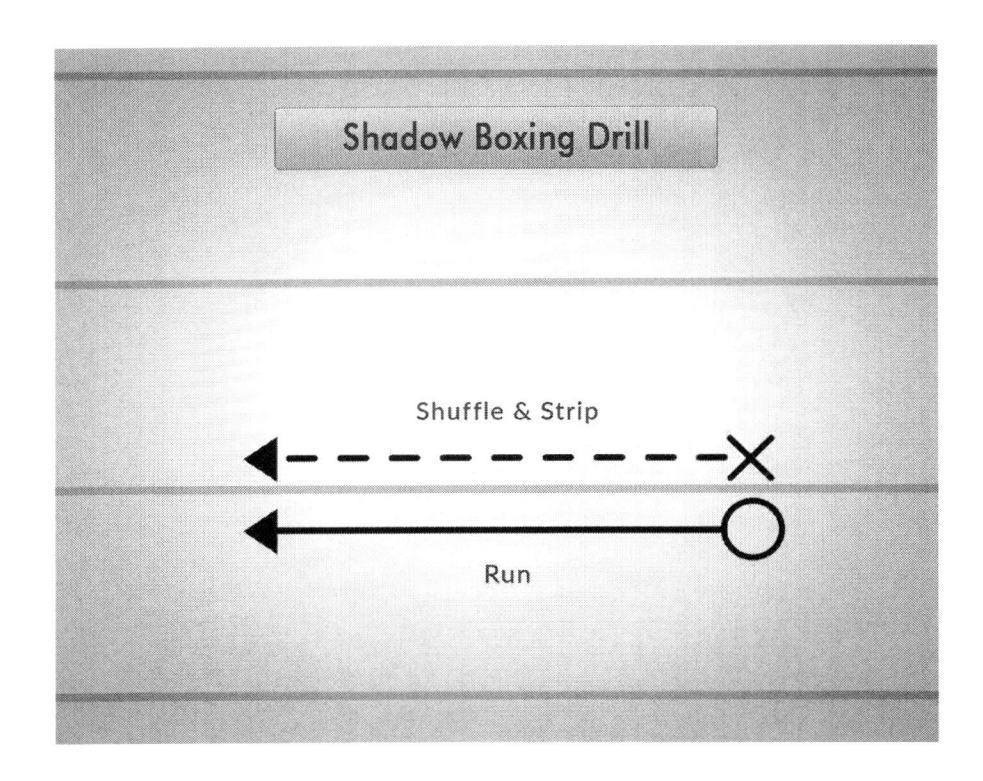

SETUP

Players partner up and use a yard line to remain horizontally parallel with each other throughout the drill.

TECHNIQUES:	BALL CARRYING
EQUIPMENT:	NONE
DRILL TYPE:	SKILL, COORDINATION

Shadow Boxing Drill

EASY   PARTNER   CONTACT

PURPOSE

The worst thing a running back can do is to fumble the football while running with it. This drill teaches good ball carrying technique and provides ball carriers with practice holding tightly onto the football while running and avoiding a strip or fumble.

DRILL DESCRIPTION

The ball carrier makes his way across the field at a slow quarter speed jog while tightly holding onto the football.

His partner, the defender, shuffles alongside him as he uses his arms to strip, rip, knock, pull, and punch the ball out of the ball carrier's grip.

The ball carrier, must use proper ball carrying technique to hold the ball high and tight across his chest, and securely hanging onto it with his fingers covering the point, his forearm across the outside, and his chest protecting the inside.

The partners trade off carrying the ball and switching sides/arms each time they go back across the field.

Pitch and Weave Drill

SETUP

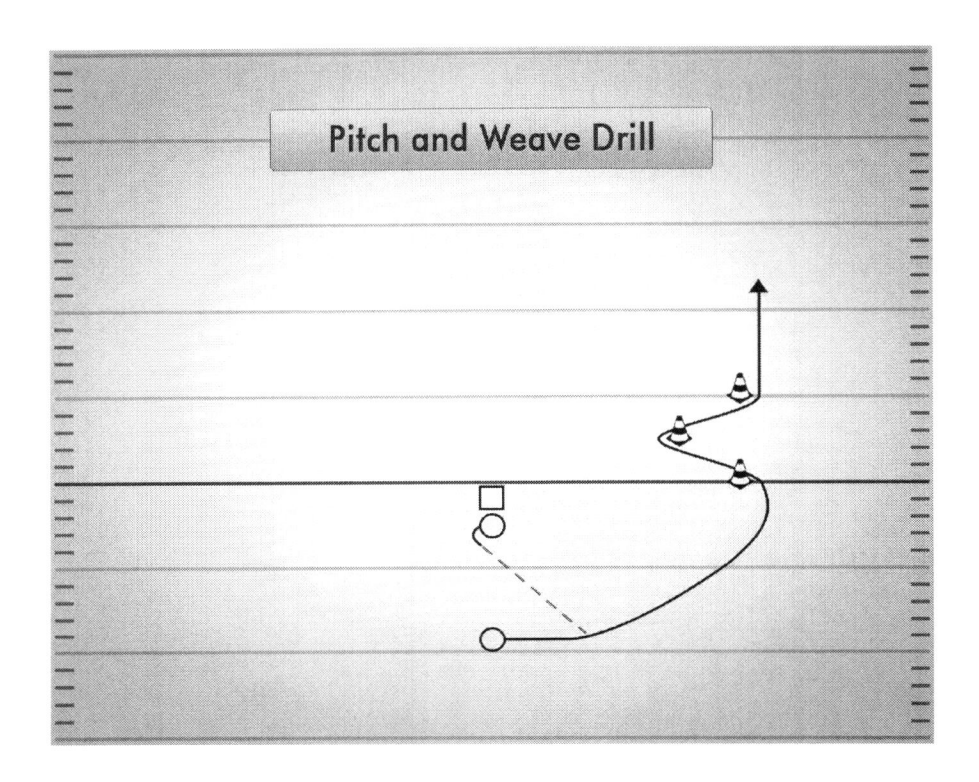

The running back and quarterback line up in their normal formation alignment in preparation for a pitch sweep play. Three cones are set up in a zigzag 5 yards away from each other starting on the far end of the line of scrimmage.

TECHNIQUES: **BALL CARRYING**

EQUIPMENT: **CONE**

DRILL TYPE: **SKILL, SPEED, AGILITY**

Pitch and Weave Drill

EASY   GROUP   NO-CONTACT

PURPOSE

The purpose of the Pitch and Weave Drill is to work on the initial phase of a pitch sweep play, and then to have the running back work on changing direction during a full sprint.

DRILL DESCRIPTION

The quarterback reverse pivots and pitches the ball to the running back on a trajectory for a sweep.

The running back receives the pitch and runs towards the sideline. Upon arriving to the first cone, the running back quickly changes direction by cutting around the cone, and then traverses around the two additional cones before finally breaking one more time to accelerate upfield.

Line Drill

(Diagram: Back Peddle → Turn and Sprint → Back Peddle → Turn and Sprint → Back Peddle)

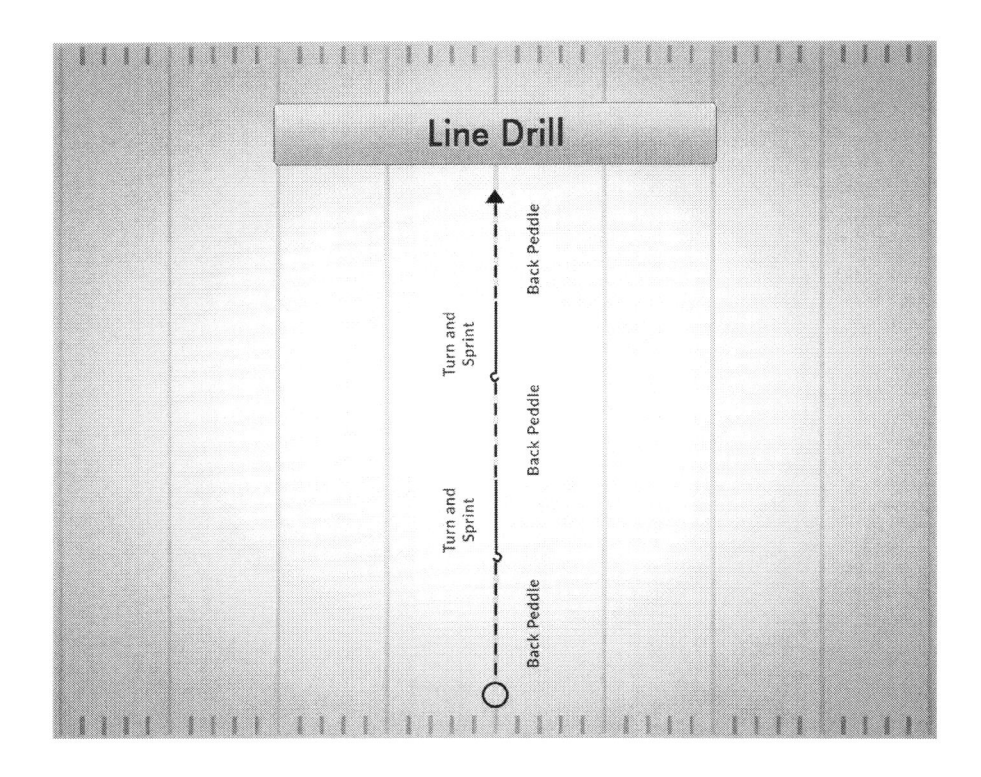

SETUP

Place players on a line and clear out all the space across the field behind the player to avoid any possible collisions.

TECHNIQUES:	PASS DEFENDING, FOOTWORK
EQUIPMENT:	NONE
DRILL TYPE:	SKILL

Line Drill

INTERMEDIATE   **INDIVIDUAL**   **NO-CONTACT**

PURPOSE

Specifically for defensive backs and defenders, the Line Drill teaches players how to flip their hips and swiftly control their backward run on the football field. It is one thing to be able to back peddle fast, but it is another level to control your movement and stay in a straight line.

DRILL DESCRIPTION

Players begin a back peddle while remaining straight on the line. After a few yards, players flip their hips into a run while keeping their eyes back at the starting point. After a few more yards, the player flips his hips back and settles into a back peddle. Continue this rotation, flipping hips each way, all the way through the extent of the drill while keeping eyes up on the starting point.

During the Line Drill, the focus is completely on having the player remain on the line and not straying out or bowing off of the line when flipping their hips.

Swim Move Drill

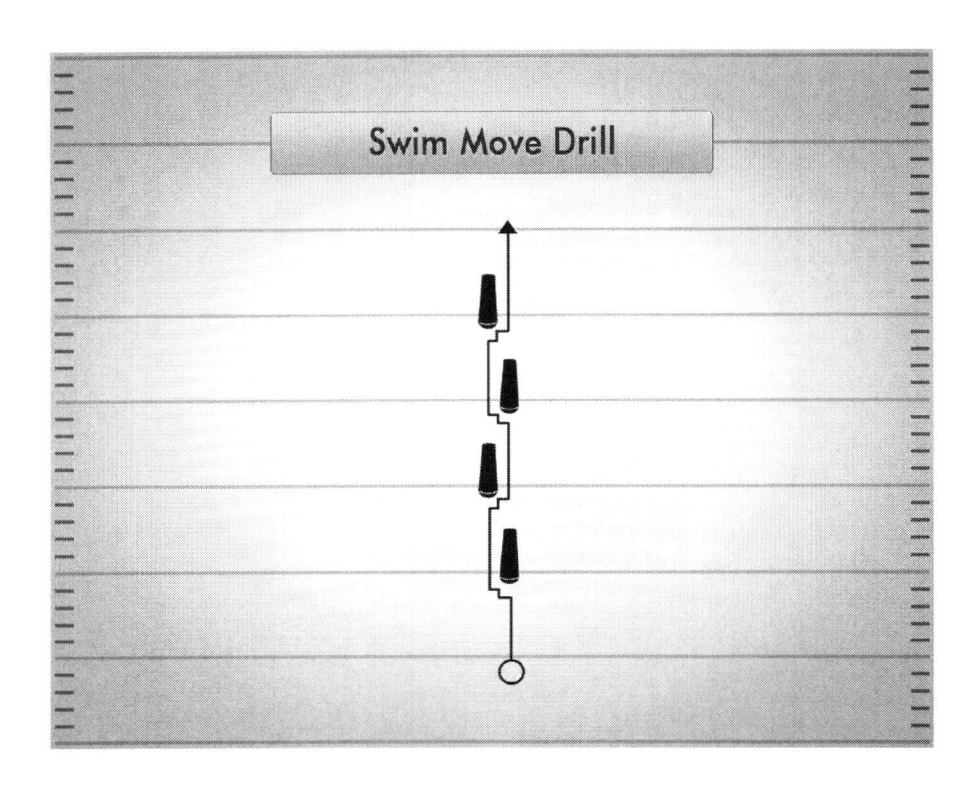

SETUP

Place a series of tackle dummies in a staggered line across the field in front of the player(s).

TECHNIQUES: FOOTWORK

EQUIPMENT: TACKLE DUMMY

DRILL TYPE: SKILL, COORDINATION

Swim Move Drill

EASY   **INDIVIDUAL**   **NO-CONTACT**

PURPOSE

Teach defensive players the technique of the swim move. Multiple repetitions of the Swim Move Drill will reinforce the muscle memory associated with successfully pulling off the swim move.

DRILL DESCRIPTION

Players start in a three point stance and run forward off of the line. As they approach the first tackle dummy, they prepare for the swim move.

To successfully pull off the swim move, players must first choose which side they are going to swim towards. If they choose the left side, they must use their left hand to swipe at waist level and push the blocker away to the right, as they bring their right hand up and over the blocker in order to quickly get their body past the block.

Making a quick head fake in the wrong direction can be a beneficial addition as players get more comfortable with the hand movement aspect of the swim move.

Drill participants alternate the direction of their swim move against each of the tackle dummies as they make their way downfield and through the drill.

Swim-Rip-Sack Drill

SETUP

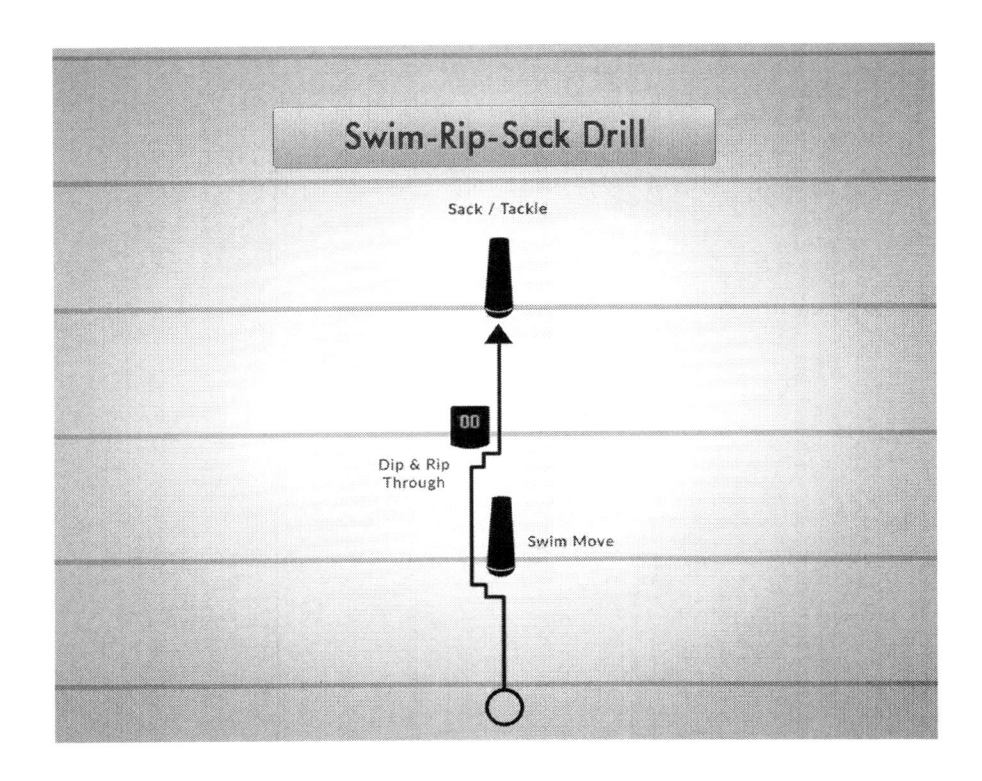

Place a tackle dummy five yards behind the line of scrimmage, someone with a blocking pad five yards behind the first dummy, and a second dummy five yards behind the blocking pad to represent the quarterback.

TECHNIQUES: TACKLING

EQUIPMENT: BLOCKING PAD, TACKLE DUMMY

DRILL TYPE: SKILL, COORDINATION

Swim-Rip-Sack Drill

EASY · INDIVIDUAL · CONTACT

PURPOSE

Combine different defensive tactics and put them all together in one drill to make a play and get a sack on the hypothetical quarterback in this drill.

DRILL DESCRIPTION

This drill combines the techniques of the Dip & Rip Drill and the Swim Move Drill. Players blast off of the line in a 3-point stance and proceed to incorporate both the swim move against the tackle dummy, and the dip & rip move against the blocking pad.

After avoiding both blockers, the player then accelerates up to and into the tackle dummy to procure the sack and finish the drill.

Roll & Go Drill

SETUP

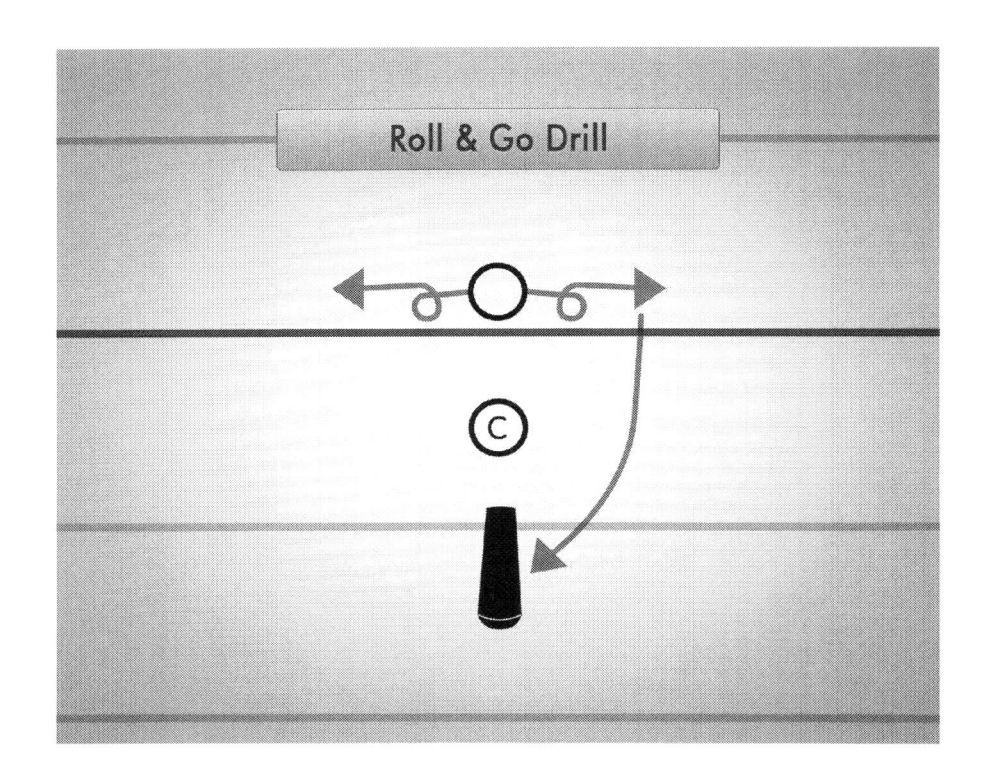

The player sets up in a 3-point stance on the line of scrimmage. A coach stands a few yards in front of the player, and a tackle dummy is placed behind the coach at 7 yards to represent the quarterback.

TECHNIQUES:	TACKLING
EQUIPMENT:	TACKLE DUMMY
DRILL TYPE:	SKILL, COORDINATION

Roll & Go Drill

INTERMEDIATE | **INDIVIDUAL** | **CONTACT**

PURPOSE

Players learn how to keep their eyes up in the backfield and react while in a three point stance, and they learn how to quickly move and recover while on the ground.

DRILL DESCRIPTION

The coach begins the drill by pointing in either the left or right direction and saying "Roll!"

When directed, the player quickly reacts and rolls onto his back and around in the direction the coach pointed. When the player finishes his roll, he regains his 3-point stance and quickly returns his eyes back up to the coach.

The coach continues pointing in various directions and instructing the player to "Roll!"

After a few rolls, the coach will then get out of the way and say "Go!"

The player then blasts off of the line of scrimmage and goes to sack the tackle dummy.

High Point Catch Drill

SETUP

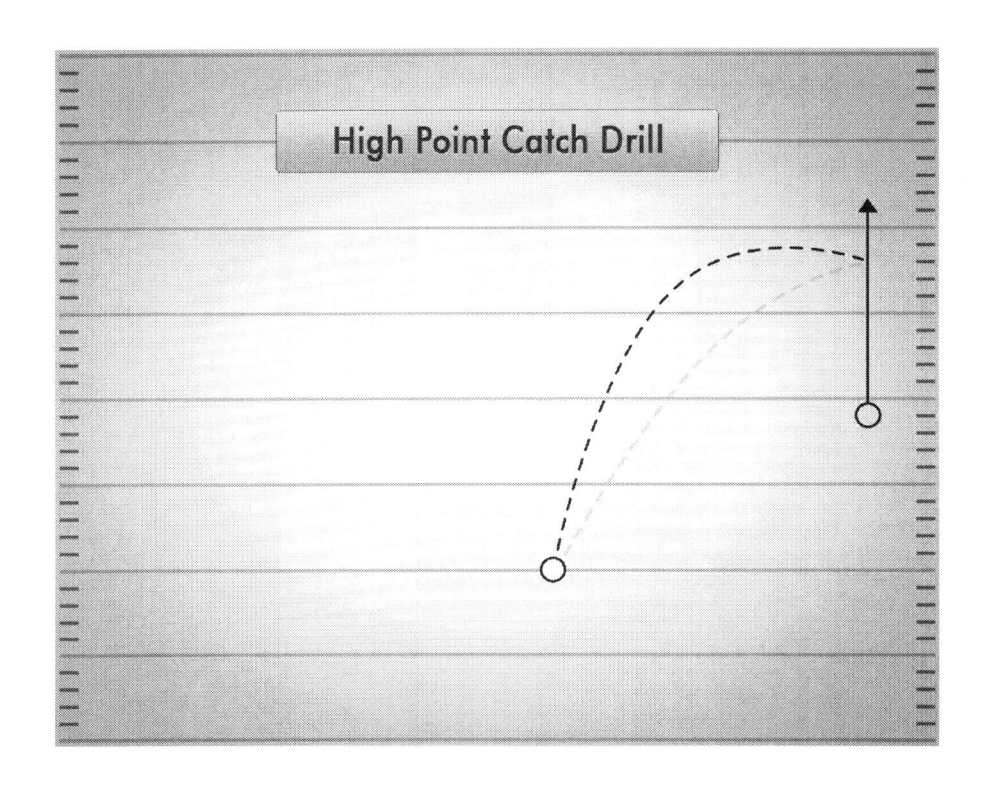

Receivers line up on the side of the field with a coach/quarterback ten yards behind the receivers.

TECHNIQUES:	CATCHING
EQUIPMENT:	NONE
DRILL TYPE:	SKILL, COORDINATION

High Point Catch Drill

INTERMEDIATE | **INDIVIDUAL** | **NO-CONTACT**

PURPOSE

Very rarely will a receiver be wide open down the sideline on a play. More often than not, the receiver will have to jump up over the defender to catch a pass.

The purpose for the High Point Catch Drill is for receivers to develop the ability to properly time their footwork to jump up as high as they can to an incoming pass and catch it at the highest possible point over a defender.

DRILL DESCRIPTION

Receivers run three-quarters speed down the sideline and identify the trajectory of a high pass coming their way.

The focus for this drill is on the footwork and timing involved with securely the catch at the highest point possible. Players jump up and extend their arms and hands up high to the sky to meet the ball at the high point.

Sometimes a successful completion in a game is determined by mere inches. This drill will help get every inch out of a players ability to go high and meet the ball at the highest point.

1 Ball - 2 Ball - 3 Ball Drill

SETUP

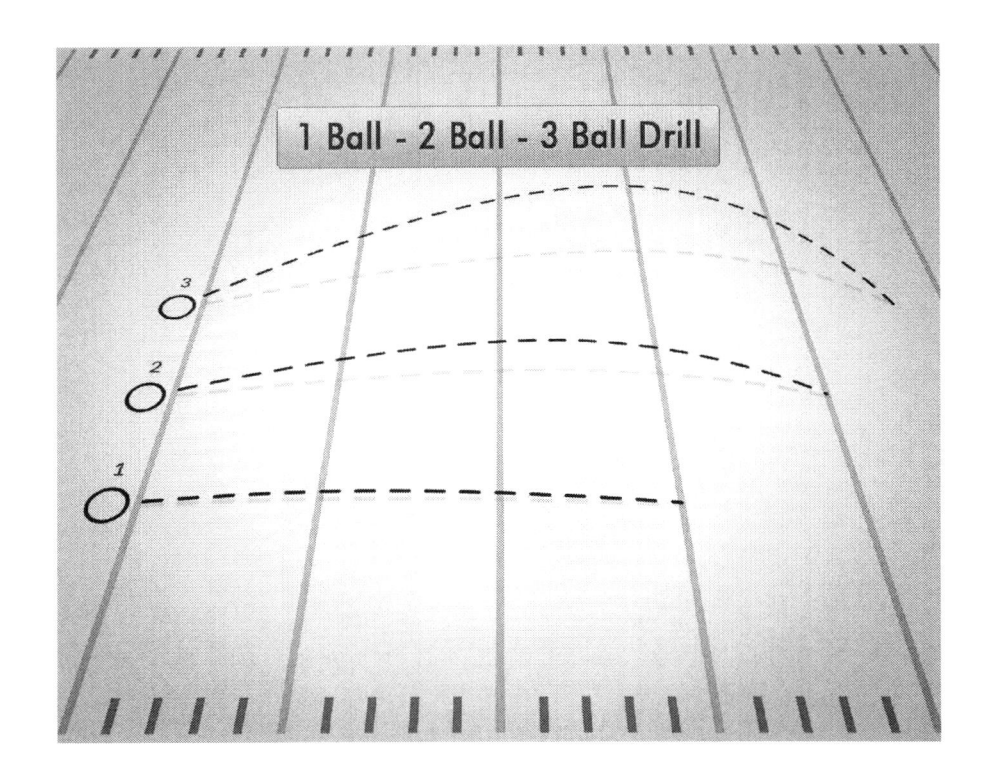

Quarterbacks partner up and play catch with each other, starting close and eventually spreading out as they rotate between the different types of throws.

TECHNIQUES: PASSING

EQUIPMENT: NONE

DRILL TYPE: SKILL

1 Ball - 2 Ball - 3 Ball Drill

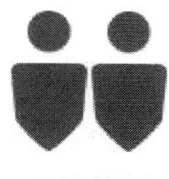

PARTNER   **NO-CONTACT**

PURPOSE

No two throws on a football field are the same. It is important for quarterbacks to learn the framework for how different throws on the field operate. Once they get a better understanding of the concepts, they can begin practicing the different types of throws in order to develop precision and accuracy.

This drill teaches the concepts and ingrains the muscle memory involved with the three different types of throw trajectory.

DRILL DESCRIPTION

Players learn to understand the three different types of throw trajectory:

1 Ball – A ball thrown on a rope with high velocity. This ball is thrown with little to no arc and is usually to a close target. 2 Ball – A ball with a firm throw, but enough of an arc to get over the hands of a linebacker, but still fall to a receiver 15-20 yards downfield. 3 Ball – A ball thrown deep downfield with a high arc.

This drill requires players to get multiple repetitions throwing each type of ball to each type of distance to get a sense for how each of the balls should be thrown.

Trap Block Drill

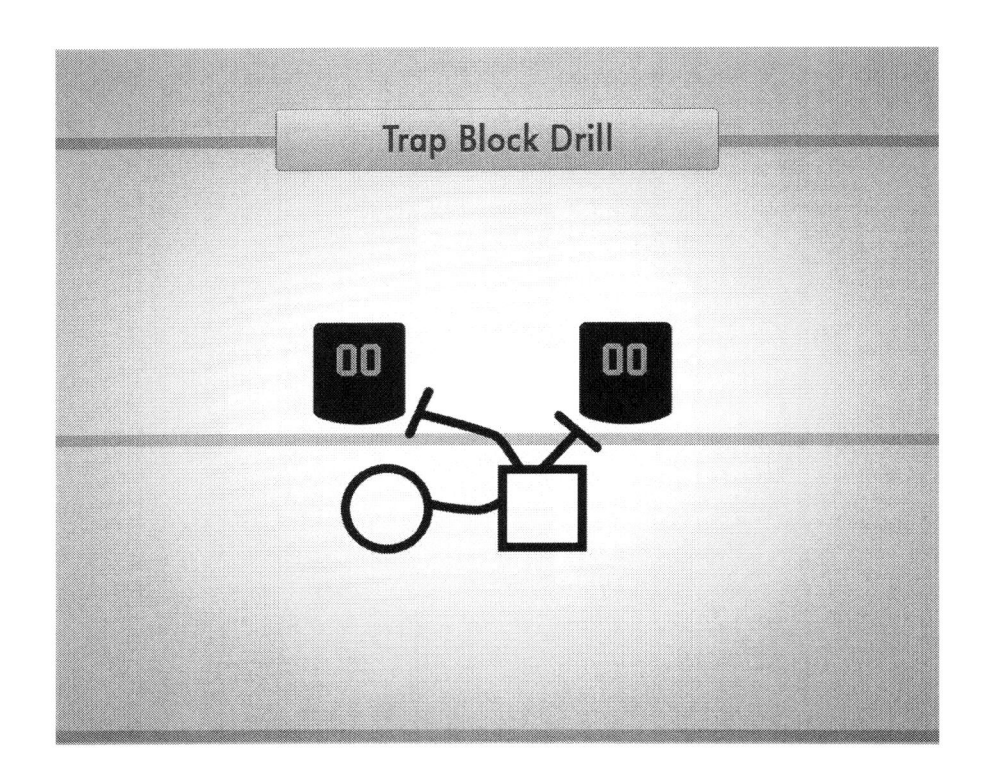

SETUP

Two offensive lineman line up across from to players holding blocking pads where the defensive lineman would line up.

TECHNIQUES:	**BLOCKING**
EQUIPMENT:	**NONE**
DRILL TYPE:	**SKILL, TEAMWORK**

Trap Block Drill

INTERMEDIATE | GROUP | CONTACT

PURPOSE

The trap block requires precise footwork and perfectly synced timing in order to successfully accomplish the intended blocks. This drill focuses the blockers' attention on the football and specific timing needed to properly perform the trap block.

DRILL DESCRIPTION

The center snaps the ball and the players perform the necessary steps needed to execute the trap block. The first blocker explodes out into his assigned block.

The most important step is the first step of the short pulling lineman. That lineman must take a quick step to open up and get around his teammate in order to reach himself around and get to where he needs to be to complete the trap block.

Multiple repetitions are useful to ingrain the muscle memory and timing needed to make the footwork and timing second nature for the trap block.

Mirror Drill

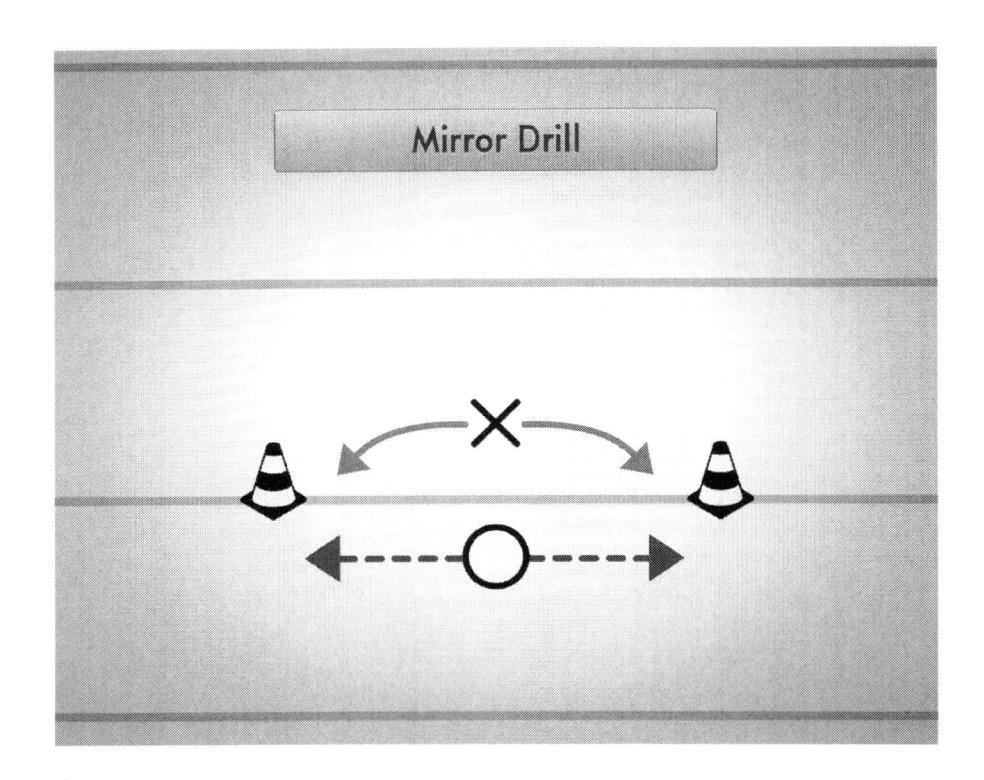

SETUP

Place two cones ten yards apart from each other. An offensive lineman lines up one side across from a player acting as the defender.

TECHNIQUES:	BLOCKING
EQUIPMENT:	CONE
DRILL TYPE:	SKILL, AGILITY

Mirror Drill

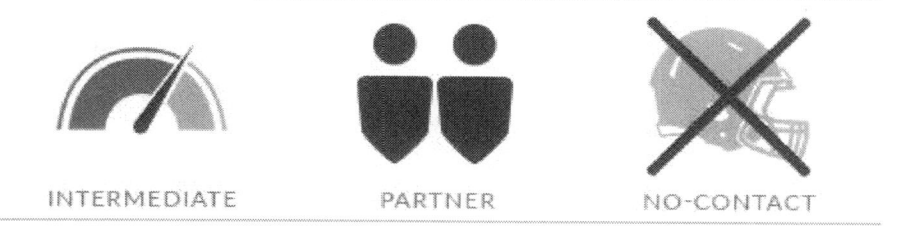

INTERMEDIATE | PARTNER | NO-CONTACT

PURPOSE

The purpose of the mirror drill is to build the offensive lineman's side shuffle speed in coordination with his reaction time to a moving defender.

DRILL DESCRIPTION

The defender attempts to run around the offensive lineman, continually changing direction and moving laterally from side to side throughout the length of the drill.

The offensive blocker must mirror the movement of the defender and stay in front of him at all time. The offensive lineman traverses the horizontal space through a side shuffle. His feet must never cross each other, as that would lead to his feet getting tangled up, and he will not be able to change direction as quickly. Instead, he should remain low in his stance, and quickly shuffle his feet to mirror the movement of the defender.

There is no contact in this drill. The goal is simply for the offensive player to mirror and stay in front of the defender, but neither player should engage in contact with each other.

Break Double Team Drill

SETUP

Mark off a 4-6 yard wide area for the boundary of the drill. Two offensive lineman line up on the line of scrimmage in front of one defensive lineman.

TECHNIQUES:	BLOCKING
EQUIPMENT:	NONE
DRILL TYPE:	SKILL, TEAMWORK

Break Double Team Drill

ADVANCED   GROUP   CONTACT

PURPOSE

The dual purposes of the Break Double Team Drill are to teach offensive lineman how to effectively execute a double team block and to teach defensive linemen how to fend off a double team block.

DRILL DESCRIPTION

Upon the start of the drill, the two offensive linemen begin the double team block of the defensive player. Due to the fact that it is two on one, they need to use their advantage to push the lineman back off the line of scrimmage to open up space. The worst thing they can do is let the defender slip in between them.

Defensively, the best thing a defender can do to fend off a double team block is to flip his shoulders parallel to the line of scrimmage in an effort to split the blocker and slip in between the double team. If the split is ineffective, then the player must attempt to hold his ground and create a cluster in the middle of the line of scrimmage, by getting low, planting his back foot into the ground and holding his place.

Find the Hole Drill

SETUP

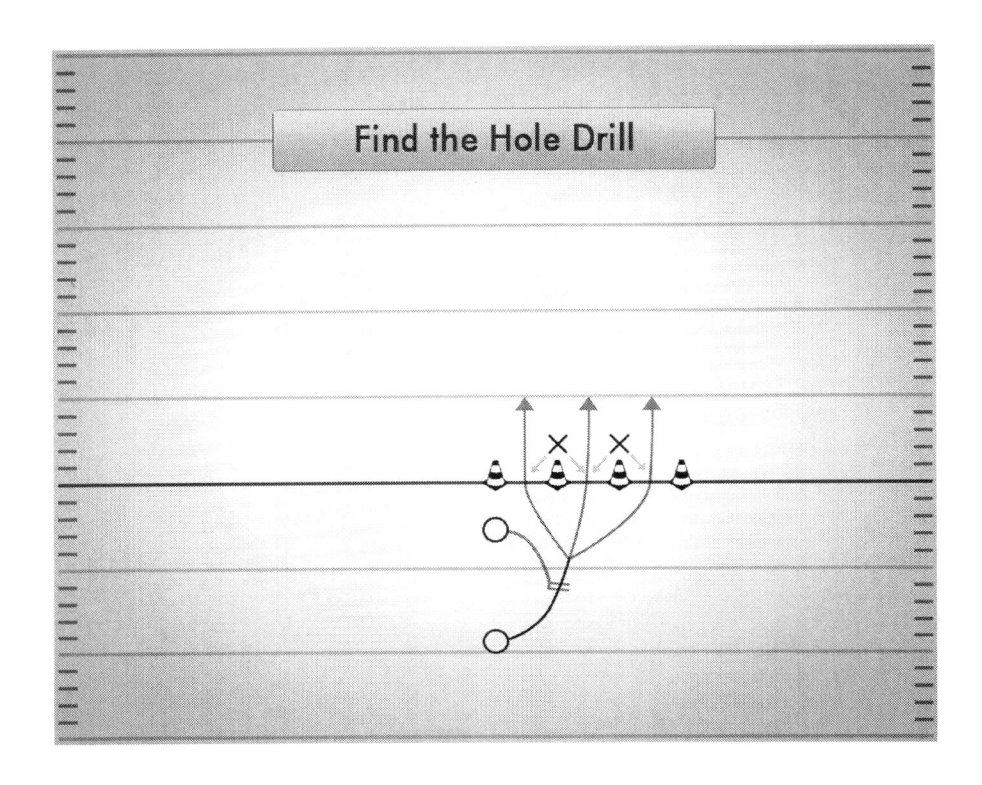

Place four cones to represent the center, guard, tackle, and tight end. Two defenders stand behind the two center cones. A coach stands behind the running back to give directions to the defensive lineman.

TECHNIQUES:	BALL CARRYING
EQUIPMENT:	CONE
DRILL TYPE:	SKILL

Find the Hole Drill

INTERMEDIATE   **GROUP**   **NO-CONTACT**

PURPOSE

In a game, if your offensive line is able to open up a hole, then it is absolutely imperative that your running back finds the hole and runs through it to gain yards.

The Find the Hole Drill forces running backs to quickly recognize and react to openings and closings at the line of scrimmage.

DRILL DESCRIPTION

Before the drill begins, the coach, standing behind the running back, gives directions to the defenders to tell them where to go. There are three options. The coach can send both of them to the right, both to the left, or have them split to leave the middle hole open.

The quarterback snaps the ball and hands it off to the running back.

The defenders delay for one second after the snap and then step into the hole that they were assigned.

The running back receives the handoff with his eyes up at the line of scrimmage to read where the open hole is going to be. As soon as he identifies the open hole, he plants his feet and propels himself through the hole and downfield. This should be a very smooth and crisp movement. The running back should work to have less and less hesitation every repetition in order to quickly and smoothly find the hole and blast through it for yards downfield.

Traffic Drill

SETUP

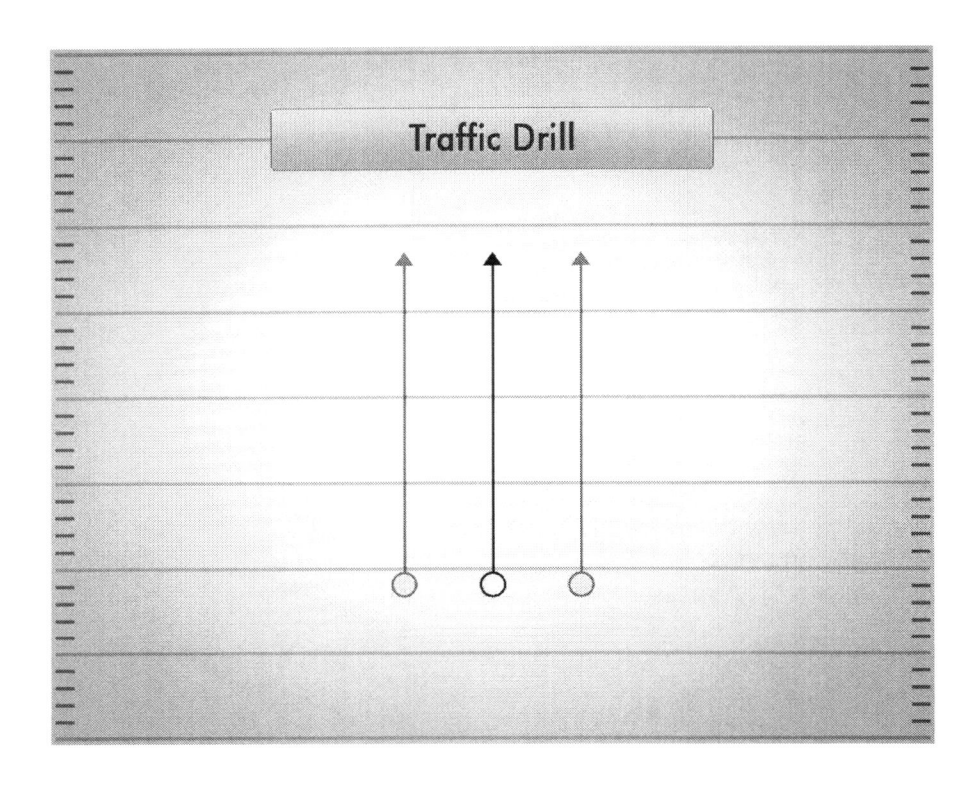

Players simply grab a football and clear out space in front of them to prepare for the drill.

TECHNIQUES:	BALL CARRYING
EQUIPMENT:	NONE
DRILL TYPE:	SKILL, COORDINATION

Traffic Drill

EASY | INDIVIDUAL | NO-CONTACT

PURPOSE

The purpose of the traffic drill is for running backs to gain a better understanding of how to handle the ball in multiple situations and how to quickly change their grip depending on the situation. Ball security is incredibly important. A team will always regret a fumble, but they will never regret devoting practice time to fumble prevention and ball security.

DRILL DESCRIPTION

Players begin jogging downfield at half speed. A coach accompanies them and gives out commands throughout the drill.

The "Traffic" command alerts the running backs that they are entering traffic and therefore must cover the ball up with both arms. When entering traffic, ball carriers must pull the ball up high into their chest and cover both the top and bottom of the football with each of their arms, and cover each point of the football with each of their hands.

The "Switch" command tells the running backs to switch the ball into their other hand. A proper ball switch requires players to briefly get into the "traffic" position in order to protect the ball during the transfer, and then smoothly transfer it into the other hand.

Coaches guide the players with these commands as they make their way downfield.

Blaster Drill

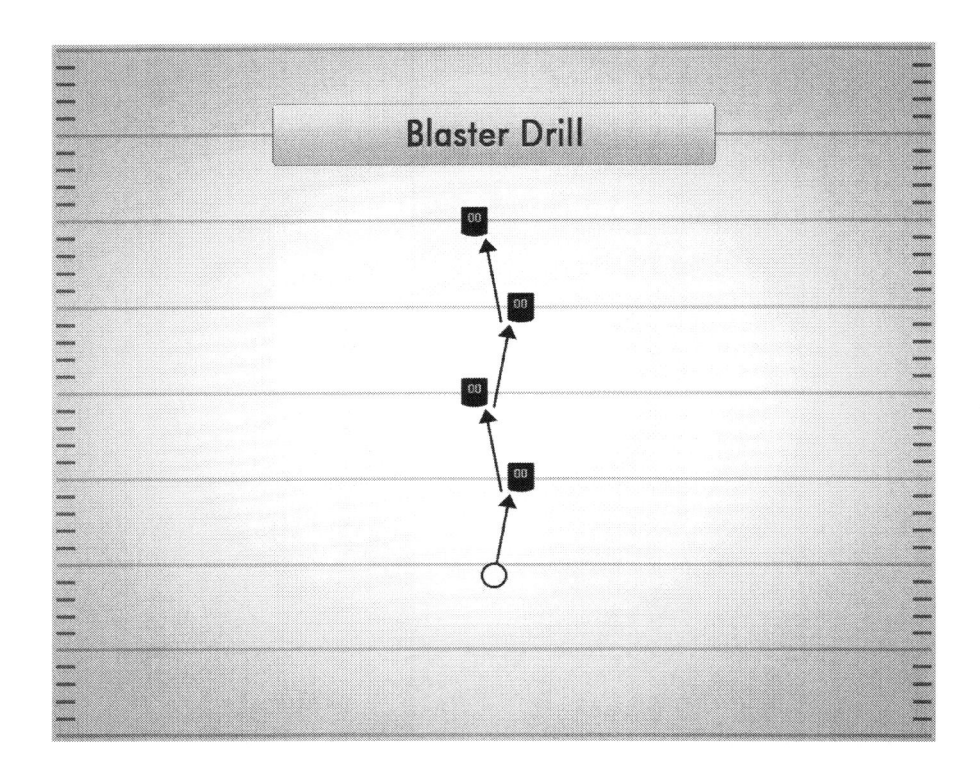

SETUP

A group of players grabs blocking pads and spreads themselves out in a staggered line in front of the ball carrier.

TECHNIQUES:	BALL CARRYING
EQUIPMENT:	BLOCKING PAD
DRILL TYPE:	SKILL

Blaster Drill

INTERMEDIATE **GROUP** **CONTACT**

PURPOSE

One of the most beneficial statistics that a running back can achieve is "yards after first contact." If the running back can get hit, break a tackle, and continue moving downfield, it means that he is racking up bonus yards.

The Blaster Drill teaches ball carriers how to take on contact and get those coveted bonus yards after contact.

DRILL DESCRIPTION

The ball carrier begins running forward. As he approaches a defender, it is incredibly important that the running back gets low to the ground and powers through the contact by keeping his legs moving. Each time he hits a blocking pad, make sure that each player is keeping his feet moving.

After lowering his shoulder into the blocking pad, the player should keep moving and continue forward to the next blocking pad.

The players holding the blocking pad step forward and provide a firm, but not abrasive, impact on the ball carrier.

Eventually, the player keeps blasting his way through the contact as he traverses throughout the entirety of the drill.

Catch and Pop Drill

SETUP

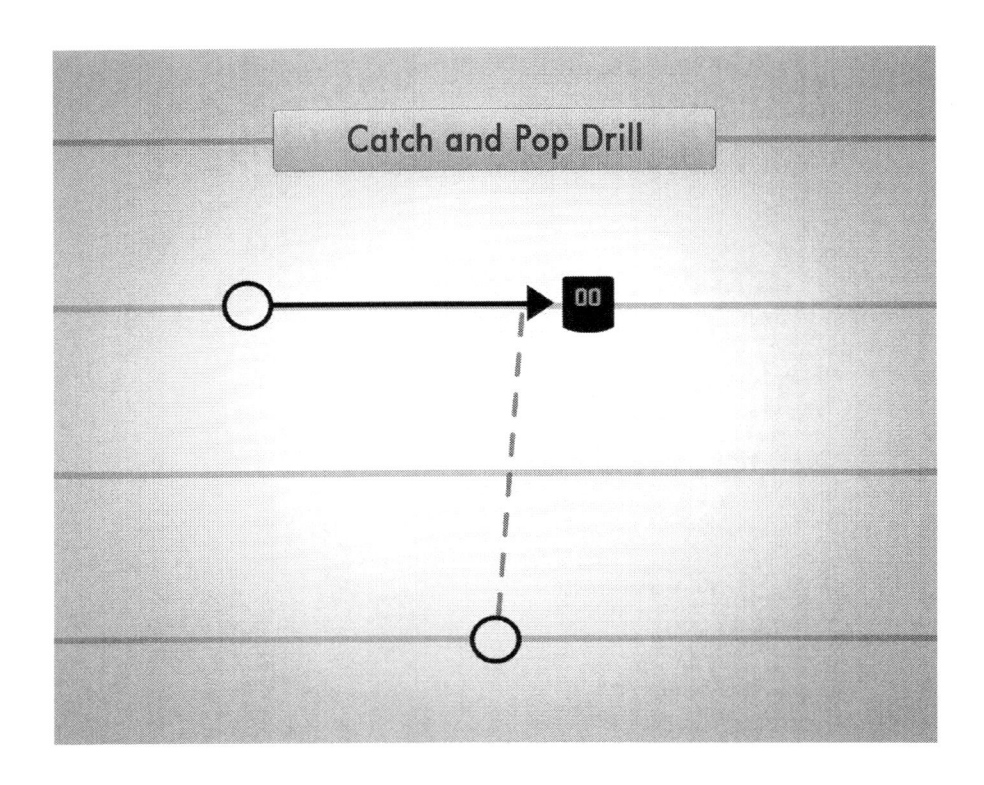

Prepare a player with a blocking pad right at the same spot where the receivers line up to catch the ball.

TECHNIQUES: **CATCHING**

EQUIPMENT: **BLOCKING PAD**

DRILL TYPE: **SKILL, COORDINATION**

Catch and Pop Drill

ADVANCED — GROUP — CONTACT

PURPOSE

Rarely do receivers ever get the change to catch the ball in the wide open field during a real game. This drill teaches receivers how to catch the ball and still bring in the catch even when they are getting popped with contact immediately after they catch the ball.

The Catch and Pop Drill will give receivers the feel for getting hit when they are bringing in a catch, without dropping the football, while they are still in the safe, learning environment of a practice, before the real thing happens to them in a game.

DRILL DESCRIPTION

The coach/quarterback sends a receiver across the field and throws them the ball right in front of a blocking pad.

The player holding the blocking pad aims to pop the receiver with contact the moment after the receiver touches the ball. The impact should be firm, but not so abrasive that it knocks the receiver to the ground.

Receivers must learn how to quickly grab the football out of the air and safely gain a firm possession of the ball as they are getting hit. Receivers must look the ball all the way into their hands and into a firm grip to their body in order to completely bring in the catch when they are getting hit.

This drill is the wide receiver equivalent to the Handoff and Pop Drill for wide receivers.

Handoff and Pop Drill

SETUP

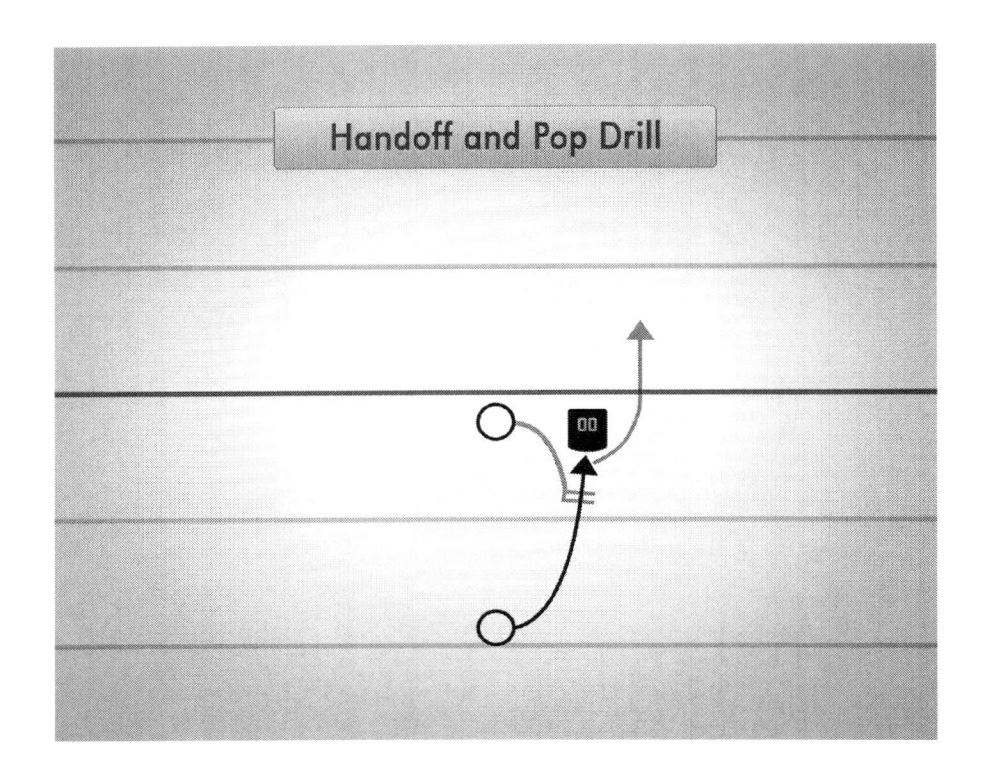

A quarterback and running back line up in their regular formation alignment for a particular run play.

A player or coach holding a blocking pad lines up near the location of where the handoff for the run play will take place.

TECHNIQUES:	BALL CARRYING
EQUIPMENT:	BLOCKING PAD
DRILL TYPE:	SKILL, COORDINATION

Handoff and Pop Drill

ADVANCED | GROUP | CONTACT

PURPOSE

Running backs must be aware that the offensive line is not going to be able to perfectly block and create a giant open hole every play. Sometimes, a defender will quickly sneak through the line of scrimmage and hit the running back as soon as he gets the handoff.

The Handoff and Pop Drill teaches running backs how to survive and react in this situation without fumbling the football.

DRILL DESCRIPTION

The quarterback goes through the cadence, snaps the football, and hands it off to the running back.

The person holding the blocking pad attempts to time his hit on the running back for the moment after the running back receives the handoff. The impact should be firm but not so violent that the player falls to the ground.

The first priority for the running back is to gain a firm possession of the ball without fumbling it. After he has secured the ball, the running back lowers his shoulders into the blocking pad or attempts to spin around the contact in order to bypass the collision and get upfield.

This drill is the running back equivalent to the Catch and Pop Drill for wide receivers.

Scoop and Score Drill

SETUP

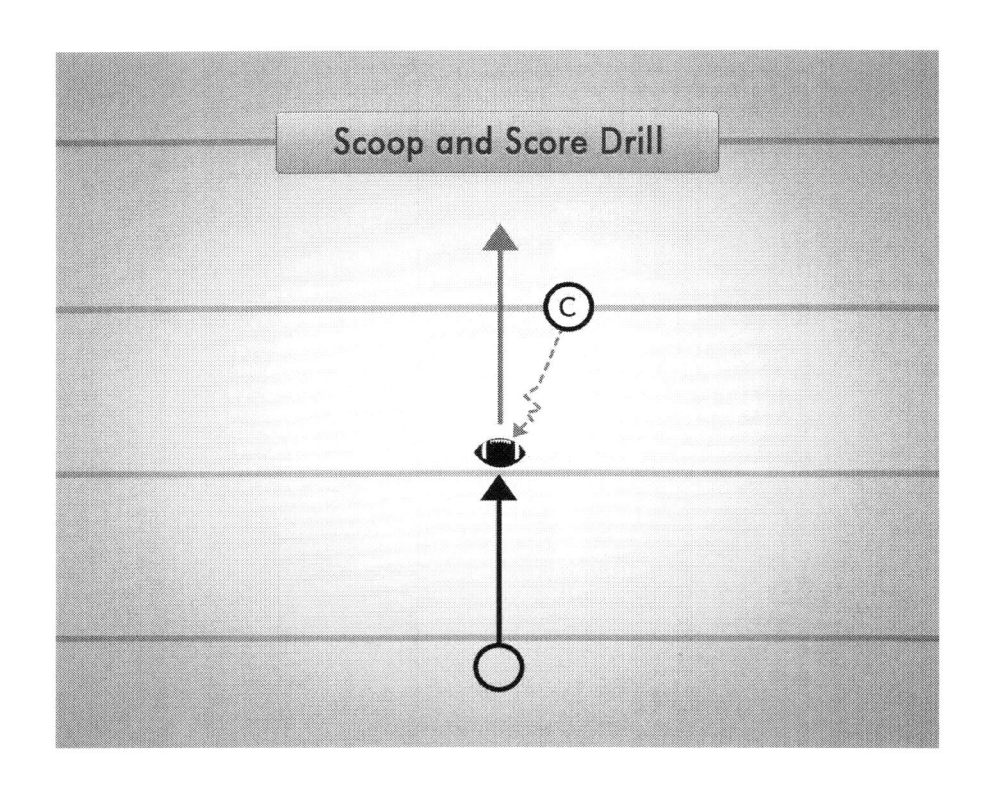

Coaches hold a football and stand ten yards in front of the players.

TECHNIQUES: BALL CARRYING

EQUIPMENT: NONE

DRILL TYPE: SKILL, COORDINATION

Scoop and Score Drill

EASY | **INDIVIDUAL** | **NO-CONTACT**

PURPOSE

Anytime the football is on the ground, it means that the next few seconds have the potential to significantly impact the game. Not only could the defense recover the football and gain possession, but if they are able to scoop it up on the run and take it the other way, the defense could easily get all the way into the end zone and score a defensive touchdown to put points on the board. The Scoop and Score Drill teaches players how to scoop up the ball on the run and take it the other way.

DRILL DESCRIPTION

The coach starts the drill by rolling the football into the open field in front of the player. As soon as the ball is on the ground, the player runs toward the football with a controlled pace. Due to the shape of a football, it can bounce in all kinds of unpredictable ways. Therefore, players must ensure that they use proper scooping form in order to secure possession of the ball while on the run. Upon getting close to the ball, the player extends both of his arms down with his fingertips just barely hovering over the ground. As he gets his hands under the football, he brings both of his arms up and into his body.

The first priority for any fumble is to jump on the ball if there are other people around, because gaining possession is more important than risking the other team getting the ball. So, if the ball is near other players or too far out of reach, then the player should just dive on the ball to secure it. But, if the ball is in the open field, then players should capitalize on the opportunity to scoop it up and take it into the end zone.

Three Man Weave

Step 1　　　　　Step 2　　　　　Step 3

SETUP

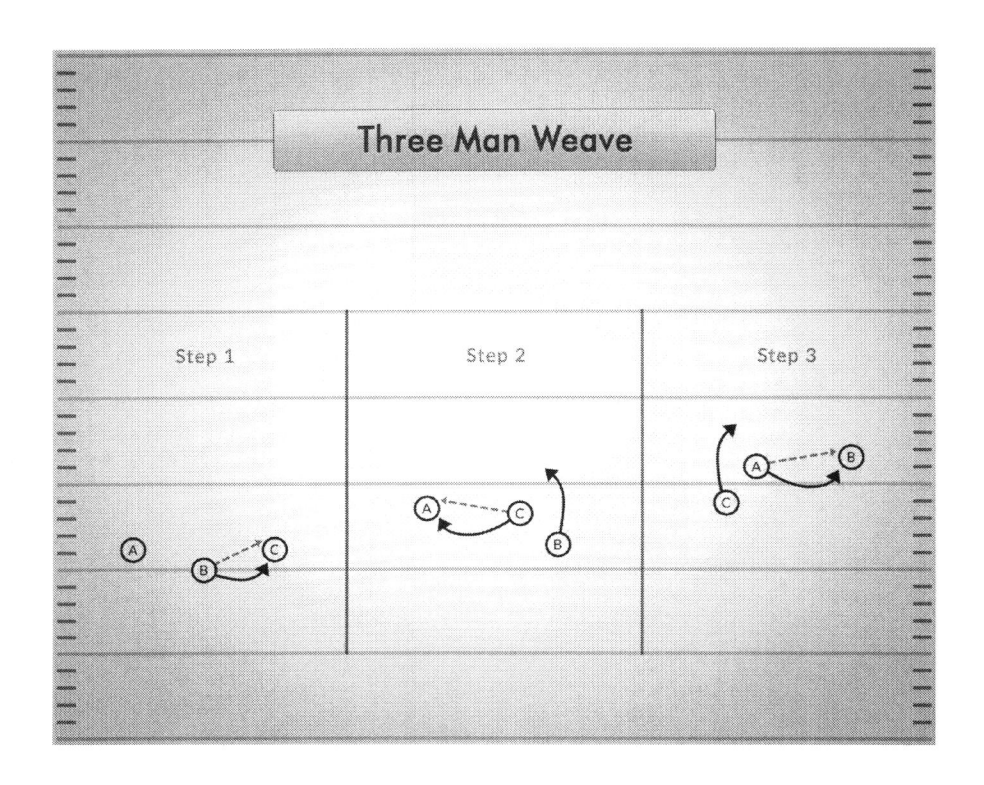

Three players space out on a line with clear space in front of them on the field. The middle player holds a football.

TECHNIQUES:	PASSING, CATCHING, BALL CARRYING
EQUIPMENT:	NONE
DRILL TYPE:	SKILL, COORDINATION, TEAMWORK

Three Man Weave

EASY   GROUP   NO-CONTACT

PURPOSE

Allow new and/or young football players to get a feel for holding, tossing, catching, and carrying and football.

Although the Three Man Weave is typically used as a basketball drill, this same concept can be used on the football field to grow a player's ability to work with the football and coordinate with teammates.

DRILL DESCRIPTION

Although the weave pattern can be confusing at first, there are two simple rules that players have to follow and these rules will always keep them straight.

Rule 1) Pass to the player on the opposite outside of you.

Rule 2) After you pass the ball, run directly behind the player you just passed to.

Continue this pattern down the field.

The pass between players can be tailored to the player's skill level. For example, you can start with simple underhand tosses, gradually spread out by pitching the ball sideways, and eventually transitioning to throwing the ball overhand.

Hot Pigskin Drill

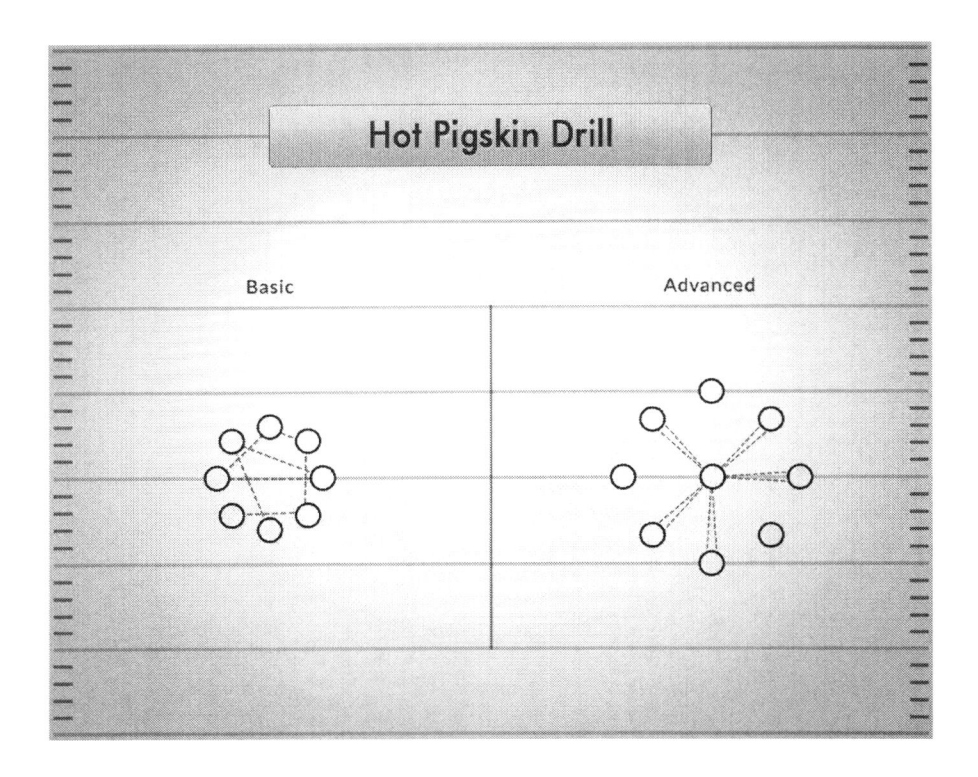

Basic | **Advanced**

SETUP

Players stand in a circle with a single football for the group, or, for the more advanced version, each player in the circle holds a football while another player lines up in the middle of the circle without a football.

TECHNIQUES:	PASSING, CATCHING
EQUIPMENT:	NONE
DRILL TYPE:	SKILL, TEAMWORK

Hot Pigskin Drill

INTERMEDIATE **GROUP** **NO-CONTACT**

PURPOSE

Based upon the simple childhood game of Hot Potato, the Hot Pigskin Drill builds players' awareness and ability to catch and handle a football.

DRILL DESCRIPTION

Easy version: Players stand in a circle and rapidly toss the pigskin (football) from player to player, transitioning the ball as fast as possible without dropping it to the ground.

Advanced Version: Player's on the outside circle randomly take turns of saying "Ball!" and tossing the ball to the player in the middle. The player in the middle must catch the ball, and toss it back to the one who threw it to him. As soon as he tosses the ball back, another player will say "Ball!" and throw it into the center. This pattern continues and forces the player in the middle to be on his toes and quickly react in order to make the catch.

Popcorn Drill

SETUP

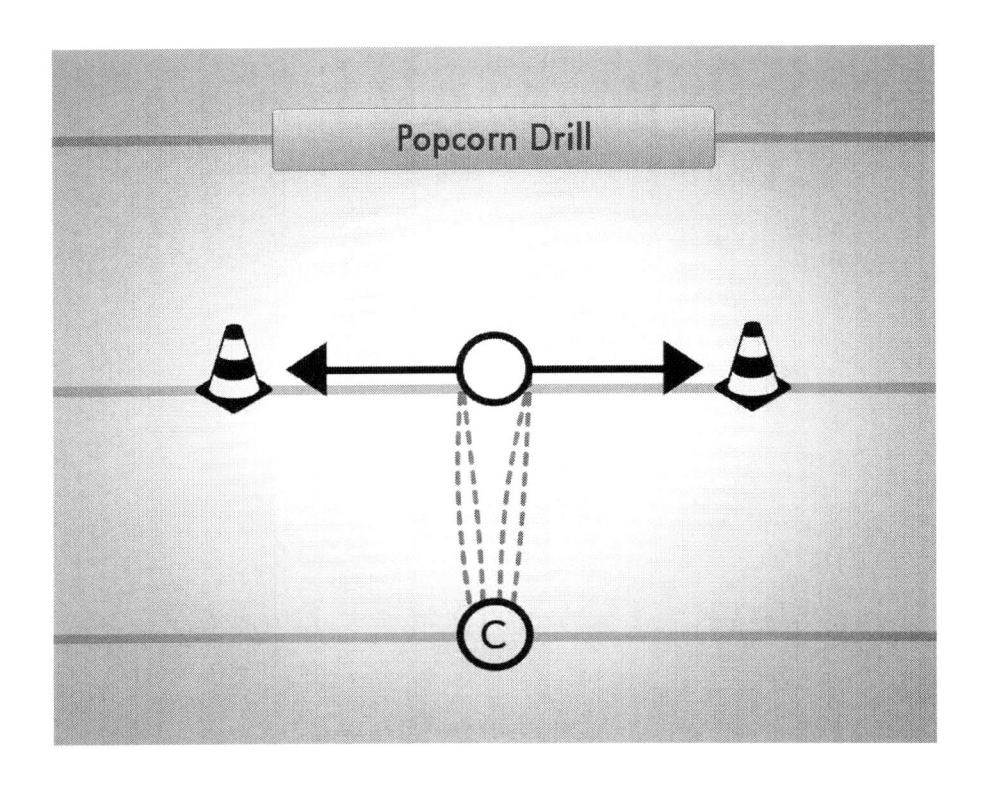

Place two cones ten yards apart and position a player in the middle of the cones. A coach stands five yards in front of the player and holds onto two footballs.

TECHNIQUES: CATCHING, BALL CARRYING

EQUIPMENT: CONE

DRILL TYPE: PHYSICAL PERFORMANCE, SKILL, AGILITY, COORDINATION

Popcorn Drill

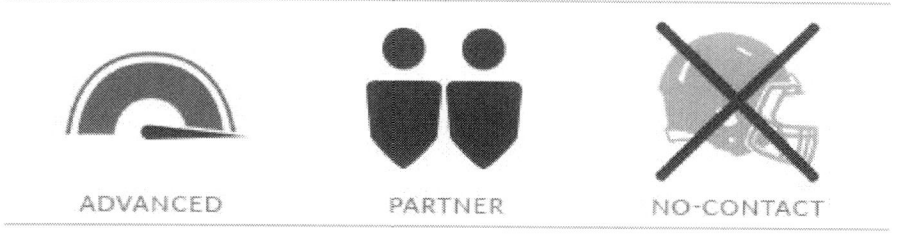

ADVANCED | PARTNER | NO-CONTACT

PURPOSE

The Popcorn drill doubles as both an agility drill as well as a ball handling and eye/hand coordination drill.

Players require intense focus and dual task management as they work on managing two separate footballs as well as quickly changing direction throughout the drill.

DRILL DESCRIPTION

The player begins the drill by shuffling laterally towards one of the cones while keeping his body facing towards the coach.

The coach tosses one of the two footballs to the player.

As soon as the player catches the ball, he stops his shuffle and begins shuffling in the opposite direction towards the other cone. As he changes his direction, the player immediately tosses the football back to the coach.

This begins the rapid-fire nature of this drill. As soon as the player tosses the first football back into the air, the coach then throws the second football back to him.

Throughout this drill, both footballs will simultaneously be in the air as they are thrown back and forth. Each time the player catches a ball, he must change the direction of his shuffle.

Shed the Block Drill

SETUP

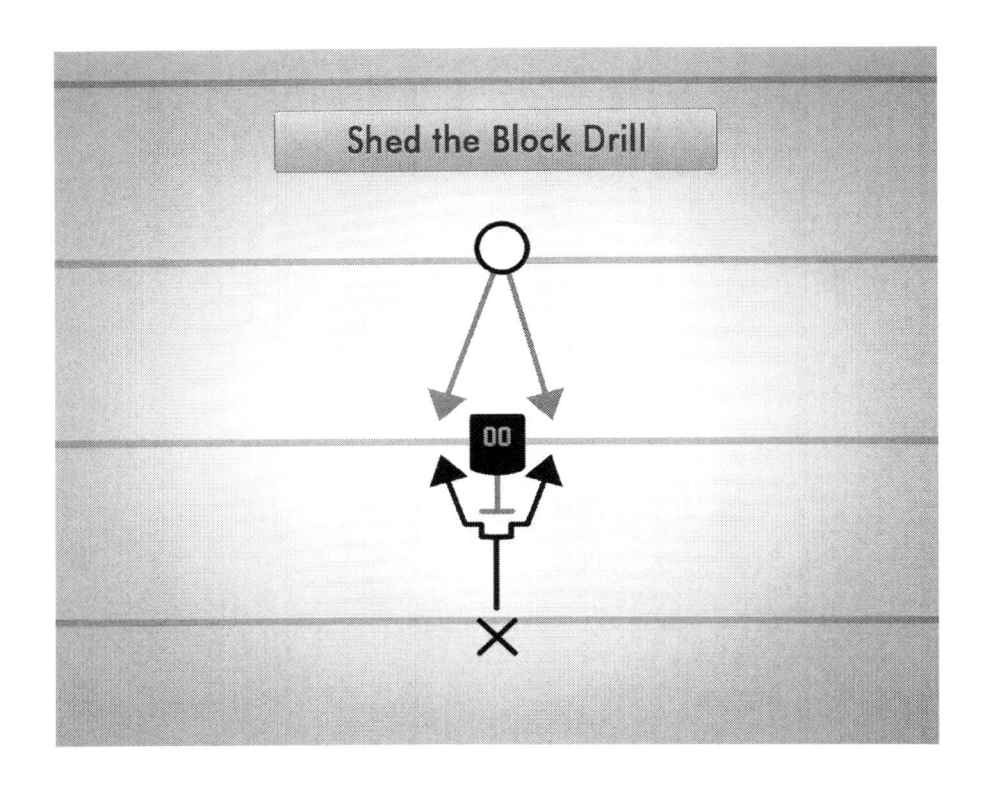

An offensive player and a defensive player stand ten yards apart with a blocking pad player in between them.

TECHNIQUES:	TACKLING
EQUIPMENT:	BLOCKING PAD
DRILL TYPE:	SKILL

Shed the Block Drill

ADVANCED   GROUP   CONTACT

PURPOSE

Teach defensive players how to engage with a blocker, shed the block, and make a tackle on the ball carrier.

DRILL DESCRIPTION

The drill begins with the defensive player engaging the blocker with the blocking pad.

The defender must meet the blocker, by firing his hands into the chest area of the blocking pad. As the defender holds up the blocker, he must make sure that his eyes are on the ball carrier behind the block.

The ball carrier runs towards one side or the other of the blocker.

The defender reads which direction the ball carrier is going, and he sheds the block by throwing the blocker/blocking pad in the opposite direction, and then engaging and wrapping up the ball carrier, but remaining on their feet.

Rotate the defender to the ball carrier and the ball carrier to the blocker in order to rotate all defenders through this drill.

Jump Ball Drill

SETUP

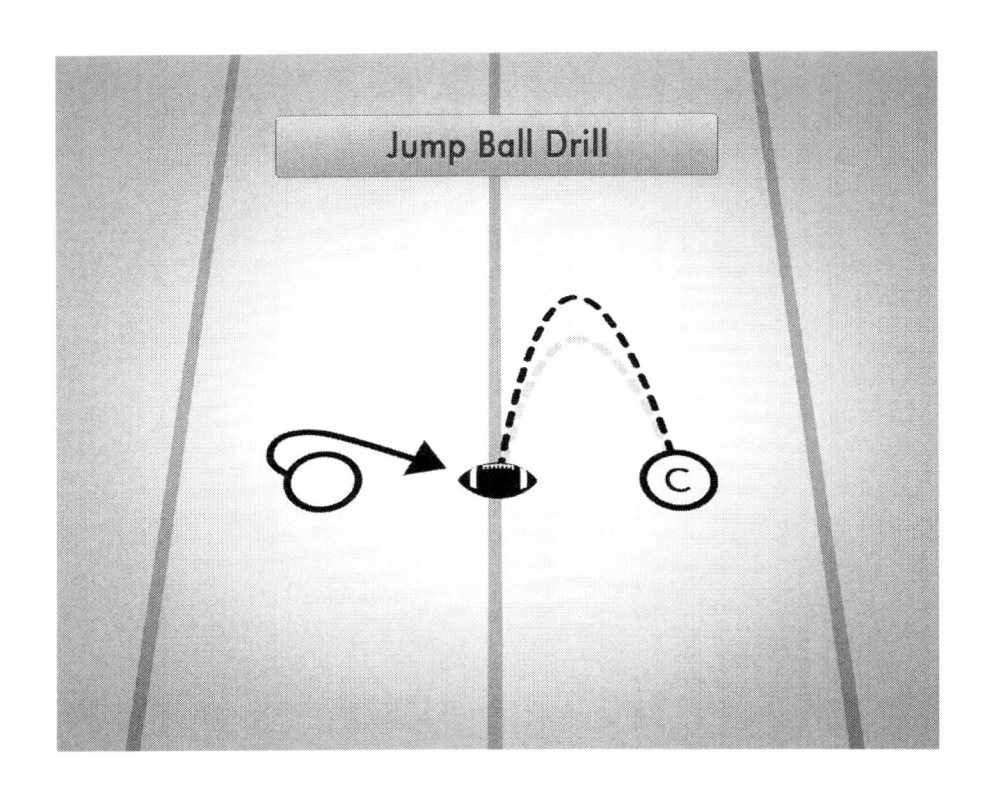

A player and a coach stand six to eight yards away from each other. Players stand with their back turned to the coach.

EQUIPMENT: NONE

DRILL TYPE: SKILL

Jump Ball Drill

EASY   INDIVIDUAL   NO-CONTACT

PURPOSE

Teach players to quickly locate the location of a fumbled football and to quickly dive on top of it.

DRILL DESCRIPTION

The coach tosses a football straight up into the air like a jump ball in basketball. As soon as the ball begins its descent, the coach says "Ball!" to the player, instructing the player to turn around.

The ball should land on the ground somewhere in between the coach and player. As soon as the player turns around, he attempts to quickly identify where the ball is and jump on top of the ball to secure the fumble recovery.

To make this drill more difficult, the coach can spin the ball in a crazy rotation for the toss in order to make it bounce in more random and unpredictable directions.

Shoot the Gap

SETUP

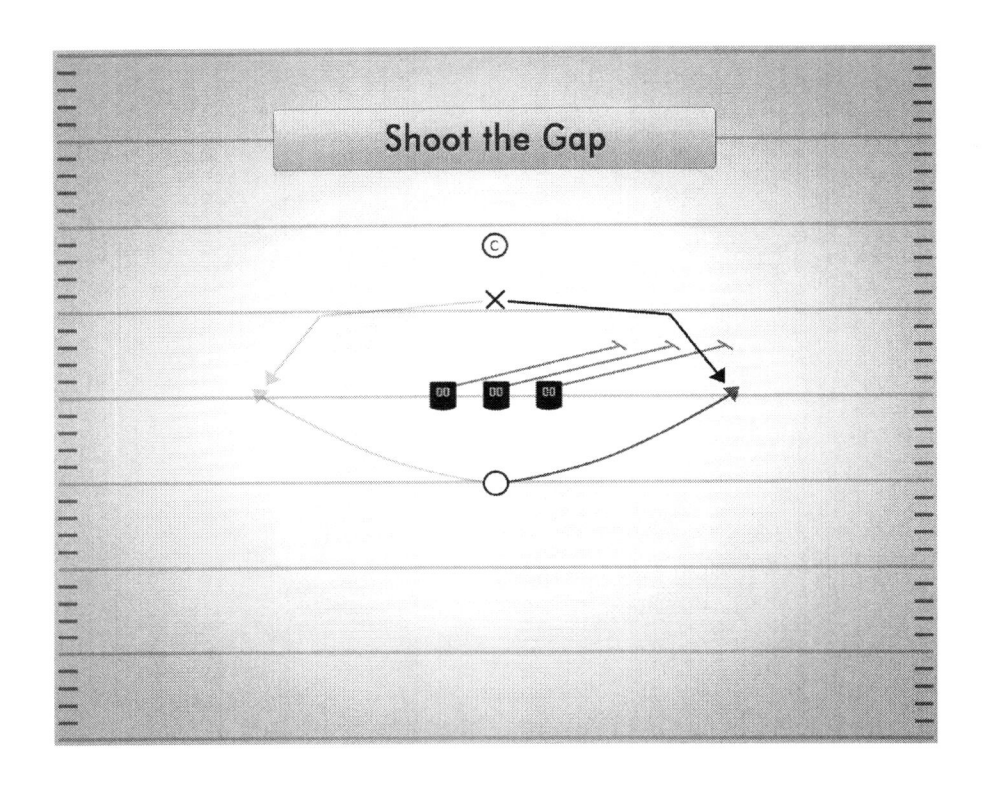

A defensive player and a ball carrier each stand five yards behind the line of scrimmage.

Three players holding blocking pads stand on the line of scrimmage with three yards of space in between each other.

TECHNIQUES:	**TACKLING**
EQUIPMENT:	**BLOCKING PAD**
DRILL TYPE:	**SKILL**

Shoot the Gap Drill

ADVANCED | GROUP | CONTACT

PURPOSE

The purpose of this drill is to teach linebackers how to "shoot the gap" in order to shoot past blockers and get to the ball carrier.

This drill is set up to provide defenders with a game-like scenario where they will have to shoot between blockers and get to the ball carrier. Shooting the gap is particularly needed when offenses deploy either a zone blocker technique or send linemen on a pull block around to the outside.

DRILL DESCRIPTION

The coach, standing behind the defender, begins the drill by indicating to the offense which direction he wants them to run (left or right).

All offensive players begin running that direction with the blockers running almost directly horizontal and parallel to the line of scrimmage.

The defender must make a quick first step and mirror the movement of the ball carrier. After a few steps, the defender must make his decision on which gap to shoot through in order to get past the blockers and get to the ball carrier.

The defender will wrap up the ball carrier without tackling him to the ground because the focus of this drill is not on the tackle itself, but on the technique needed to shoot through the gaps of the blockers.

First Step Drill

SETUP

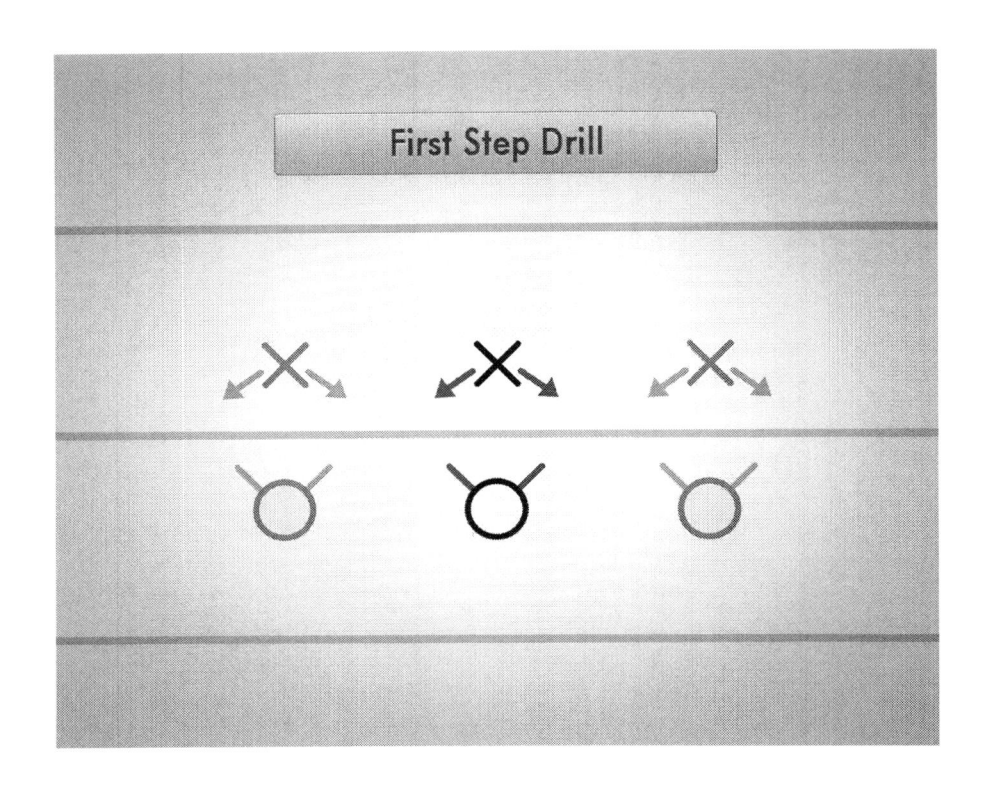

Players partner up and stand facing each other in an athletic stance with their feet shoulder-width apart.

TECHNIQUES:	**FOOTWORK**
EQUIPMENT:	**NONE**
DRILL TYPE:	**SKILL**

First Step Drill

EASY — PARTNER — NO-CONTACT

PURPOSE

One of the worst moves a defender can make on the football field is to make a false step. A false step is when the offense makes a move, but the defense slowly reacts to that move by either moving backward or moving in the wrong direction. This is particularly wasteful for linebackers who must quickly match the steps of the running backs in the backfield to defend against the run.

The purpose of the First Step Drill is to eliminate false steps and increase defensive reaction times.

DRILL DESCRIPTION

One player is selected to act as the offensive player, with the other acting as the defender.

The offensive player makes a jab step in one direction. The defender must quickly react and take a step in the same direction. It is absolutely critical that the defender does not take any false steps and that his first step is quick and in the correct direction.

Players rotate and repeat the drill while randomly mixing up which direction the offensive player steps in.

Pick Up Drill

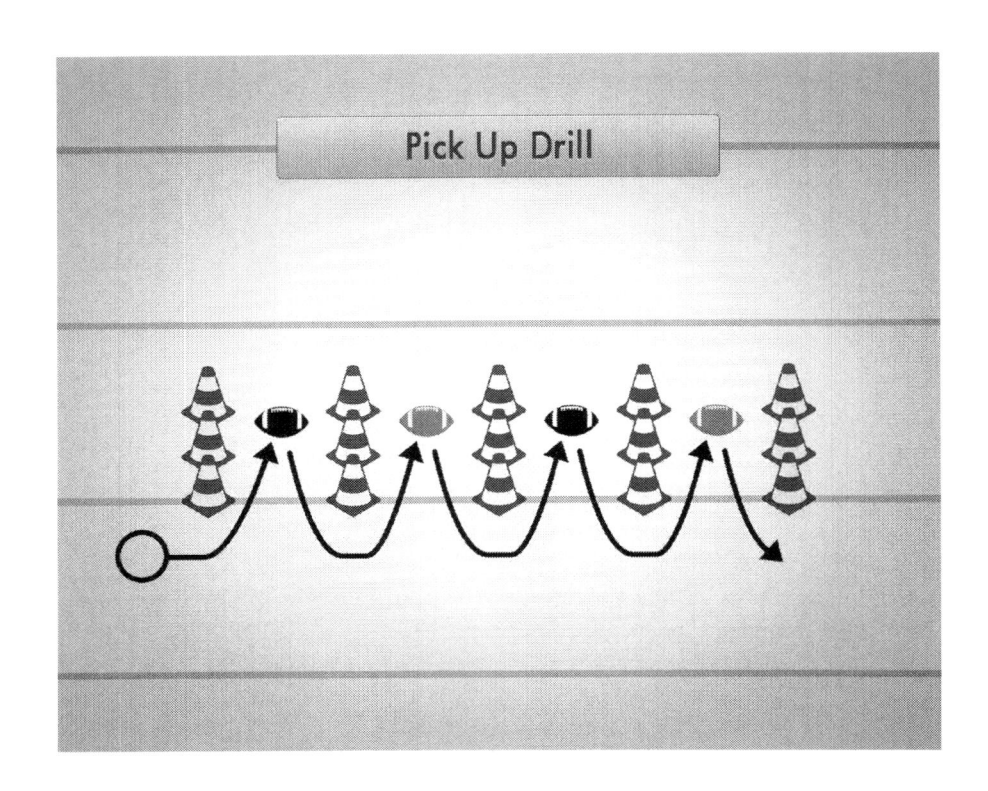

SETUP

Place a series of cones or bags that make four lanes of space, three yards wide. A football is placed in the first and third lane.

TECHNIQUES:	**FOOTWORK**
EQUIPMENT:	**CONE**
DRILL TYPE:	**SKILL**

Pick Up Drill

INTERMEDIATE | **INDIVIDUAL** | **NO-CONTACT**

PURPOSE

The Pick Up Drill teaches players to remain low while encountering different play situations. Getting low to the ground allows players to gain an advantage by being in a powerful position to explode up and through contact. Picking up the football, and setting it down forces players drop their hips and keep low throughout the drill.

For defenders, they must remain low when shielding off a block or engaging in a tackle. For offensive players, they must remain low when executing a block or running with the football through a hole or contact in the middle of the field.

DRILL DESCRIPTION

When entering a lane, players concentrate on dropping their hips and keeping their bodies in a low, powerful position. Players keep their bodies facing the forward throughout the entirety of the drill as they enter in and out of each lane. Players get low to pick up the football in the first lane, and then they get low to set the football down in the second lane. They repeat this maneuver again by transferring the ball in the third lane to the fourth lane.

After backing out of the fourth lane, players continue the drill by repeating the same maneuvers, but his time going in reverse from right to left, transferring the ball from lane four to lane three, and again from lane two to lane one. After completing the drill, the two footballs should be in the same locations as when the drill was started so that the next player up can begin without having to reset any portion of the drill.

Bubble Bounce Drill

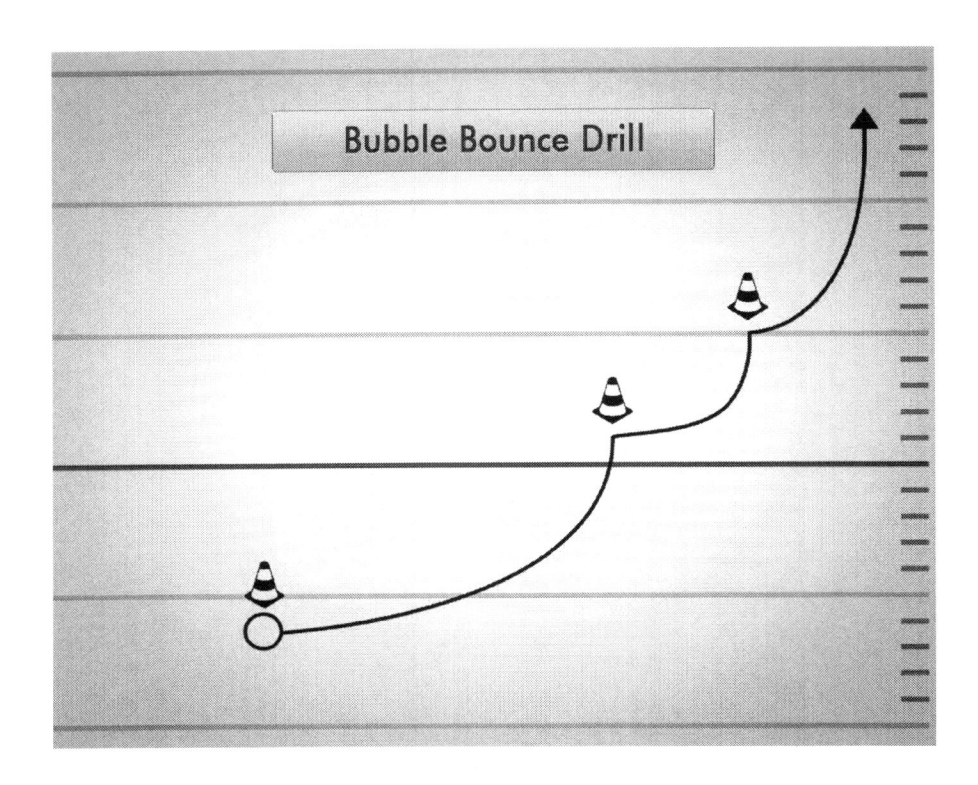

SETUP

Place one cone in the middle of the field placed five yards deep in the backfield where a ball carrier would begin the play. Place two more cones a few yards past the line of scrimmage towards the sideline where a linebacker and a defensive back would meet the ball carrier on some sort of outside run play.

TECHNIQUES:	BALL CARRYING, FOOTWORK
EQUIPMENT:	NONE
DRILL TYPE:	SKILL

Bubble Bounce Drill

EASY   INDIVIDUAL   NO-CONTACT

PURPOSE

Teach ball carriers a simple but effective tactic to outmaneuver a defender in the open field.

When running towards the outside in the open field, the number one advantage that the defense has over the offense is that their angle of pursuit can force the offense to run out of room on the sideline. The Bubble Bounce move is a simple maneuver that creates extra space to the outside by allowing the ball carrier to force the defense to sacrifice their angle by slowing down to square up on the ball carrier.

DRILL DESCRIPTION

Players begin running with a football to the outside of the field. They visualize a defender running with them to the outside, and square that defender up by changing their angle to momentarily run straight upfield, directly at the defender (represented by the cone). This is the "bubble" part of the maneuver.

Once the defender slows his pursuit to square up on the ball carrier, then the ball carrier simply does the "bounce" part of the maneuver by cutting back outside. Repeat the Bubble Bounce one more time before accelerating up the sideline.

Performing the Bubble Bounce is an effective way to teach beginner players how to manipulate the angles and speed of the defense while inherently creating extra space outside and down the sideline for them.

Peel Drill

SETUP

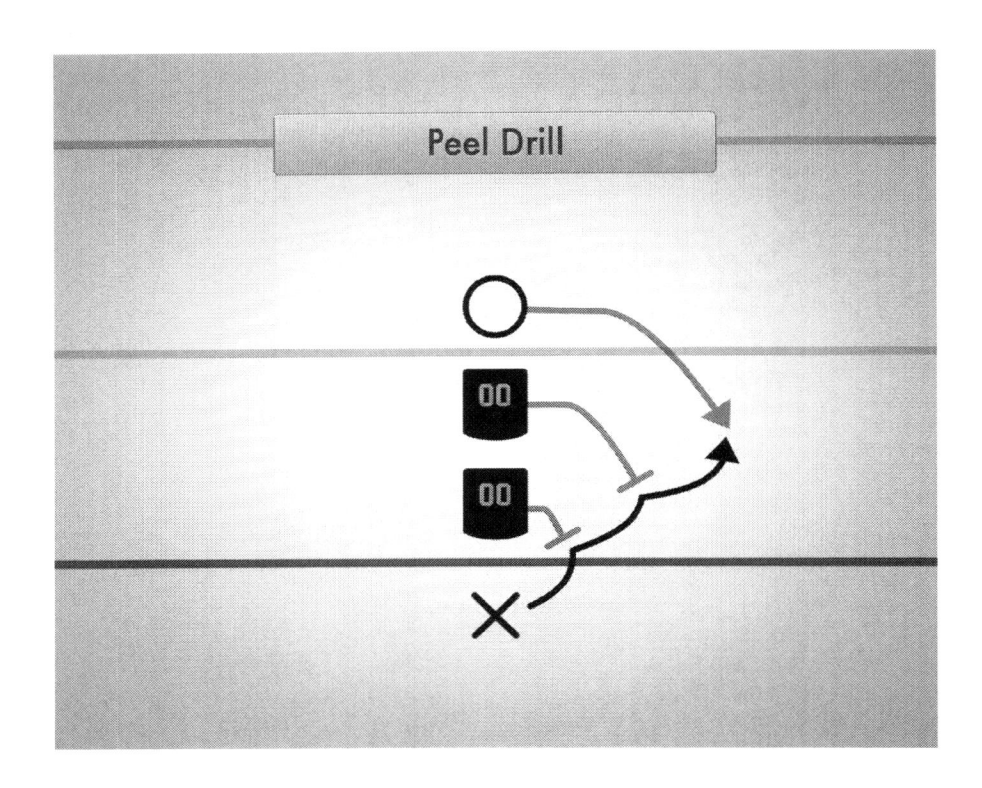

One defender lines up in front of two players holding blocking pads. One ball carrier lines up behind the two blocking pads.

TECHNIQUES:	TACKLING
EQUIPMENT:	BLOCKING PAD
DRILL TYPE:	SKILL

Peel Drill

GROUP   CONTACT

PURPOSE

Teach players how to peel off of blocks and get to the ball carrier.

Anytime there is a ball carrier on the field, it means that he has up to ten of his teammates blocking for him. The Peel Drill teaches players how to fend off those blocks and get to the outside in order to bring down the ball carrier.

DRILL DESCRIPTION

The coach gives the offense a direction and initiates the drill with a command. The offensive players start moving in that direction. As the blocking pads approach the defender, they thrust the pad at the waist of the defender.

The defender must fend off the blocks by pushing them down and away, one at a time, as he peels off to the next level outside.

Upon reaching the runner, the defender will wrap him up and drive through him for a few yards without bringing him to the ground.

Players rotate through the responsibilities.

Cage Fight Drill

SETUP

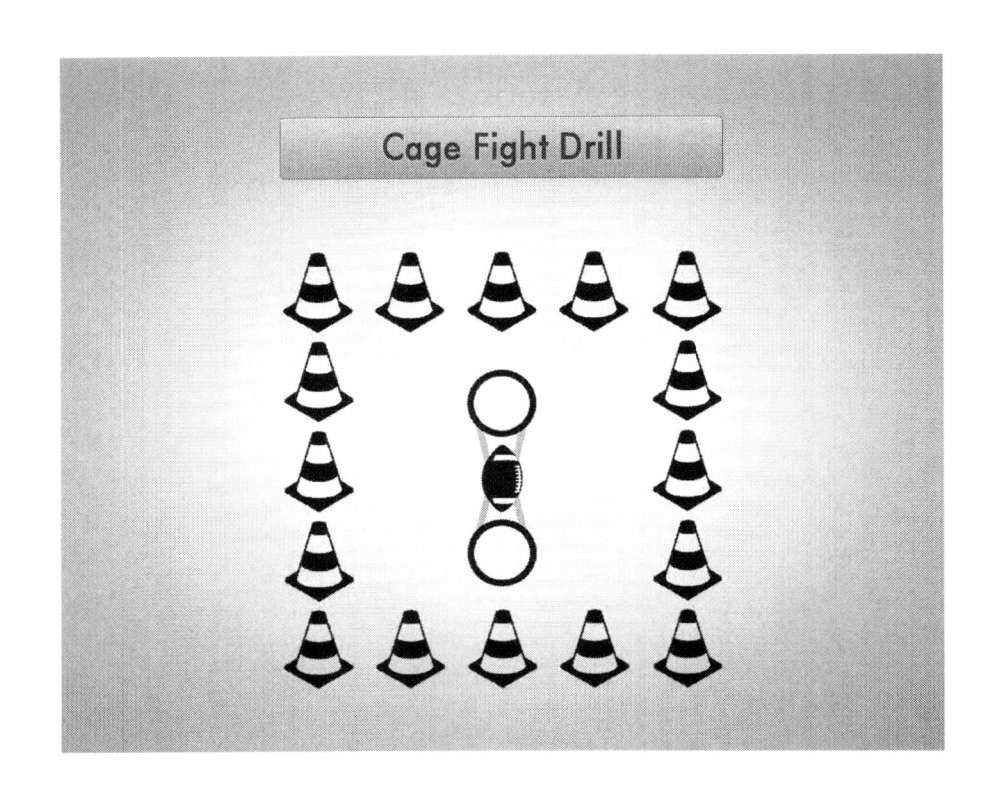

Line up a square area to contain the cage fight competition.

TECHNIQUES:	BALL CARRYING
EQUIPMENT:	NONE
DRILL TYPE:	SKILL, COMPETITION

Cage Fight Drill

INTERMEDIATE   PARTNER   CONTACT

PURPOSE

The Cage Fight Drill gives players the opportunity to compete and showcase their tenacity to obtain possession of the football.

DRILL DESCRIPTION

Prepare the competition by allowing each player to get an equal grip on the football. Each player's grip must start on their half of the football without crossing over into their opponent's half.

Upon initiating the competition, each player fights to rip the ball out of their opponent's hands, and secure the ball for themselves. The player who is able to grab and obtain full possession of the football wins the Cage Fight competition.

If the ball falls to the ground, then the first player to jump on the ball wins.

Triple Punch Drill

SETUP

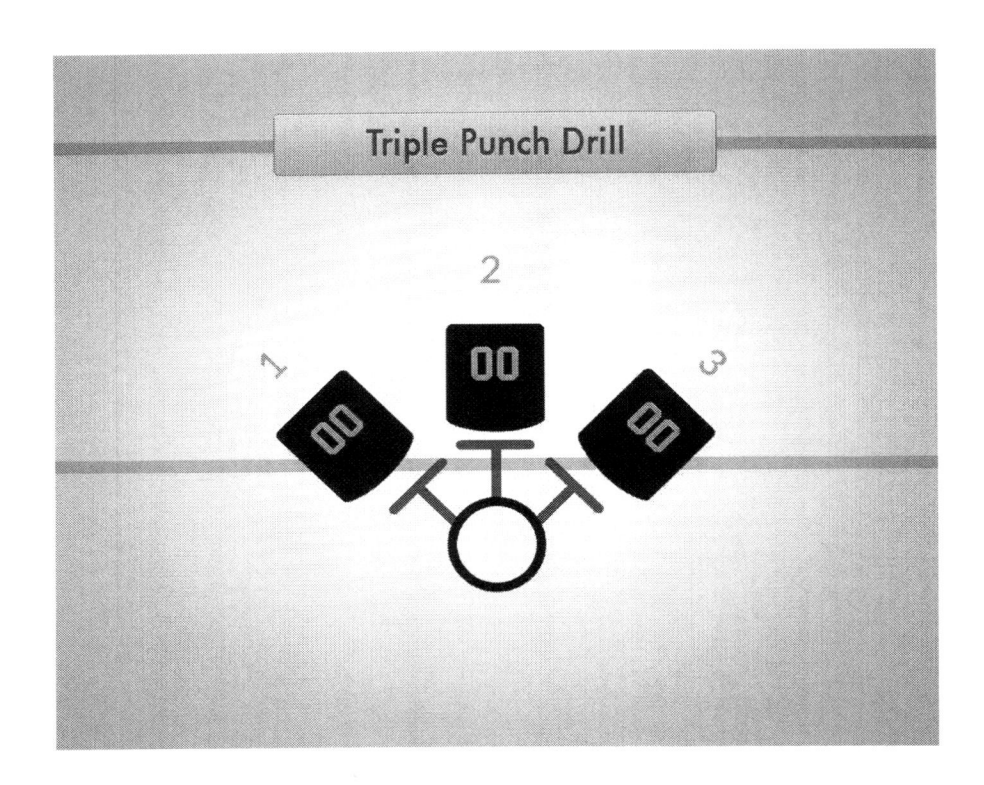

Position three players with blocking pads around the player. One blocking pad should be directly in front, while the other two are angled around the player on each side.

EQUIPMENT: **BLOCKING PAD**

DRILL TYPE: **SKILL**

Triple Punch Drill

INTERMEDIATE   GROUP   CONTACT

PURPOSE

Teach players to quickly react and punch their hands into their opponents' chests.

DRILL DESCRIPTION

A coach guides the player through the drill by randomly calling out different numbers. Each of the three bags is assigned a number from 1 to 3.

Each time that the coach calls a number, the player quickly punches his hands into the associated pad.

The player stands in a powerful low position with his feet shoulder-width apart. He punches with both his hands open and making contact on the pad at the same time, by starting low and pushing up. Each time a pad is punched, it should be brought up from low to high.

Repeat calling out random numbers for multiple repetitions before the players rotate through the drill.

Drills

Execution Drills

Oklahoma Drill

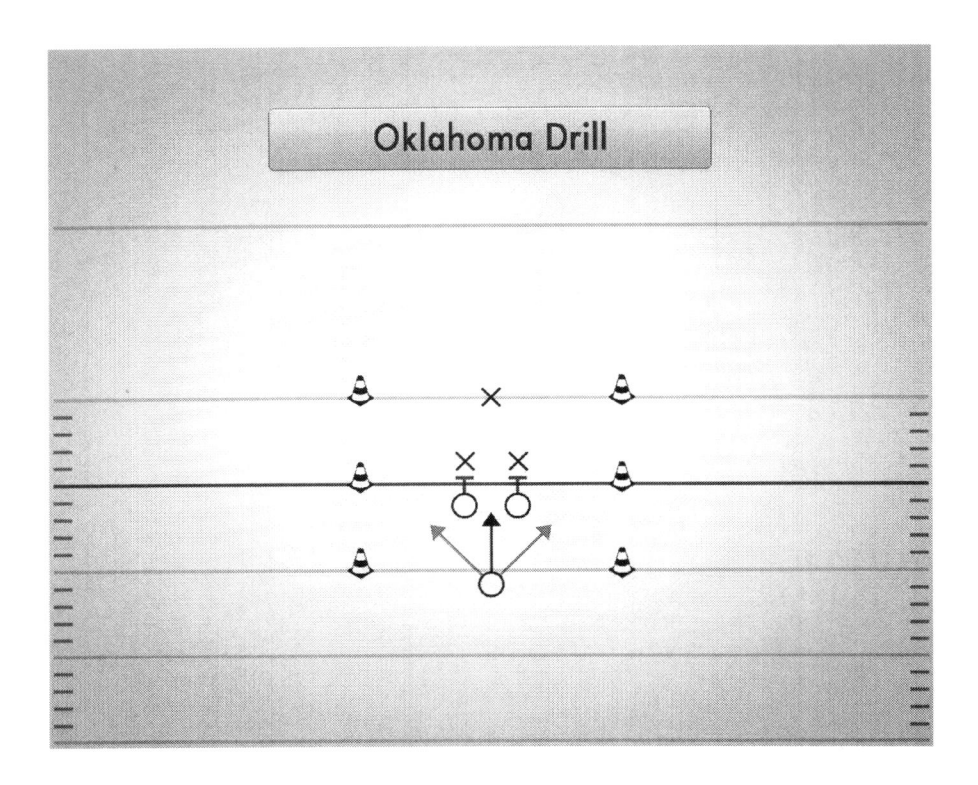

SETUP

Place boundaries about 15 yards apart to represent the sidelines of a condensed field. The line of scrimmage for this drill should be the five yard line, so indicate that the goal line is only five yards from the line of scrimmage.

TECHNIQUES:	BALL CARRYING, BLOCKING, TACKLING
EQUIPMENT:	CONE
DRILL TYPE:	EXECUTION, TEAMWORK

Oklahoma Drill

INTERMEDIATE — GROUP — CONTACT

PURPOSE

Simulate a condensed portion of a full speed play by pitting three offensive players against three defensive players.

DRILL DESCRIPTION

The Oklahoma Drill is a classic contact football drill. It pits three offensive players vs. three defensive players. Each side has two linemen facing off at the line of scrimmage. The defensive has a linebacker behind the line in opposition to the running back behind the offensive line.

At the start of the drill, the lineman clash at the line of scrimmage will the running back makes his move for the end zone. The running back must find and select one of the three gaps amidst his blockers while keeping in mind that he will have to face the linebacker behind the line.

The offensive linemen do their best to block their man, while the defensive lineman will do their best to shed to block and make the tackle. The linebacker will start with his feet on the goal line and mirror the running back while trying to meet him as close to the line of scrimmage as possible since he has no room to give up behind him before the end zone.

This drill does a great job of simulating a condensed portion of a play in a goal line situation.

Pursuit Drill

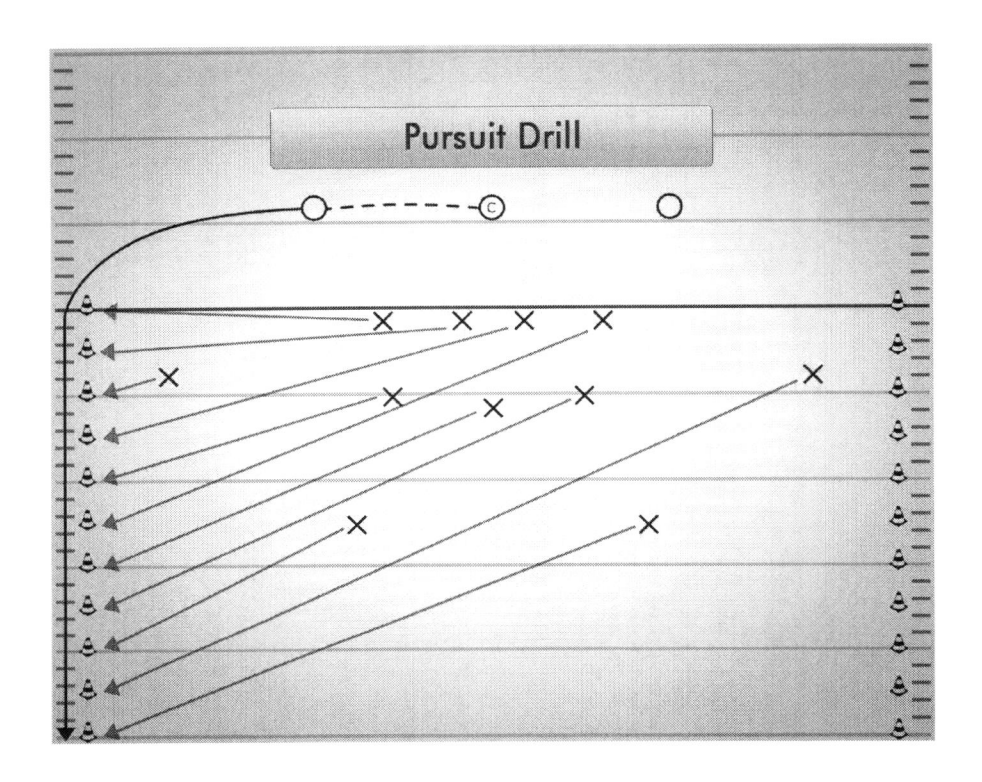

SETUP

The defense lines up in their base defensive formation. One coach will run the drill in the position of the Quarterback and will need one player, or "rabbit," flanking each side of him.

Optionally, line up eleven cones down each sideline, spaced 2 and a half yards apart, to indicate the spots your defense will run to.

EQUIPMENT: **CONE**

DRILL TYPE: **EXECUTION, CONDITIONING, TEAMWORK**

Pursuit Drill

INTERMEDIATE | TEAM | CONTACT

PURPOSE

Teach the defense the correct angles to take as they pursue a ball carrier down the sideline. A defense with a great pursuit will come up with more tackles and this drill teaches the proper way to do just that.

DRILL DESCRIPTION

The coach begins the drill be simulating a snap. Upon starting the drill, all members of the defense begin running in place. The coach will then throw the ball out to one of the players, or "rabbits," beside him. These players are called rabbits because after they catch the ball, they will begin running as fast as they can down the sideline while the defense chases them.

As soon as the ball is thrown, all defenders begin pursuing towards the rabbit. Coaches should ensure that players are taking proper angles in order to cut off the rabbit.

The teamwork portion of this drill means that each player needs to match themselves up with a cone. If a cone is already covered, then they will need to locate the nearest available cone. Once at the cone, players continue chopping their feet in place until the coach blows a whistle to end the drill.

The Pursuit Drill requires a lot of running so it is best used towards the end of practice as a precursor to or replacement of conditioning.

Scramble Drill

SETUP

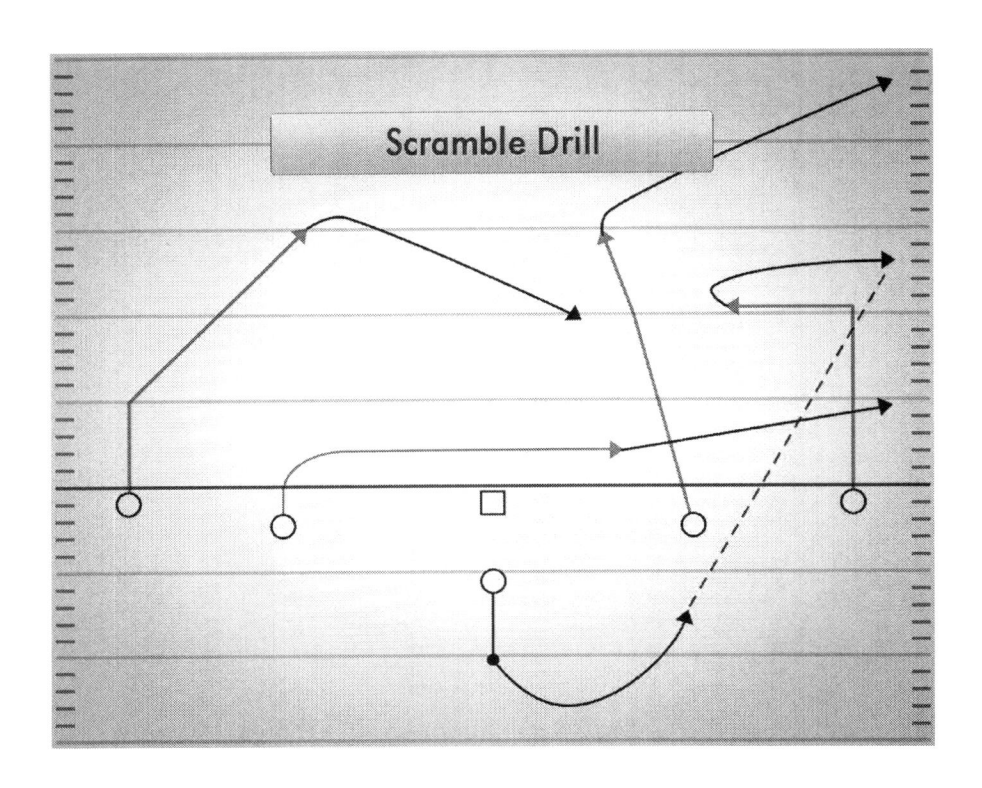

The quarterback and wide receivers line up in an offensive formation in order to be prepared to run the routes of a pass play.

TECHNIQUES: PASSING, CATCHING

EQUIPMENT: NONE

DRILL TYPE: EXECUTION, TEAMWORK

Scramble Drill

ADVANCED **GROUP** **NO-CONTACT**

PURPOSE

The purpose of the Scramble Drill is for your quarterbacks and wide receivers to develop the foundation of chemistry and strategic knowledge that is needed when a pass play breaks down and the quarterback begins running around and scrambling in the offensive backfield. Wide receivers need to learn the principles of what they should do when this situation arises in order to work together to put the team in the best possible situation to succeed.

DRILL DESCRIPTION

Call an entire pass play from your playbook and have the wide receivers run their routes as normal. After roughly three seconds, the Quarterback begins scrambling either to the right or to the left. The receivers must then identify which direction the quarterback is rolling out to, and proceed to get open for the quarterback.

There are two primary principles that the wide receivers must know when this situation arises. 1) If the receiver is already on the side that the quarterback is rolling out to, then they must find unoccupied space on the near sideline. Spreading out is key to the Scramble Drill so that two receivers are not both in the same place. 2) If the receiver is on the opposite side of the field, then they must jet across the middle of the field and find a hole in the defense where the quarterback may be able to find them.

After the foundational principles of this drill have been developed, you can begin adding defensive players to take this drill up a notch.

Pass Pursuit Drill

SETUP

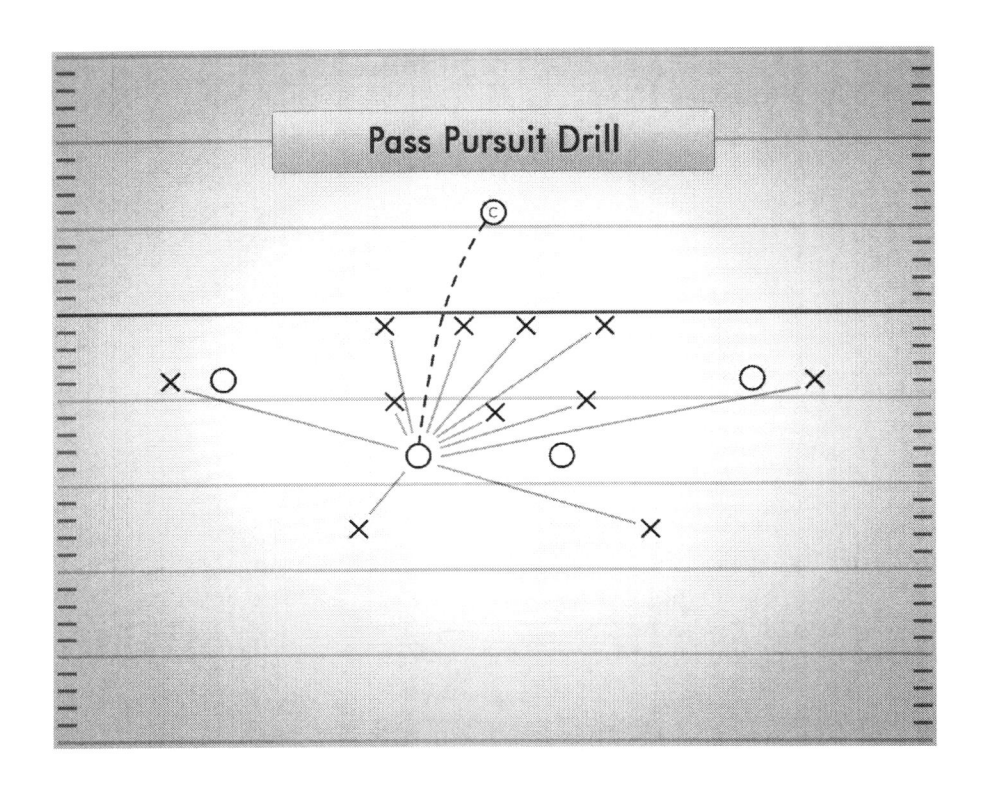

The defense lines up in their base defensive formation. The coach lines up as the quarterback for the offense and selects 3 to 4 players/helpers/coaches to position themselves at various locations within the defensive secondary.

TECHNIQUES:	PASS DEFENDING
EQUIPMENT:	NONE
DRILL TYPE:	EXECUTION, TEAMWORK

Pass Pursuit Drill

INTERMEDIATE   **TEAM**   **NO-CONTACT**

PURPOSE

The purpose of the Pass Pursuit Drill is to equip defenders with the ability to identify where the quarterback throws a pass and quickly pursue to the location of the targeted receiver.

DRILL DESCRIPTION

This drill is the passing play version of the Pursuit Drill. Instead of taking an angle to pursue a running back down the sideline, this drill requires defenders to identify where the ball was thrown and pursue the receiver.

A coach acts as the quarterback and simulates a snap. Once the play has begun, all defenders run in place while keeping their eyes on the quarterback/coach. The coach then throws the ball to one of the stationary receivers.

Immediately upon the throw, all defenders rally to the location of the receiver and run in place next to the receiver (without tackling him) until all players have arrived at that location and the coach whistles the play dead.

Find the Window

SETUP

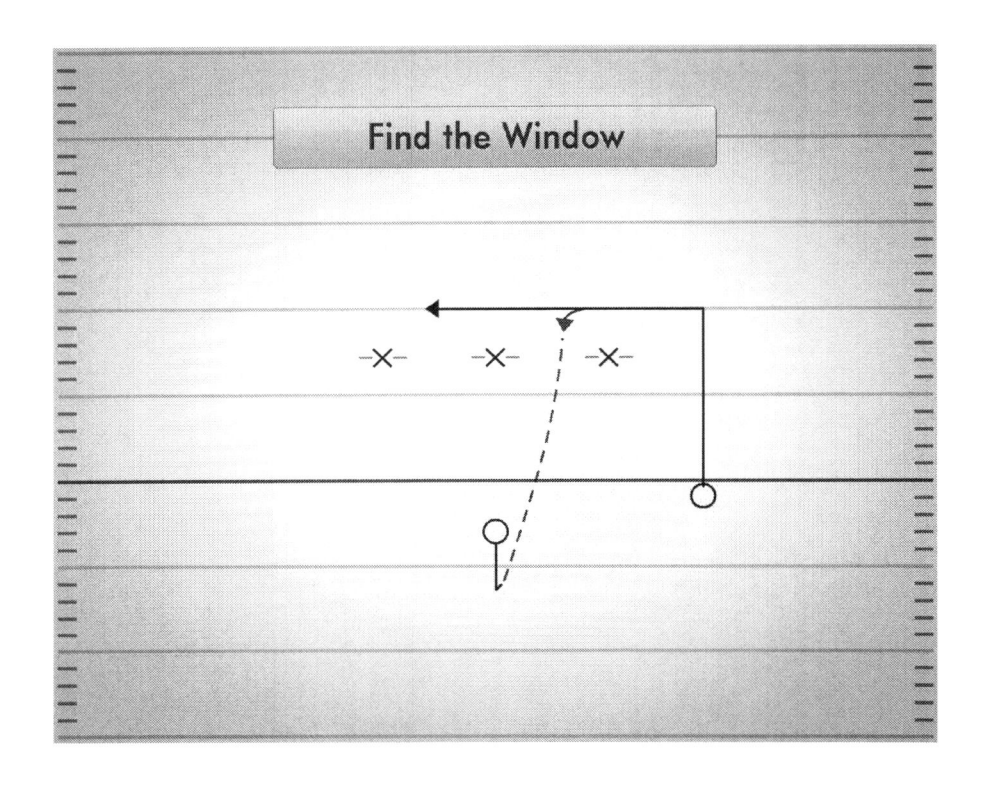

The quarterback and the wide receiver line up in formation on the offensive side of the ball. Three players line up as linebackers on the defensive side of the ball about seven yards deep.

TECHNIQUES:	PASSING, CATCHING
EQUIPMENT:	NONE
DRILL TYPE:	EXECUTION, TEAMWORK

Find the Window

ADVANCED   GROUP   NO-CONTACT

PURPOSE

Finding an open zone to settle into is one of the most difficult skills for wide receivers to learn in football. This drill teaches receivers how to find the open window in order to get themselves open for the quarterback. The quarterback also gets to build his chemistry with the receivers as they work in tandem to complete a pass in the open window.

DRILL DESCRIPTION

A wide receiver runs a 10 yard in route across the middle of the field and watches the linebackers in order to find the best place to settle down in an open area.

The quarterback takes the snap and drops back while reading the linebackers and the trajectory of his receiver.

As the receiver runs his route, the players acting as the linebacker randomly take a couple of steps either to the right of the left, in order to make the receiver and quarterback react.

It is the receiver's job to locate an open area to position himself for the quarterback, and it is the quarterback's job to provide a throw to his receiver that slices in between the defenders and hits his receiver in the numbers.

Two Minute Drill

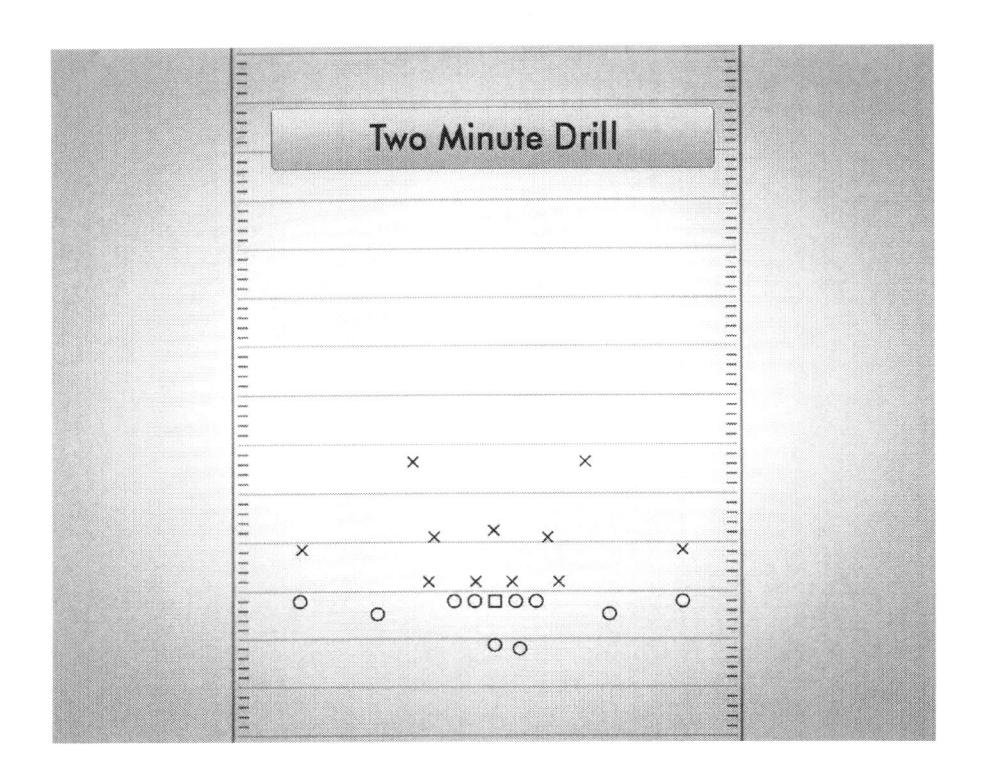

SETUP

The two minute drill requires the entire offense to line up against the entire defense. Usually, you will want to place the ball on the 20 yard line to simulate the start of a fresh offensive drive.

TECHNIQUES: PASSING, CATCHING, BLOCKING, TACKLING, PASS DEFENDING

EQUIPMENT: TIMER

DRILL TYPE: EXECUTION, TEAMWORK, COMPETITION

Two Minute Drill

ADVANCED　　　　TEAM　　　　CONTACT

PURPOSE

Practice the unique "two minute" situation where your offense gets the ball with only two minutes left on the clock before the end of the half or end of the game.

DRILL DESCRIPTION

Run this drill in a manor that simulates a full game scenario as closely as possible. Often times, when the clock is running out at the end of a half in a real game, and the seconds start ticking down, things can begin to feel very chaotic for both players and coaches. This drill provides an opportunity to practice the proper procedures and principles that players and coaches must follow in order to put points up on the scoreboard before the scoreboard ticks down to 0:00.

The offensive coach continuously calls plays to march his team down the field. One coach is in control of a clock and loudly declares the time remaining regularly throughout the course of the drill. Once you start the drive, there should be absolutely no pauses or resets, because you will not be able to pause and reset in a real game. Optionally, the offense can be given one timeout to utilize as they see fit.

One key principle that players need to keep in mind is that if they are running with the ball, they need to try their absolute hardest to not get tackled in bounds, but should instead seek to run out of bounds in order to stop the clock. Additionally, this is a great opportunity to teach your team how to "spike" the ball in order to stop the clock, if a player is tackled in bounds.

Inside Drill

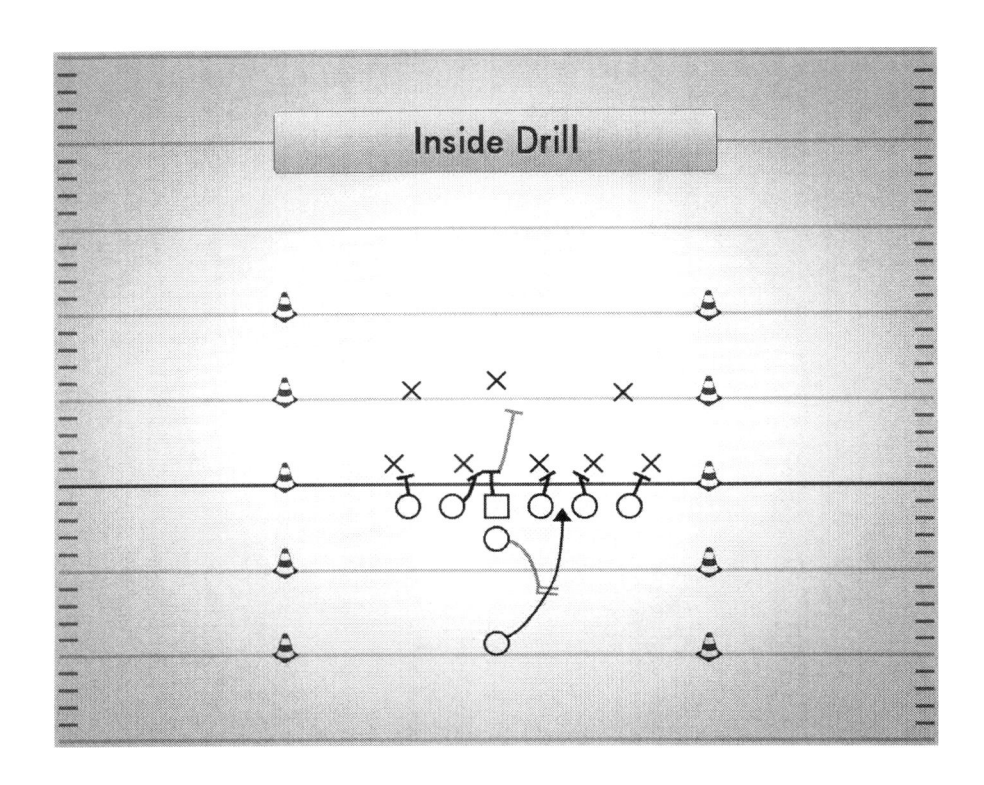

SETUP

Grab all the players in the positions that comprise the "inside" of a play. Namely, your lineman, linebackers, quarterbacks, and running backs. Create boundaries for the drill that contain the drill to the central inside portion of a play.

TECHNIQUES:	BALL CARRYING, BLOCKING, TACKLING
EQUIPMENT:	NONE
DRILL TYPE:	EXECUTION, TEAMWORK, COMPETITION

Inside Drill

ADVANCED   TEAM   CONTACT

PURPOSE

Focus specifically on the run plays with the players on the "inside" of the play. This drill is where you can get really detailed work and repetitions with the personnel responsible for implementing run plays on offense and stopping run plays on defense.

DRILL DESCRIPTION

Continuously call run plays to have the inside of the offense face off in full speed against the inside of the defense. After each play, allow the offense to reset and huddle back up before running the next play.

Both the offense and defense can mix up the play calls and formations to add variety to the types of plays they are working on throughout their playbook.

This drill allows for coaches to get specific with their coaching points between each play since the drill is boiled down to just the inside personnel. Take advantage of the opportunities in the drill to make sure that every player knows exactly what his techniques and responsibilities are for each play.

In a way, this drill is almost the exact opposite of the 7-on-7 Drill, which focuses on the outside personnel with purely passing plays.

7-on-7 Drill

SETUP

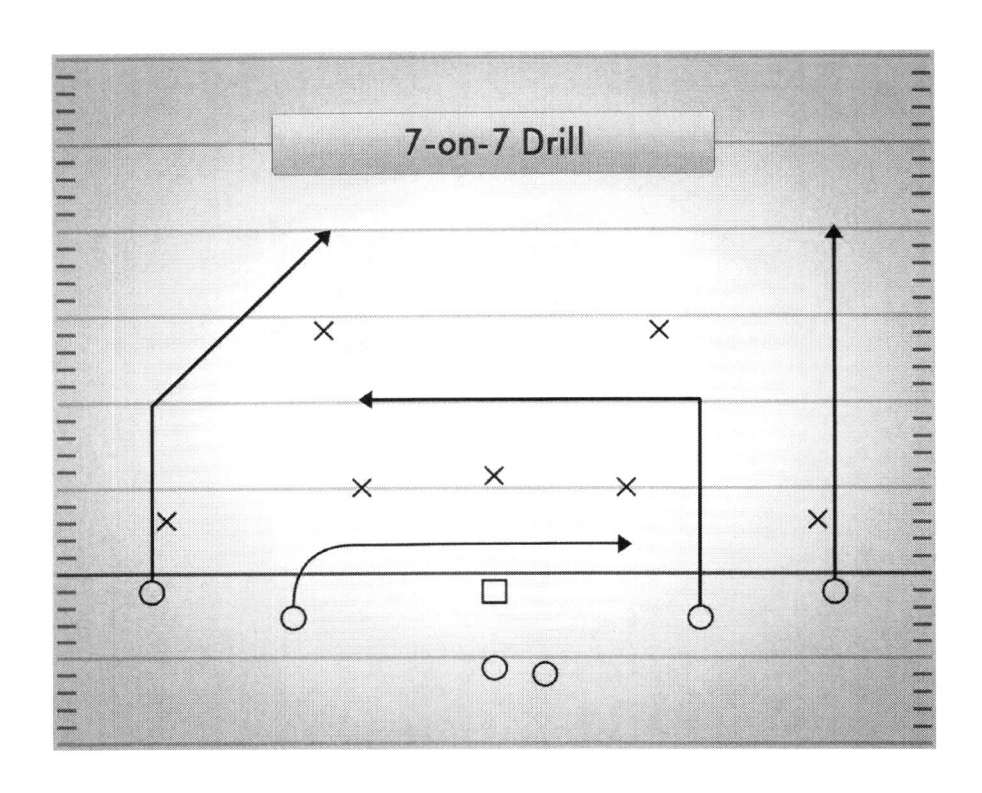

Seven defensive players line up against seven offensive players. The seven players needed for this drill are from the seven skill positions (backfield players, with the exception of the center on offense.)

TECHNIQUES:	PASSING, CATCHING, PASS DEFENDING
EQUIPMENT:	NONE
DRILL TYPE:	EXECUTION, TEAMWORK, COMPETITION

7-on-7 Drill

ADVANCED | TEAM | NO-CONTACT

PURPOSE

The purpose of the 7-on-7 drill is to focus on the passing concepts, strategies, and techniques for your team. With 100% percent of the repetitions comprising of pass plays, this drill specializes in the passing game.

DRILL DESCRIPTION

The offense competes against the defense through a series of pass plays. Coaches call passing plays on offense for the quarterback, running back, and wide receivers. Coaches call pass defense plays on defense for the linebackers, cornerbacks, and safeties.

Due to the fact that this drill specializes in the passing game, coaching points can be made in between repetitions to ensure that all players are clear on their roles and responsibilities for the given play calls.

This drill focuses on the exterior of offensive and defensive formations making it a good companion drill for the Inside Drill which focuses on the interior of formations.

Hands Team Drill

SETUP

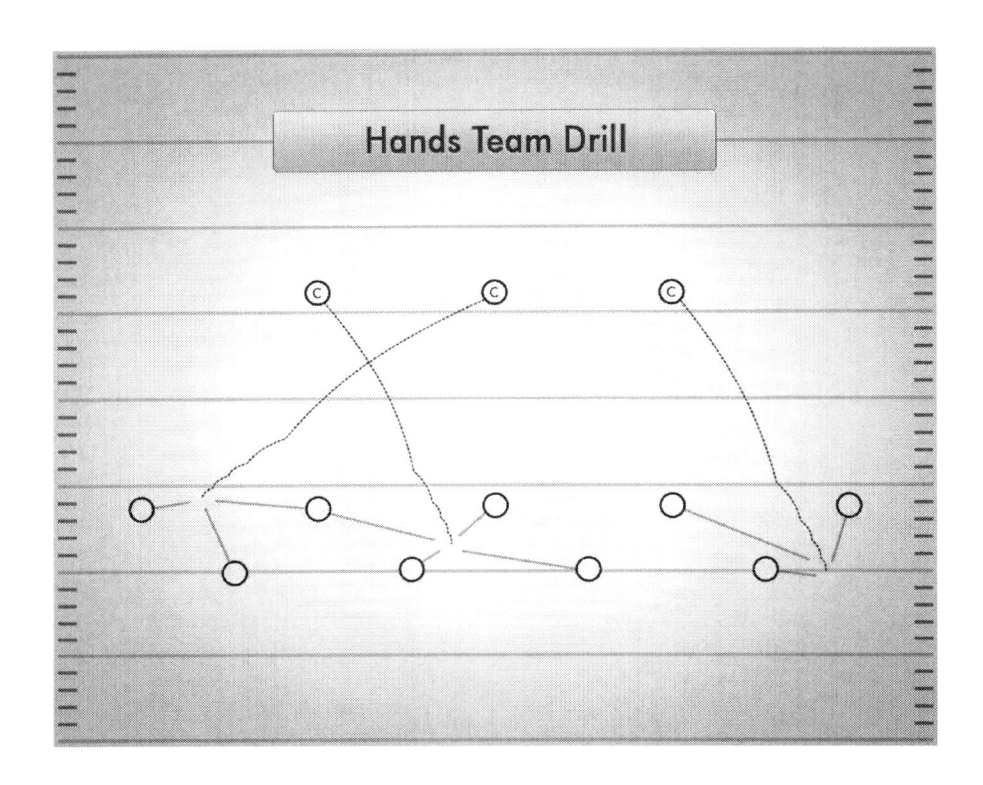

Place your "hands team," or your onside kick return team, in formation on the football field. Distribute three coaches with footballs to run the drill where a hypothetical kicker would line up to kick an onside kick.

TECHNIQUES: **CATCHING**

EQUIPMENT: **NONE**

DRILL TYPE: **EXECUTION, COORDINATION, TEAMWORK**

Hands Team Drill

ADVANCED   TEAM   NO-CONTACT

PURPOSE

Work on your team's ability to successfully recover an onside kick by repeatedly simulating onside kicks. Teach your team the techniques required to successfully procure possession of the football when the game is on the line.

DRILL DESCRIPTION

Simulate an onside kick by having coaches throw footballs hard and low into the ground. By placing three separate coaches to run this drill, you can both increase the number of repetitions during the span of the drill while also forcing your players to constantly be ready and alert for a football flying their way.

Your "hands team" is the unit of players on your team that has the best catching and coordination ability to secure the football at the final stages of a game when a team is attempting an onside kick.

Proper protocols for an onside kick recovery is for the nearest player to dive onto the football after it has traversed ten yards. The second closest player should protect his teammate by covering him up to prevent the other team from sneaking in and stealing the football. All other players should quickly run in front of the recovery and block any opponent who is still trying to run in and dive on the pile.

Chase Down Drill

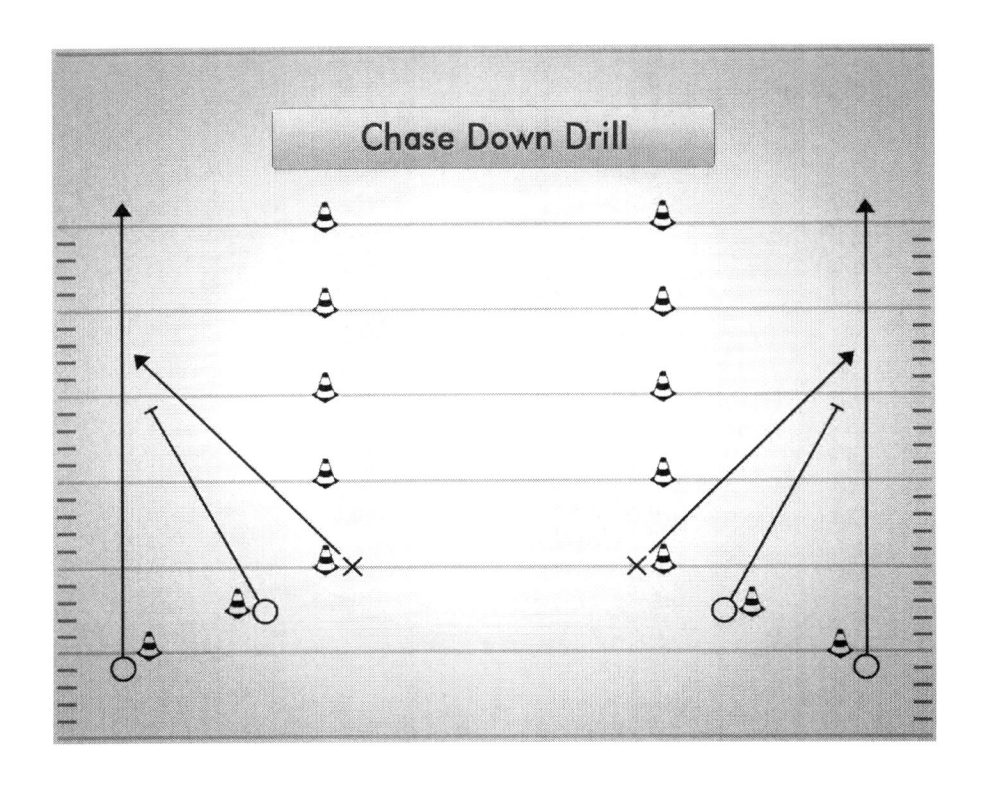

SETUP

Place three cones that signify the staggered starting location of the drills three participants. The first cone (for the ball carrier) is placed on the 25 yard line, five yards from the sideline. Each starting location after that is five more yards inside and two and a half yards further upfield.

TECHNIQUES: BALL CARRYING, BLOCKING, TACKLING

EQUIPMENT: CONE

DRILL TYPE: EXECUTION, SPEED, CONDITIONING, TEAMWORK, COMPETITION

Chase Down Drill

ADVANCED   GROUP   CONTACT

PURPOSE

The Chase Down Drill has three participants with three purposes. The ball carrier works on his ability to navigate past the last defender on his way to the end zone. The blocker works on his ability to make an open field block in space. The defender practices the very tough situation of having to be the sole player in charge of making a touchdown-saving tackle.

DRILL DESCRIPTION

Upon starting the drill, all three players begin sprinting downfield at an angle that helps them best play out their purpose. The defender will have to take an accurate angle downfield to cut off the ball carrier. Players can use their creativity to score, block, and tackle, but the ball carrier is not allowed to ever go backward, or go back too far across the field.

This drill truly is pitted in favor of the offense, but it helps all three participants with a very critical, often overlooked aspect of the game. There are a lot of yards at stake for the offense, and they need to learn how to maximize the space available to them. The defender needs to find out how to do whatever it takes to make a touchdown-saving tackle all alone, even if it means sacrificing up some yards to do so.

Backed Up Drill

SETUP

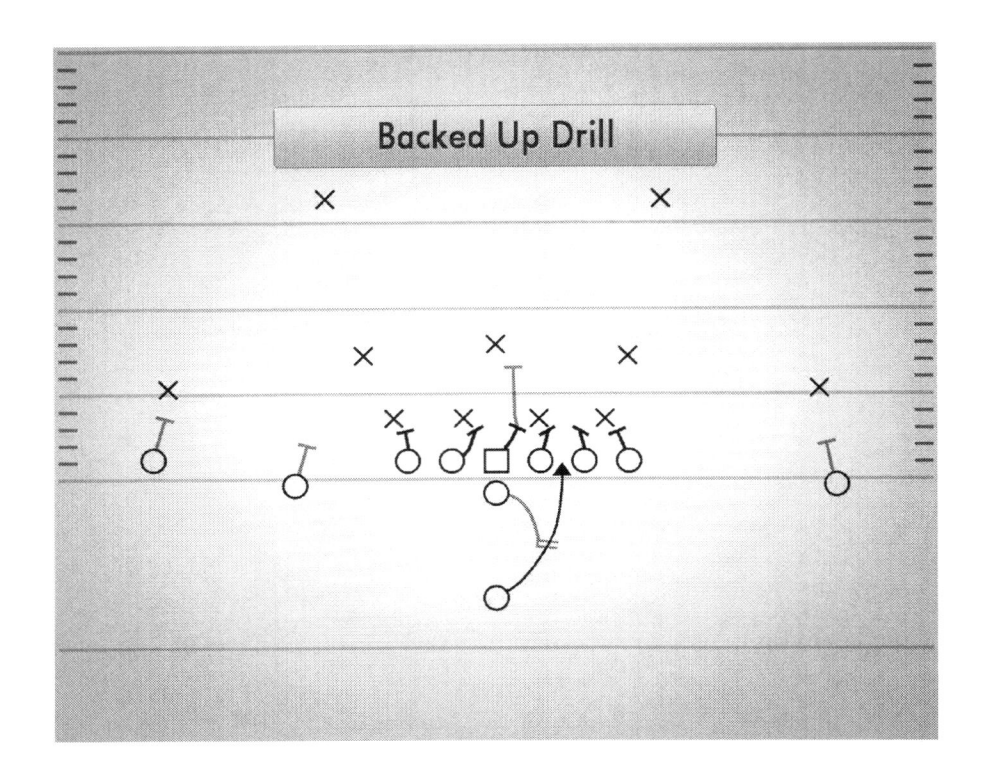

Position the offense and defense to line up on the line of scrimmage at the 2 yard line. This drill features a scenario where the offensive backfield is backed up into their own end zone.

TECHNIQUES: PASSING, CATCHING, BALL CARRYING, BLOCKING, TACKLING, PASS DEFENDING

EQUIPMENT: NONE

DRILL TYPE: EXECUTION, TEAMWORK, COMPETITION

Backed Up Drill

INTERMEDIATE   **TEAM**   **CONTACT**

PURPOSE

Give both the offense and the defense situational experience when the ball is backed up into the end zone.

The strategy can be different for the defense when there is a safety to be gained and for the offense when there is a safety at risk. Therefore, giving your team experience in this situation during practice can pay dividends in a game.

DRILL DESCRIPTION

Call full plays for the offense and defense against each other with the ball on the 2 yard line, directly in front of the goal line.

When your offense executes run plays, your running backs must ensure that they get the ball back out past the goal line, while your defense tries to push through and stuff him for a safety.

When your offense executes pass play, your quarterback must ensure that he get rid of the ball quickly to avoid a sack in the end zone, while your defense pins their ears back to get that sack and procure a safety.

3rd & Long Drill

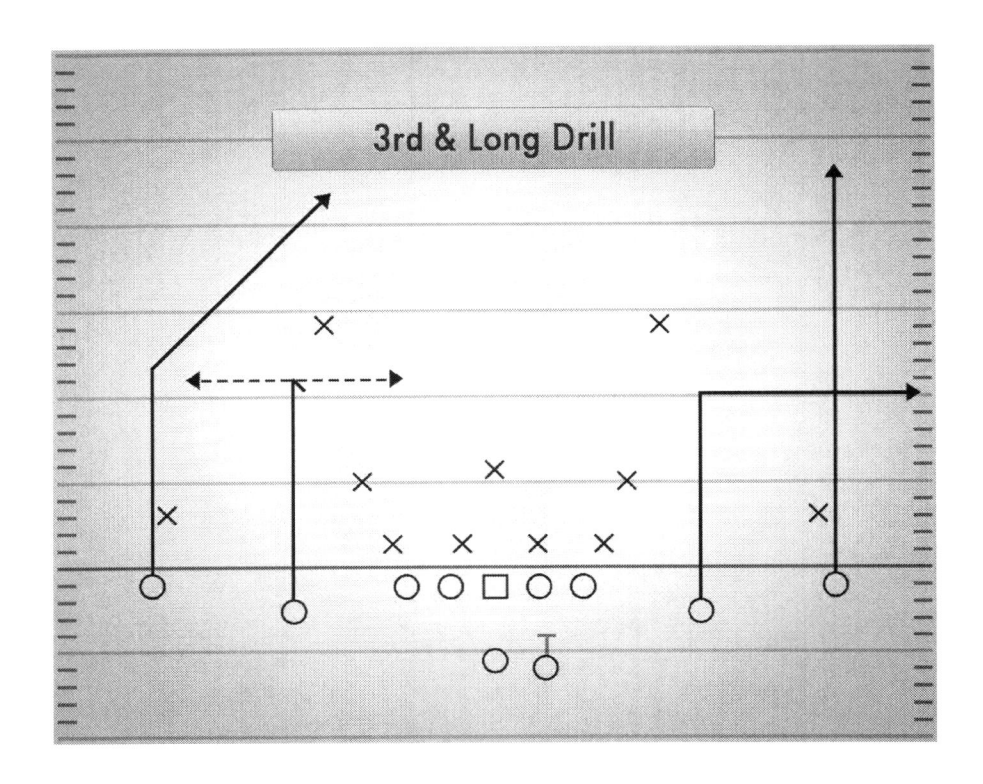

SETUP

Indicate the line of scrimmage and the first down line. Generally, a good distance for this drill is 10 yards, so that the team gains experience with a 3rd & 10 situation.

TECHNIQUES:	PASSING, CATCHING, BLOCKING, TACKLING, PASS DEFENDING
EQUIPMENT:	NONE
DRILL TYPE:	EXECUTION, TEAMWORK, COMPETITION

3rd & Long Drill

EASY   TEAM   CONTACT

PURPOSE

Provide situational awareness to players by having them get repetitions of a 3rd & Long situation. The offense must keep in mind how many yards they need for the first down, and the defense must keep in mind what yard line they need to protect in order to stop the offense from procuring the first down.

DRILL DESCRIPTION

Call offensive plays that give the offense the best chance of gaining the necessary yards to overcome the third and long situation. Teach the receivers to tailor their routes in order to get deep enough to procure the first down if the ball is thrown to them.

The defense must keep in mind the first down line in order to keep the offense in front of them and keep them short of the sticks.

Two Point Conversion Drill

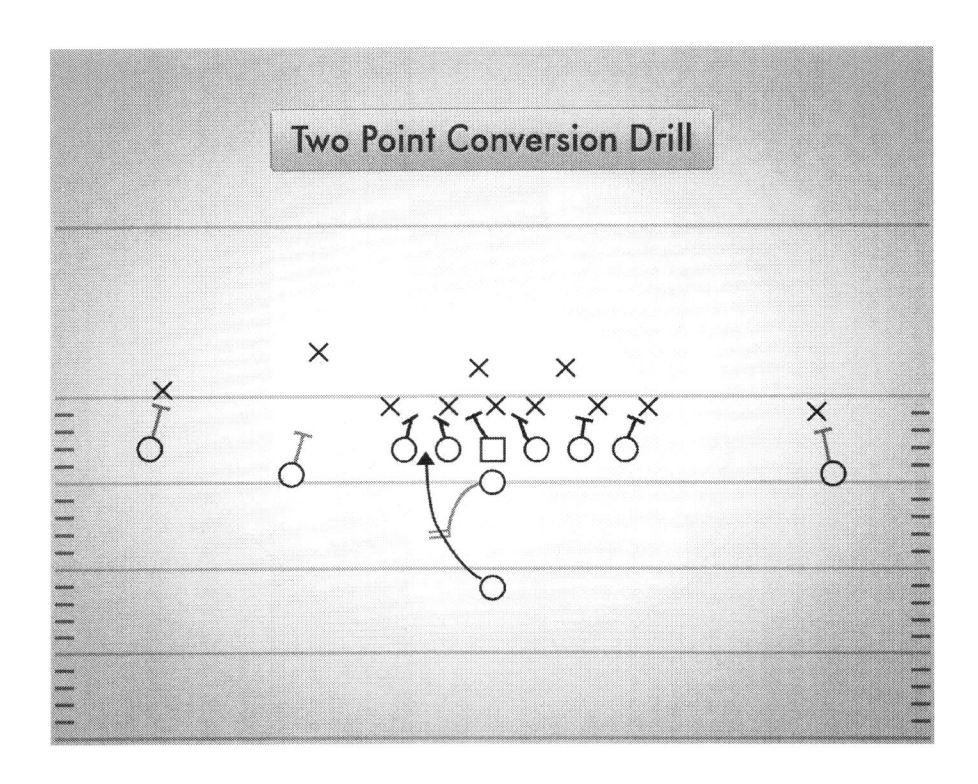

SETUP

Place the ball on the two point conversion line, which is usually the two yard line. Both offense and defense will use this as the line of scrimmage for the two point conversion attempt.

TECHNIQUES: PASSING, CATCHING, BALL CARRYING, BLOCKING, TACKLING, PASS DEFENDING

EQUIPMENT: NONE

DRILL TYPE: EXECUTION, TEAMWORK, COMPETITION

Two Point Conversion Drill

INTERMEDIATE | TEAM | CONTACT

PURPOSE

Players gain experience executing a two point conversion. A two point conversion can be responsible for making for breaking an entire game. Giving your team repetitions of this situation in practices can make the difference between wins and losses in games.

DRILL DESCRIPTION

The defense competes against the offense on the goal line during a simulated two point conversion attempt. This gives your team experience running (and defending) various types of plays in this do or die situation.

You only have one try at any given two point conversion, so it is imperative that your team practices their best plays and gets comfortable executing their responsibilities during this do or die situation.

Hail Mary Drill

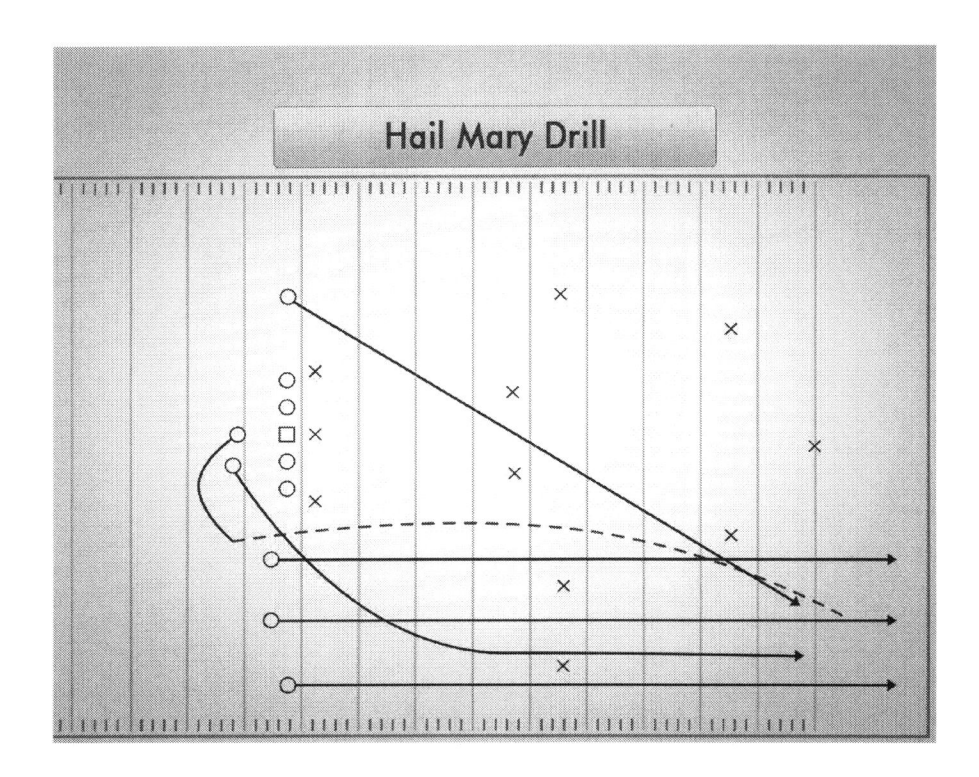

SETUP

Depending on your quarterback's arm strength, place the line of scrimmage at the furthest location possible where your quarterback can still throw the ball to the goal line.

TECHNIQUES:	PASSING, CATCHING, PASS DEFENDING
EQUIPMENT:	NONE
DRILL TYPE:	EXECUTION, TEAMWORK, COMPETITION

Hail Mary Drill

ADVANCED | TEAM | CONTACT

PURPOSE

The Hail Mary situation has a very low success rate, so anything your team can do to prepare for this situation to increase their chances of success can pay huge dividends. This drill prepares your team to execute when the game is on the line and one last heave from the quarterback will affect the outcome of the entire game.

DRILL DESCRIPTION

Successfully executing a hail mary requires a proper plan and a whole lot of luck. Put the luck in your favor by sending as many of your receivers to the same spot in the end zone in hopes that one of them can come down with the ball. In case the ball gets tipped backward, consider having at least one of your players act as "trailers" who don't try to jump for the ball, but instead remain in front of the group of players and watch for the ball to get tipped down into their arms.

Your quarterback will need to buy time in the backfield to allow your receivers to get far downfield before he hurls the ball as high and as far as he can.

The defense needs to move their players back into the end zone and bat the ball straight down into the ground out of the air so that the offense does not pull off the miraculous feat.

A few repetitions of this drill is important so that your players can get a feel for how to properly perform in this situation.

Double Trouble Drill

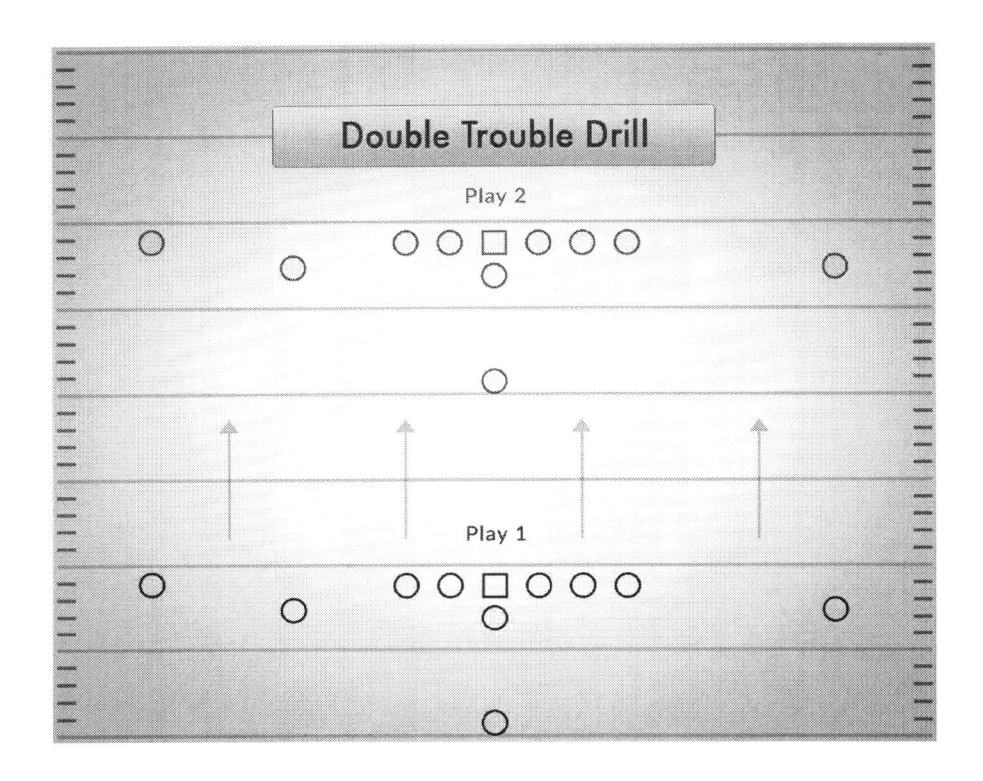

SETUP

The offense huddles up and the coach sends two plays into the huddle at once.

EQUIPMENT: NONE

DRILL TYPE: EXECUTION, TEAMWORK

Double Trouble Drill

ADVANCED | TEAM | NO-CONTACT

PURPOSE

In time-critical situations, coaches may need to deliver two plays into the huddle at once. This is called a double play call and requires the team to remember both plays to quickly run them in sequence without having to huddle again in between plays. Rapidly moving into the next play can often throw the defense off and result in picking up some easy yards, if the offense can keep both play calls in their mind at once.

This drill trains the team to both remember and execute a double play call.

DRILL DESCRIPTION

Two plays are given in the huddle to be run one after the other. The offense breaks the huddle and runs the first play. A coach runs downfield and acts as the referee to set up the ball on the new line of scrimmage.

The offense then quickly resets on the new line of scrimmage and runs the second play as quickly as possible in hopes of catching the defense off guard.

No defense is needed for this drill. The plays can simply be run against air, because the focus of the drill is not on competition, but instead on remember two different play calls and executing them back to back.

Zone Alone Drill

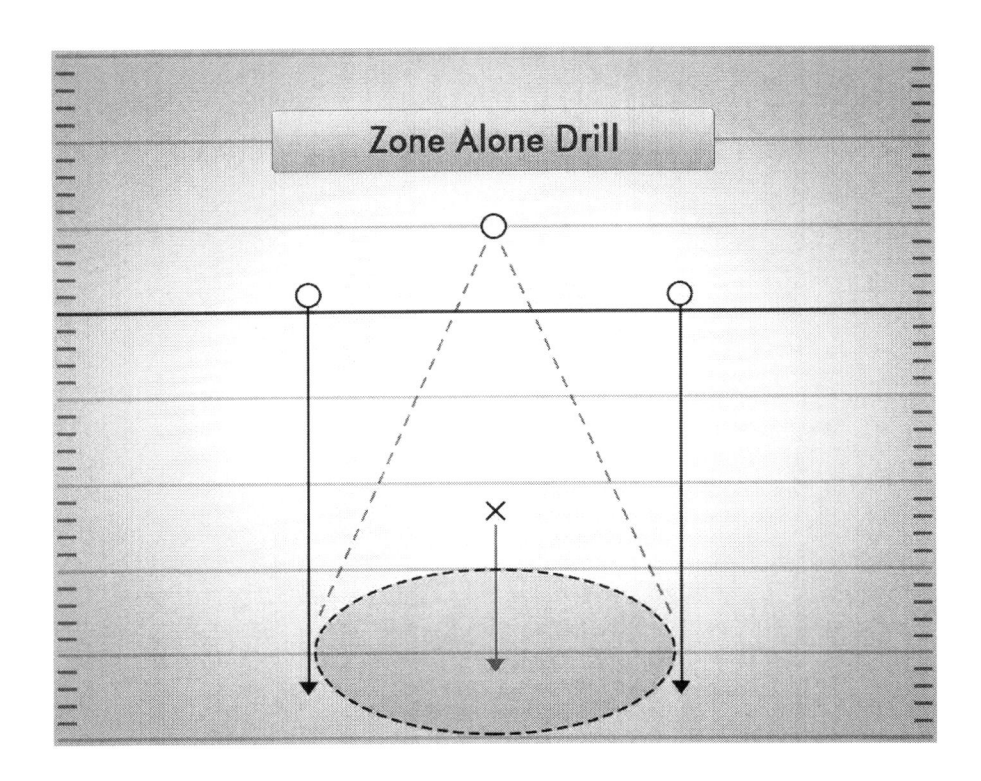

SETUP

Two receivers or tight ends line up close to the hashes in the middle of the play. A safety lines up in the middle of the field, about 12-18 yards deep.

TECHNIQUES:	PASSING, CATCHING, PASS DEFENDING
EQUIPMENT:	NONE
DRILL TYPE:	EXECUTION

Zone Alone Drill

ADVANCED　　　　GROUP　　　　NO-CONTACT

PURPOSE

This drill focuses on a particular game situation where there are two vertical routes going down the center of the defense.

The Cover 1 safety must manage multiple players entering his deep zone and read the quarterback's throw. The quarterback, on the other hand, must read the movement of the safety and fit the ball into one of his receivers without the safety intercepting the pass.

DRILL DESCRIPTION

The quarterback snaps the ball and drops back to pass as his receivers make their way downfield. The safety drops into his deep Cover 1 zone as he feels the presence of the two receivers entering his zone, and watches the eyes of the quarterback.

The quarterback attempts to deliver a pass to one of his receivers at a depth of 15-25 yards. He can use his eyes to look off the safety to one side, and then throw it to the other.

The safety tries to make a play on the ball to knock it down or intercept it.

Screen Block Drill

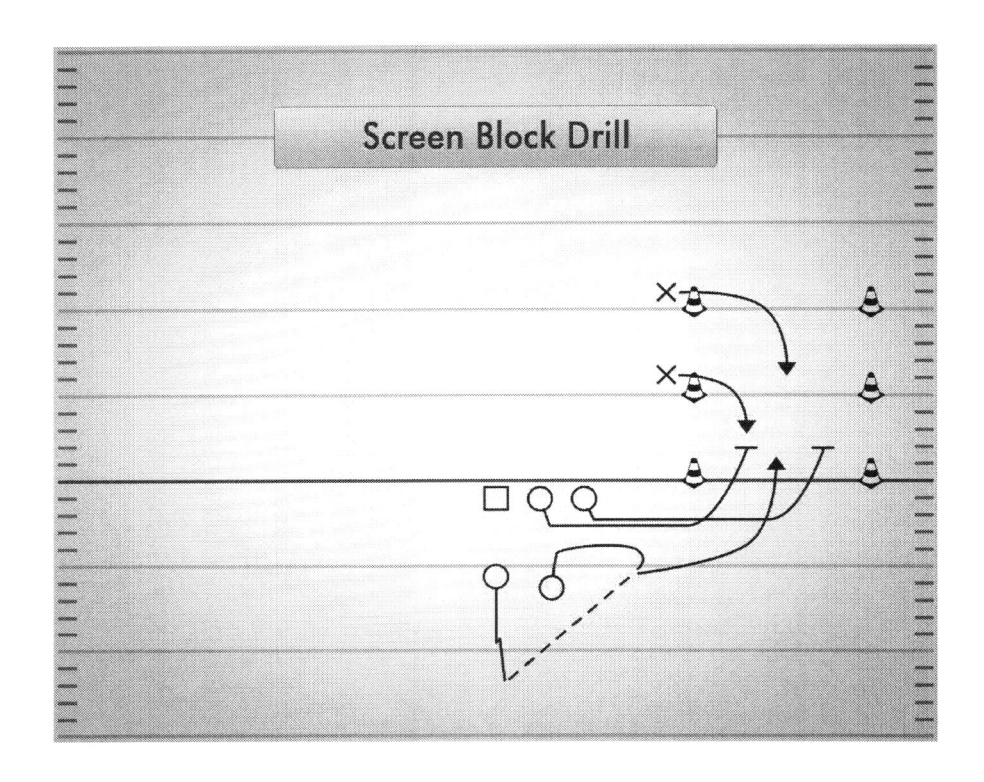

SETUP

Place a series of cones on one side of the field that indicate a 10 yard wide strip of field that contains the players in the drill.

A linebacker lines up inside the cones five yards away from the line of scrimmage, and a safety lines up inside the cones ten yards away from the line of scrimmage.

TECHNIQUES:	TACKLING
EQUIPMENT:	CONE
DRILL TYPE:	EXECUTION, TEAMWORK, COMPETITION

Screen Block Drill

ADVANCED — GROUP — CONTACT

PURPOSE

Simulate the open field blocking and tackling of a screen pass play. The offensive line learns how to run in space and make a block in the open field. The defenders learn how to avoid blocks and make tackles on the running back during a screen play in the open field. The running back and quarterback both work on their footwork, timing, and responsibilities for a screen pass play.

DRILL DESCRIPTION

The offensive players (quarterback, running back, one guard, and one tackle) run throw the progression of a screen pass play in the backfield.

The defenders must wait inside the cones until the running back catches the ball. As soon as the running back catches the ball, the defenders step inside the cones and release to make a tackle on the ball carrier.

All drill participants must stay inside the boundaries of the cones throughout the drill. If the running back makes it ten yards downfield, then the offense wins the competition, but if he gets tackled or steps outside the cones, then the defense wins the drill.

To increase the size of this drill, incorporate the center as another blocker with a cornerback starting outside the cones as another defender.

Fade Drill

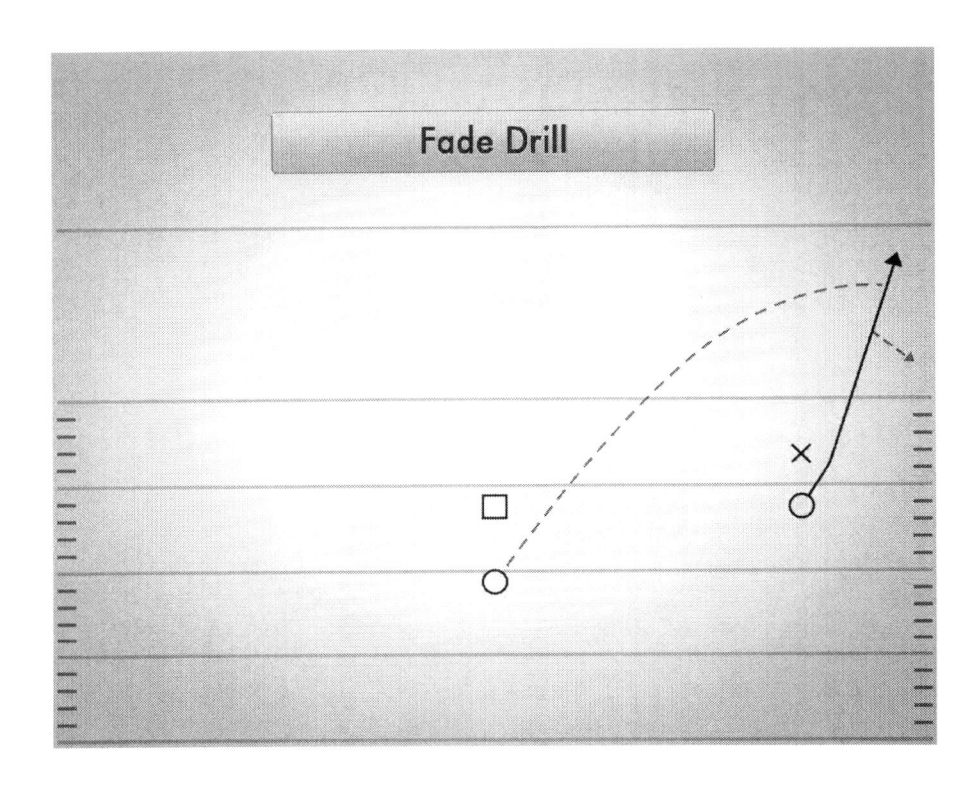

SETUP

A cornerback and a receiver line up across from each other near the end zone on the outside of the line of scrimmage.

TECHNIQUES:	PASSING, PASS DEFENDING
EQUIPMENT:	NONE
DRILL TYPE:	EXECUTION, TEAMWORK, COMPETITION

Fade Drill

ADVANCED   GROUP   CONTACT

PURPOSE

When close to the end zone, the successful execution of a fade route can mean the difference between scoring a touchdown and settling for a field goal.

This drill allows both the offense and the defense to get experience executing and defending a fade route into the end zone.

DRILL DESCRIPTION

The quarterback and the receiver must exhibit teamwork to successfully convert a fade route into the end zone. The receiver must cleanly get to the proper location, and the quarterback must perfectly place the ball up high where only his receiver can get to it.

Depending on the positioning of the cornerback, the quarterback may select to throw the fade to the back shoulder of the receiver. Therefore, the quarterback/receiver combo must have great teamwork and chemistry to pull off this play.

The quarterback will either put to the ball up high over the cornerback in the back of the end zone or fire it on a line to the outside for the receiver to cut back and get to.

The cornerback will play up close to the receiver and attempt to stick his hands in between the receivers hands to prevent the catch.

Blitz Detection Drill

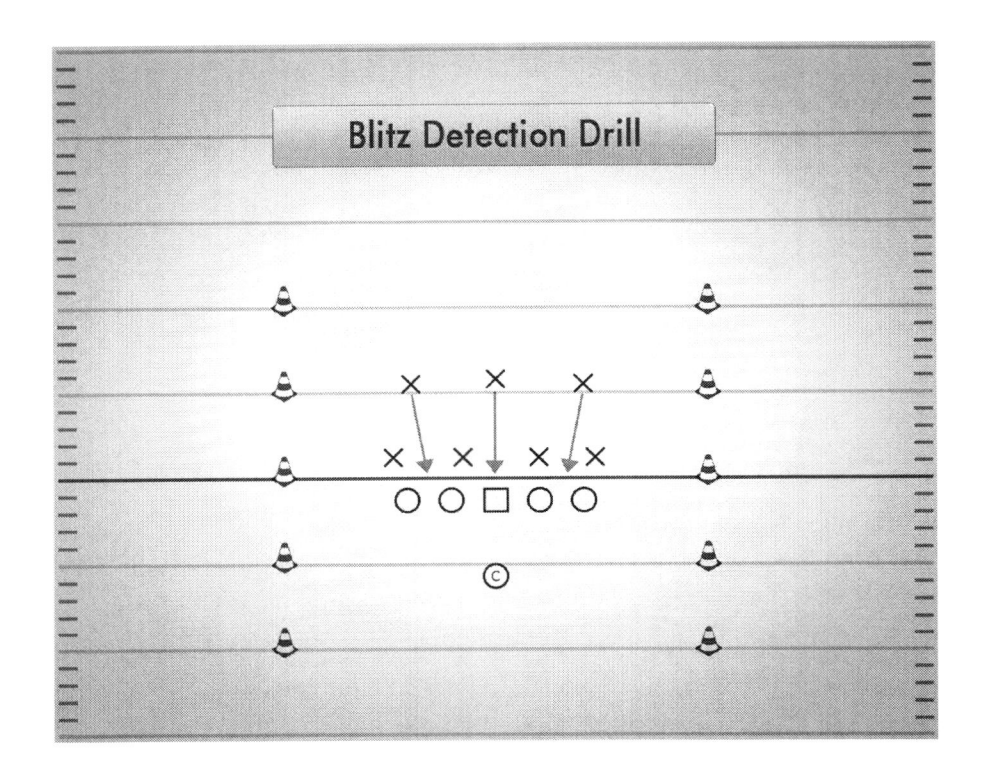

SETUP

Position the five players of the offensive line in formation on the line of scrimmage. Place seven player in a defensive formation to act as the defensive front seven.

EQUIPMENT: **NONE**

DRILL TYPE: **EXECUTION, TEAMWORK**

Blitz Detection Drill

| ADVANCED | GROUP | CONTACT |

PURPOSE

Teach offensive lineman how to pass block while working together as a unit. Specifically, this drill teaches your offensive line how to detect a blitz from the linebackers, and use teamwork to make sure that they pick up and block all five players.

Offensive lineman are the biggest, brawniest players on the football field, but they also must utilize an incredible amount of their brain, to work as a unit to make blocks and execute their assignments while also looking out the corner of their eyes to detect blitz attempts.

DRILL DESCRIPTION

A coach stands behind the offensive line and indicates by pointing to the defense which of the linebackers should blitz, and where they should blitz.

The coach then gives the cadence and the members of the offensive line work together to not only block all four of the defensive lineman, but also to spread out and pick up the blitzing linebacker.

Coaches can increase the difficulty level by instructing certain lineman to back off into pass coverage and sending multiple linebackers in on a blitz.

Turnover Turnaround

SETUP

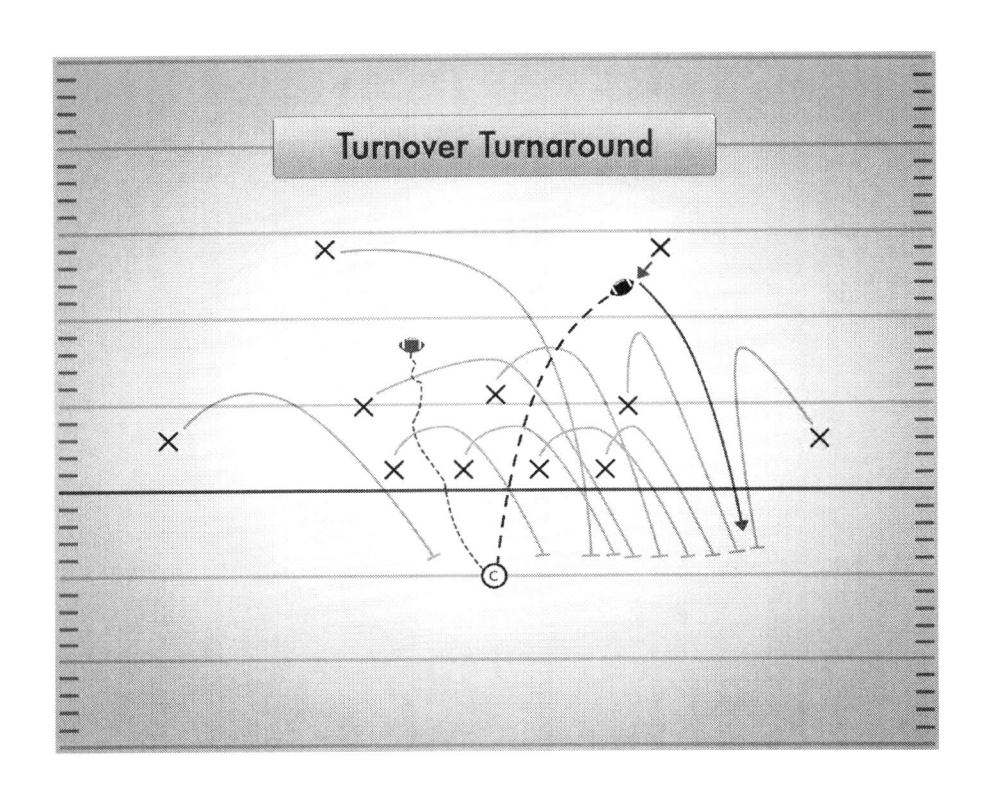

The entire defense lines up in their defensive formation on the field.

TECHNIQUES: **BLOCKING**

EQUIPMENT: **NONE**

DRILL TYPE: **EXECUTION, TEAMWORK**

Turnover Turnaround Drill

EASY TEAM NO-CONTACT

PURPOSE

One of the most exciting times for a defense is when they secure a turnover and begin running the ball down the field back the other way. Sometimes, in the midst of the excitement, some of the other defensive players do not do a good enough job of turning around and blocking for their teammate taking the ball the other way.

The Turnover Turnaround teaches your team to turnaround and run down the field as a unit to lead block for the ball carrier holding the football as he makes his way toward the end zone whenever a turnover is secured.

DRILL DESCRIPTION

A coach stands in the offensive backfield and instructs the defense to run in place by firing their feet. The coach then either throws the football up into the air for the defense to intercept and take the other way. Or the coach rolls the football hard into the ground to force the defense to scoop up the fumble and take it the other way.

As soon as the turnover is secured, all players start running down the field to lead block for their teammate on the way to the end zone.

The Turnover Turnaround principle can be inherently implemented as a part of any team defense drill. Simply instruct your team to turnaround and run down the field as a team whenever a turnover naturally occurs in the midst of a team drill.

Cutoff & Cleanup Drill

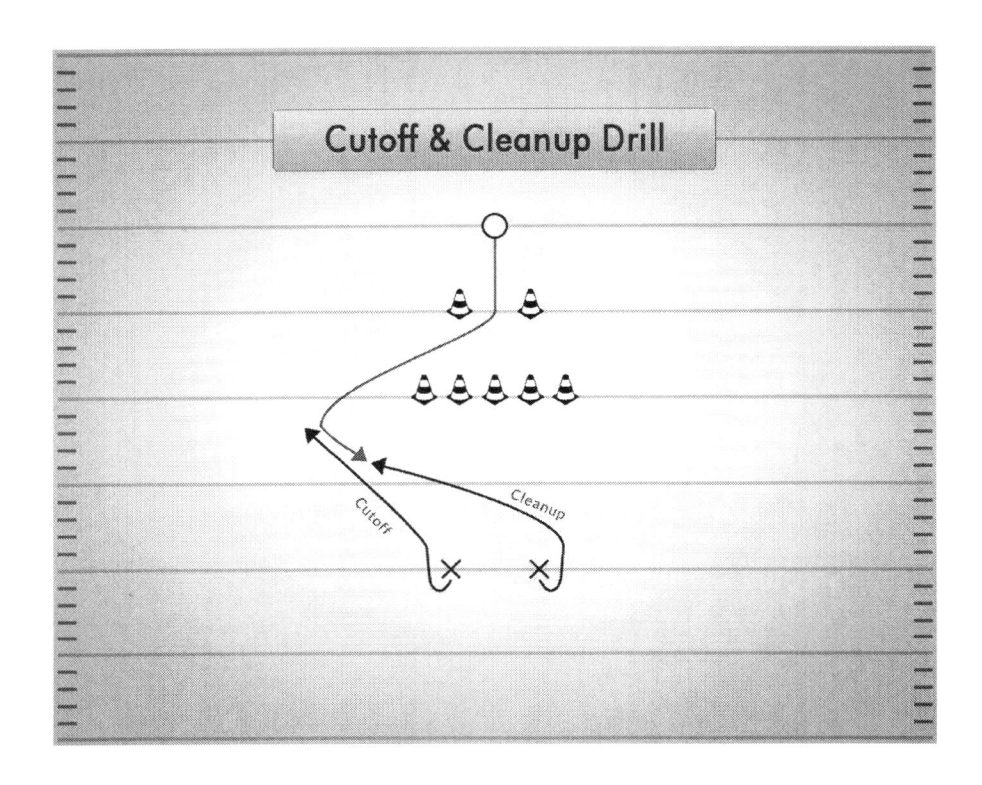

SETUP

Cones are placed as pictured in the diagram above. One offensive player with a football stands ten yards away from the center of the drill.

Two defensive players lay face down on the ground, ten yards away from the center of the drill, pointing away from the drill.

TECHNIQUES:	BALL CARRYING, TACKLING
EQUIPMENT:	NONE
DRILL TYPE:	EXECUTION, TEAMWORK, COMPETITION

Cutoff & Cleanup Drill

ADVANCED   GROUP   CONTACT

PURPOSE

Teach defensive players how to work in unison to "cutoff" the ball carrier from the outside, and "cleanup" the tackle when the ball carrier cuts back into the inside.

DRILL DESCRIPTION

A coach starts the drill with a verbal command and the ball carrier runs in between the first set of cones and then selects to run around the next line of cones to one side or the other. After the runner gets to the line of scrimmage, he may use his creativity to avoid tackles and get past the defenders.

The defenders jump up off of the ground and run to meet the ball carrier close to the line of scrimmage. The defender on the side that the ball carrier runs to must realize his position on the field and aim to cutoff the ball carrier from getting around him to the outside.

The defender opposite of the ball must trail towards the runner and prepare to cleanup the tackle after his teammate redirects the runner back to the inside.

Both defenders must be aware of their position on the field, be aware of their cutoff/cleanup responsibilities, and work in coordination to either execute a solo or group tackle.

Pylon Drill

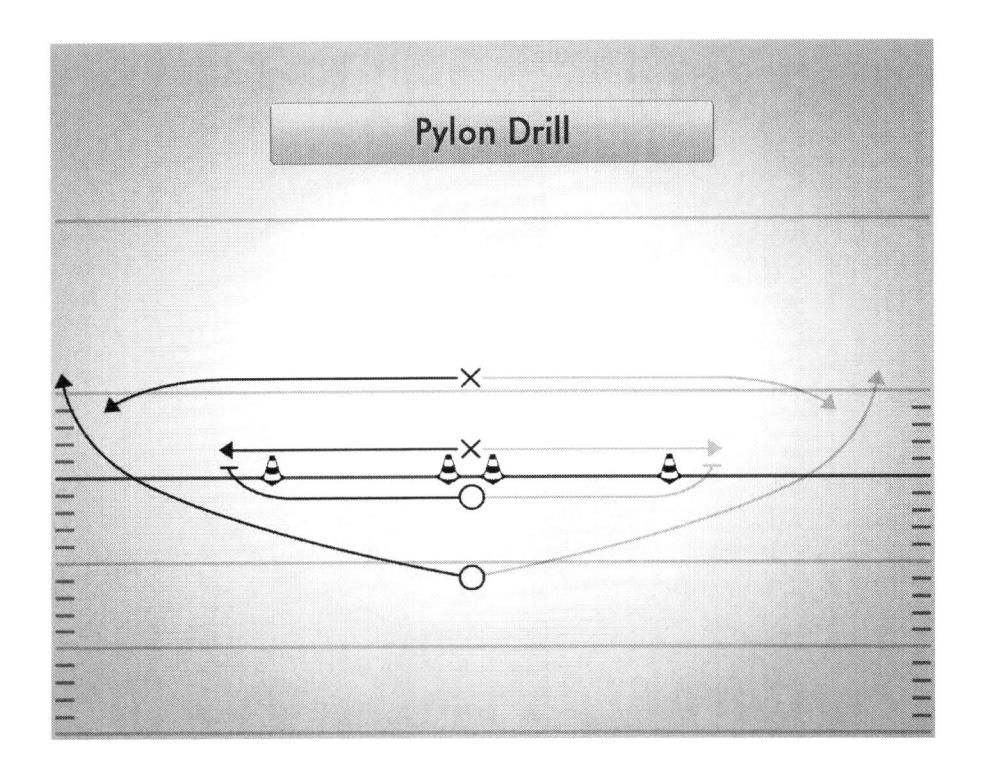

SETUP

Place two cones in the center of the field on the five yard line to indicate where players start the drill. Place another two cones on the outside of the five yard line that splits the distance between the center cones and the sideline.

A defensive player and an offensive player each line up on the line of scrimmage. A ball carrier lines up five yards behind the line of scrimmage, and a defensive counterpart lines up on the goalline.

TECHNIQUES:	BALL CARRYING, BLOCKING, TACKLING
EQUIPMENT:	CONE
DRILL TYPE:	EXECUTION, COMPETITION

Pylon Drill

ADVANCED   **GROUP**   **CONTACT**

PURPOSE

Give your offensive players realistic experience trying to score while running on an angle towards the pylon.

Give your defensive players realistic experience trying to stop the offense from scoring while running on an angle towards the pylon.

DRILL DESCRIPTION

A coach begins the drill by indicating to the offensive players which direction they should run. The offensive players immediately begin running in an attempt to block and score. The defenders must react and then fend off the blocker and tackle the runner.

All players are allowed to use any legal means necessary during the course of the drill, but since the focus of the drill is to work on the angle of pursuit towards the pylon, all player must stay on their side of the line of scrimmage until they have gone outside and around the outside cone.

The offense wins the drill if they convert a score into the endzone, and the defense wins the drill if they are able to stop the offense from scoring.

Index

Equipment

No Equipment
24, 30, 44, 46, 56, 58, 60, 72, 74, 78, 80, 86, 92, 94, 96, 100, 102, 106, 108, 122, 130, 132, 134, 136, 142, 150, 152, 154, 156, 158, 160, 162, 164, 166, 170, 178, 180, 182, 186, 190, 198, 200, 202, 208, 212, 216, 220, 230, 232, 234, 238, 240, 242, 246, 248, 250, 252, 254, 256, 260, 262, 264, 266

Cone Drills
12, 14, 16, 18, 20, 22, 26, 28, 32, 34, 36, 38, 40, 42, 48, 50, 52, 54, 62, 64, 66, 76, 82, 84, 98, 110, 112, 116, 120, 128, 144, 148, 168, 184, 188, 204, 214, 226, 228, 244, 258, 268

Blocking Pad Drills
90, 104, 124, 126, 146, 174, 192, 194, 196, 206, 210, 218, 222

Tackle Dummy Drills
82, 84, 110, 114, 116, 118, 120, 128, 138, 172, 174, 176

Timer Drills
12, 14, 22, 32, 68, 236

Technique

Passing Drills
90, 92, 94, 138, 140, 142, 162, 180, 200, 202, 230, 234, 236, 240, 246, 248, 250, 252, 256, 260

Catching Drills
76, 106, 130, 132, 134, 136, 138, 142, 154, 156, 162, 178, 194, 200, 202, 204, 230, 234, 236, 240, 242, 246, 248, 250, 252, 256

Ball Carrying Drills
76, 96, 98, 108, 110, 112, 114, 122, 124, 126, 128, 146, 158, 166, 168, 188, 190, 192, 196, 198, 200, 204, 216, 220, 226, 238, 244, 246, 250, 266, 268

Blocking Drills
118, 120, 148, 158, 164, 182, 184, 186, 226, 236, 238, 244, 246, 248, 250, 264, 268

Tackling Drills
82, 84, 110, 112, 114, 116, 118, 120, 160, 174, 176, 206, 210, 218, 226, 236, 238, 244, 246, 248, 250, 258, 266, 268

Pass Defending Drills
100, 102, 106, 144, 170, 232, 236, 240, 246, 248, 250, 252, 256, 260

Footwork Drills
12, 14, 16, 18, 20, 22, 24, 26, 28, 34, 36, 38, 40, 44, 62, 64, 86, 92, 94, 100, 116, 128, 150, 154, 170, 172, 212, 214, 216

Difficulty

Easy Drills
12, 14, 20, 24, 26, 28, 30, 32, 44, 46, 52, 56, 58, 62, 64, 70, 74, 78, 80, 82, 84, 96, 100, 102, 110, 112, 116, 136, 146, 148, 150, 152, 160, 166, 168, 172, 174, 190, 198, 200, 208, 212, 216, 248, 264

Intermediate Drills
16, 18, 22, 34, 36, 40, 42, 48, 50, 54, 60, 66, 68, 72, 86, 90, 92, 94, 98, 104, 106, 108, 118, 138, 142, 164, 170, 176, 178, 182, 184, 188, 192, 202, 214, 220, 222, 226, 228, 232, 246, 250

Advanced Drills
38, 76, 114, 120, 122, 124, 126, 128, 130, 132, 134, 140, 144, 154, 156, 158, 162, 186, 194, 196, 204, 206, 210, 230, 234, 236, 238, 240, 242, 244, 252, 254, 256, 258, 260, 262, 266, 268

Size

Individual Drills
12, 14, 16, 18, 20, 22, 24, 26, 28, 30, 32, 34, 36, 38, 40, 48, 50, 52, 56, 58, 62, 64, 68, 70, 72, 74, 78, 80, 82, 84, 86, 90, 92, 98, 100, 102, 116, 124, 130, 132, 136, 170, 172, 174, 176, 178, 190, 198, 208, 214, 216

Partner Drills
54, 60, 66, 76, 94, 96, 110, 112, 114, 118, 120, 122, 134, 140, 144, 148, 152, 160, 164, 166, 180, 184, 204, 212, 220

Group Drills
42, 44, 46, 94, 104, 106, 108, 126, 128, 138, 142, 146, 150, 154, 156, 158, 162, 168, 182, 186, 188, 192, 194, 196, 200, 202, 206, 210, 218, 222, 226, 230, 234, 244, 256, 258, 260, 262, 266, 268

Team Drills
228, 232, 236, 238, 240, 242, 246, 248, 250, 252, 254, 264

Contact Level

No-Contact Drills
12, 14, 16, 18, 20, 22, 24, 26, 28, 30, 32, 34, 36, 38, 40, 42, 44, 48, 50, 52, 54, 56, 58, 60, 62, 64, 66, 68, 70, 72, 74, 76, 78, 80, 86, 90, 92, 94, 96, 98, 100, 102, 104, 106, 116, 128, 130, 132, 134, 136, 138, 140, 142, 150, 152, 156, 162, 168, 170, 172, 178, 180, 184, 188, 190, 198, 200, 202, 204, 208, 212, 214, 216, 230, 232, 234, 240, 242, 254, 256, 264

Contact Drills
46, 82, 84, 108, 110, 112, 114, 118, 120, 122, 124, 126, 144, 146, 148, 154, 158, 160, 164, 166, 174, 176, 182, 186, 192, 194, 196, 206, 210, 218, 220, 222, 226, 228, 236, 238, 244, 246, 248, 250, 252, 258, 260, 262, 266, 268

Drill Type

Evaluation Drills
12, 14, 24, 32, 52

Speed Drills
14, 18, 22, 26, 32, 34, 38, 40, 44, 66, 70, 74, 80, 98, 128, 150, 168, 244

Agility Drills
12, 14, 16, 18, 20, 22, 26, 28, 34, 36, 38, 40, 44, 48, 50, 52, 62, 64, 66, 76, 80, 82, 84, 86, 98, 102, 116, 128, 150, 168, 184, 204

Conditioning Drills
30, 36, 54, 56, 58, 60, 68, 72, 78, 228, 244

Coordination Drills
74, 76, 86, 96, 104, 106, 108, 122, 124, 134, 140, 152, 154, 156, 166, 172, 174, 176, 178, 190, 194, 196, 198, 200, 204, 242

Teamwork Drills
42, 46, 60, 96, 106, 138, 142, 152, 158, 162, 182, 186, 200, 202, 226, 228, 230, 232, 234, 236, 238, 240, 242, 244, 246, 248, 250, 252, 254, 258, 260, 262, 264, 266

Competition Drills
42, 54, 60, 66, 112, 114, 118, 120, 144, 148, 220, 236, 238, 240, 244, 246, 248, 250, 252, 258, 260, 266, 268

About the Author

DILLON HESS

Dillon Hess feels awkward writing this section about himself. He supposes that he should just write about football since that is what this book is all about.

Dillon was a two-time Texas All-State Quarterback at Colleyville Covenant Academy in Colleyville, Texas. He threw for over 5,000 yards passing and scored 70 total touchdowns during his high school football career. He played four seasons of college football at Beloit College where he was the captain his senior year and played just about every single position on the field, including rewriting the school's record book for punting yards.

If the Best Flag Football Plays for Defense book sells enough copies to make him a multi-billionaire, Dillon plans on buying an NFL football franchise and making himself the starting Quarterback.

In addition to writing books for football coaches, Dillon also created a football playbook maker website for coaches to draw football plays and manage their football playbook all in one place. This tool is called Playbook Hut and can be found at playbookhut.com

Printed in Great Britain
by Amazon